UNITY
BEGINS WITHIN

Spiritual Healing Meets the
Four-Petaled Flower

ANNIE FULLER

Spiritual Healer and Teacher

ART BY EMILY K. GRIEVES

Unity Begins Within
Spiritual Healing Meets the Four-Petaled Flower

Published by Yanantin Press
www.FullcircleSpiritualHealing.com

Original artwork by Emily K. Grieves
Book design by Chris Molé

Library of Congress Control Number: 2022916337
ISBN: 979-8-9866555-0-5
First Edition
Printed in the United States of America

NOTE TO READER: This publication is meant as a source of valuable information for the reader; however, it is not meant as a substitute for direct expert assistance. The author is not a licensed mental health professional, and her advice is not intended as a substitute for consultation with a licensed practitioner. If such a level of assistance is required, the services of a competent professional should be sought.

For Susan

Table of Contents

A Letter to You

Dear Reader,

In 2011, one of my spirit teachers said: *Your planet is in a turbulent situation and cannot continue to exist in the ways it has been going.* Was he prophesizing our current political, socio-economic, and racial crises? Climate change disasters? The global pandemic? Vaccine polarization? Rampant gun violence? Immigration chaos? War? Choose any topic and recall a conversation you recently participated in or a report you watched on the news. Greed and self-righteousness are being placed ahead of the welfare of humanity, and there doesn't appear to be much agreement or Unity about anything.

Why has life become so polarized? Why is separation thriving?

Here's my perspective:

Too many people have forgotten that we are One being.

This collective amnesia of the Oneness of our spiritual roots creates a void within the soul and generates a fertile environment for states of separation to take root, emerge, and proliferate. While one person might become depressed and another feeds their emptiness with food or alcohol, it's when we fall down the well of extreme spiritual amnesia that internal disunity implodes and becomes outwardly destructive. We see these manifestations daily in the egocentric abuse of people, animals, and our planet.

Does having power over others fill the emptiness within? One person alone cannot awaken the entire collective, but one person *can* awaken oneself and play their part—however small it might seem—in shifting collective consciousness.

Separation was a hallmark of my abusive upbringing. It seeded within my soul when I was young, was generously fertilized by my parents, and grew to become a deep-rooted tree. I didn't realize it existed until my early thirties when Janice, my partner at the time, and I were camping at the Yuba River in Northern California.

On the first day of our trip, while bushwhacking along the river's edge and exploring off-the-beaten-track trails, by some miracle, we found ourselves in a magnificent gorge where we spent the day. I loved sunbathing on the giant rocks and refreshing myself in the cool, flowing water. But when the setting sun came all too soon, reminding us it was time to return to camp, because of our creative explorations, we didn't have a fix on how to get there. When Janice said, "It looks like we have to go through the river," I, a fire sign who fears drowning, transmuted from expansive relaxation to contracted tension. And even though Janice championed me all the way back, I coped with my vulnerability by emotionally shutting down and snapping at her.

That evening, I found myself in a ferocious inner battle—me fighting me. Since my mother had never acknowledged accountability for anything (according to her, she was always right, and my father agreed), I learned from a young age that being wrong was the worst possible character flaw. I knew I needed to apologize for my rude behavior, but admitting I'd made a mistake felt unbearable.

Janice was a saint. She witnessed my anguish, never pushed me to speak, and even though my suffering had traveled outside of me and visited her with the sturdy thickness of a glacial wall, she didn't take it personally. After hours of agonizing self-torment, I realized I had to melt the wall and surrender my internal war. At this point, it was dark and we were in our warm, homey tent. Janice was reading a short story aloud, and in the middle of a sentence, I blurted, "I am so sorry!" and collapsed into her loving arms.

Author Anaïs Nin wrote, "And the day came when the risk to remain tight in a bud was more painful than the risk it took to blossom."

My battle was finally over, and Unity—both inner and outer—had won. This profound experience of being so *disunified* within myself that I'd created a barrier to separate me from a person I loved frightened me, and on that chilly night nestled among the trees with the river's soothing melody in the background, I began uprooting my childhood tree.

Traumatic life experiences often land us in survival, separation, and spiritual amnesia. Do you feel separate—even from yourself? Alone? Unable to find purpose or meaning? Are you suffering from physical, emotional, or energetic disharmony? In my Spiritual Healing practice, I've seen how inner disunity—warring against oneself as I did at the river—can be so pronounced as to manifest physically as an auto-immune disease, when our body, which is meant to support us, turns against us instead.

How do we awaken from the trance of separation? Remember our spiritual identity? Unify within ourselves? Mother Nature is a nurturing catalyst for me. Every day, I take two long walks with Apu, my corgi-mix companion. Rain, shine, wind, or heat, this dog-enforced routine consistently reminds me of my Oneness with the Earth and inspires inner knowings and creativity. Can you fit one walk into your day? What about leaning against the tree in the local park during your lunch hour? Or, one of my favorites: go to the beach and immerse yourself in the expansiveness of the ocean. The refined energy of the natural world does wonders to clear our noisy heads, melt survival defenses, and reveal emotional fragilities.

In 1938, naturalist John Muir wrote in his journal, "The clearest way into the Universe is through a forest wilderness." As we attend to our suffering in healthy ways—spending time in nature, going to counseling, participating in Spiritual Healing—the power of our wounds diffuses and rouses us from the separation trance. Then, as we awaken, our personal "forest wilderness" will lead us "into the Universe" and remind us of our unified spiritual identity.

A huge aspect of my awakening has been the gifts I've received from people of varied cultural backgrounds and distinctive spiritual paths. From being invited to attend a traditional Native American Healing Ceremony in Oakland, California, which completely altered the course of my life, and a Sundance on the Navajo reservation in New Mexico, where I supported the dancers for three years in a row, to the Hungarian shamanic practitioners who honored me by requesting my presence at their drumming circles, to the Indian teacher in Bodh Gaya, who wouldn't let us leave town until we sat in the cave where Buddha had meditated for seven years, to the Tibetans who opened their homes and shared their spiritual lineage through huge hearts and yak butter tea—each person, ceremony, and teaching enhanced my awareness, healing abilities, and life.

I've spent the most time with the Q'ero of Peru—Indigenous peoples of the Andes mountains and direct descendants of the Inka—whose profound-yet-simple teachings infuse this book. Known as keepers of ancient knowledge and wisdom, the Q'ero see everything as living energy and consciously coexist with the Earth—whom they call Pachamama (as do I)—and the entire cosmos. Since 1996, when I first began traveling to Peru, I've become friendly with a few families, participated in dozens of ceremonies with spiritual leaders who willingly share their knowledge, and have been brought and introduced to more sacred sites than I can count. One of my most memorable experiences was being invited to attend a wedding at a 15,000-feet-above-sea-level village as the honored family godmother or *madrina*.

These multi-cultural events, teachings, and individual heart offerings stand alone and blend together as natural dyes within the unique tapestry of my spiritual life and healing work. They create a dimensionality and "rightness" that infuse my "medicine," which I share from the unified wellspring from which they arose.

Since this book is replete with "my medicine," I suppose I should define Spiritual Healing, a venerable healing style that some find "new age" and others are aware has existed since the beginning of time. Its foundation lies within our innate identity as sacred beings and weaves the mystical, energetic realms with the dense, physical world. If you asked a roomful of Spiritual Healers to describe what this fabric looks like, you'd likely receive as many answers as there are healers. Each of us partners with spirit allies—evolved *disincarnate* beings whose paths include helping us here on Earth—in distinctive ways, all outgrowths of our experiences and gifts. I imagine everyone would agree that as *incarnated* beings, we serve as vehicles for universal, cosmic forces to move through the landscapes of our souls for the purpose of restoring emotional wholeness and physical vitality to the landscapes of our clients' souls. Can Spiritual Healing cure everything? No. But it can get to the root cause of most disturbances and either relieve them (ideally) or at the very least, offer insight regarding the purpose of their presence.

I was a practicing Spiritual Healer for fifteen years before I traveled to the ruins of Teotihuacan, Mexico, in 2006 and encountered the Four-Petaled Flower. In a flash, this mysterious ancient symbol activated something deep within my soul and became an image I couldn't get enough of. A few years later, as I was co-leading a group journey at the ruins with my artist friend, Emily—whose visions grace this book—I met Sarayna, my Teotihuacana spirit teacher. She shed light on what the symbol meant in ancient times:

The Four-Petaled Flower is a symbol of the Unity of All Life. It is Wholeness, Beauty, Fragrance, Bounty, Harvest, and Union. The energy of each petal imparts its own unique quality, and the center of the flower is a fusion of all four petals and creates the energy of the entire flower, which is Unity.

Receiving this teaching enhanced my preoccupation with the Four-Petaled Flower, which by then, I was unable to imagine living without. Then, eleven years after that first sighting and energetic infusion, as I was in the process of writing this book, its presence took me by surprise— it felt like a sudden visitation. Images from the Temple of the Feathered Conches began dancing in my mind, and Sarayna's words became a constant chant. A few days later, while walking with

Apu one hot, sunny morning, the Four-Petaled Flower showed me what it wanted. I rushed home, immediately found a large sheet of white paper, and with brightly colored markers, drew what became a Medicine Wheel!

Medicine Wheels are sacred symbols of Native American culture. Each wheel is divided into quadrants that embody the special energies of the four directions (East, South, West, North) and their relationship to the four stages of life (birth, youth, adulthood, death) as well as states of being (physical, emotional, mental, spiritual). Indigenous peoples create and interpret the Medicine Wheel in their traditional ways, determining the colors, elements, animals, and plants associated with each direction. The emphasis of all Medicine Wheels is balance within the self and interconnection with Mother Nature.

Jamie Sams, a Native American author of Cherokee and Seneca descent and respected member of the Wolf Clan, wrote several books about Native American spirituality. In *The Sacred Path Cards*, she says, "The Stone Circle of the Medicine Wheel is a symbol of Sacred Ceremonial Space that has been honored by our people for centuries as a place to come and experience the beauty of the cycles of physical life. These cycles of planting, gestation, birth, growth, change, death, and rebirth are the life lessons of the Sacred Hoop."

Like the Native American Medicine Wheel, the Four-Petaled Flower is not a time-fixed idea or experience. Both are life-long (and beyond) processes. We can step into the East at any time, walk around the petals all the way to the North, enter the Center, look up and notice another flowered wheel awaiting our feet. And then another…

Join me on a journey to—as Jamie Sams states—"experience the beauty of the cycles of physical life." It begins pre-birth, in the pure Spirit Realm of Unity and Oneness, travels to Earth, where duality and suffering are commonplace, and returns full circle, at death, to the Unity of spirit. This four-petaled exploration seeks to awaken—person by person—the collective amnesia of the Oneness of our spiritual roots. Each petal along the way offers opportunities to rouse from the slumber of spiritual separation, rediscover our primal legacy, and recognize and heal inner disunity. The union of Spiritual Healing with the Four-Petaled Flower creates a mystical alchemy that has the potential to move us out of exclusive emptiness and into inclusive Unity.

Imagine yourself sitting on a cozy couch or chair in my living room surrounded by like-minded spiritual seekers. There's a wooden table in the center of our circle—a group altar that's covered with a beige-and-brown, handwoven alpaca Peruvian cloth—filled with items you and the rest of the group have brought from home. A crystal that someone's deceased mother gave her. A photo of another person's young son. A rock from a sacred mountain that the owner carries in her purse. An owl feather. Your special object.

A white, unlit candle sits in the middle.

Let's light it. Open our ceremony.

And step into the Four-Petaled Flower together.

We'll enter in the traditional starting place of all Medicine Wheels—the East, where Grandfather Sun rises every day—and explore Unity in a circular fashion, the style in which I teach and the shape of the petaled path. Allow the teachings, stories, explorations, and paintings within each petal to broaden your awareness and free you from whatever might be keeping you from living your uniquely unified Four-Petaled-Flower potential. And even though we're exploring collectively, make sure to take all the individual time you need. There's no rush. A petal might take you by surprise, and you may linger. Then, when you reach the Center, sit down for a while, and enjoy a cup of hot tea or a glass of your favorite wine. Receive. Integrate. And most important, honor yourself for the commitment and work it took to arrive there.

Every chapter in *Unity Begins Within* is enhanced by Emily's magnificent artwork. I ask that you not only admire it, for each painting stands alone, but absorb the images into your soul. Emily's artistic expressions are rays of light that will help you assimilate teachings, fertilize the earth of your memories, and enrich your spiritual awakening. I encourage you to keep a journal as a reminder of your discoveries.

As an empirical learner, I believe that whatever knowledge I attain is not just for me; it's for everyone, so after I integrate an experience, the gained wisdom becomes an educational story in my healing and teaching practice. All the narratives here are real and purposefully placed to enhance the circular teachings of the flower (although I've changed most names to protect privacy).

This brings me to reciprocity.

The Q'ero have a fundamental aspect of their cosmovision called *Ayni*. Simply put, it means sacred reciprocity. We live from our hearts and do what we can because we want to, and the positive energy of these actions will return to us in one form or another. It's not,

"I'll take you out for dinner tonight and you can take me out tomorrow" (although it can be). It's more like, "I'll take you out for dinner tonight because it's something I want to do, and I expect nothing in return." But there will be a return because Ayni is universally stored. So, you might receive it as an abundance of good luck, a healthy physical exam, or a bountiful garlic crop—nothing you would relate to the dinner.

In the spirit of Ayni, I offer this book to every person who has crossed my path. Where would I be without you? And I offer it to each group who shared their culture and spirituality with me, wisely understanding that *all* paths lead to remembering and living Unity. By unifying their diverse teachings, I hope to help you unearth a treasure chest of buried knowledge, explore new thoughts, and experience a rebirth of Self. Everything here is my truth—one person's experiences and the resulting knowledge. It is not The Truth, for what human being can know that?

My prayer is for you to awaken to *your* truth.

Separation and disunity can be a little like a privet tree, an invasive species in Northern California that constantly reseeds itself. Is there something like it where you live? Let's be vigilant, notice new sprouts, and pull them out by the roots. One by one, we can do our part to change a "turbulent situation" into something stable and sustainable. And here's the magic: Each awakening—yours, mine, and everyone's—becomes an elixir that permeates the collective spiritual amnesia and inspires it to rub its sleepy eyes and begin remembering, living, and seeing Unity everywhere.

Open-hearted Blessings,

April

CHAPTER ONE

The Unfolding of a Spiritual Healer

A medicine man shouldn't be a saint. He should experience and feel all the ups and downs, the despair and joy, the magic and the reality, the courage and the fear, of his people. He should be able to sink as low as a bug or soar as high as an eagle. Unless he can experience both, he is no good as a medicine man.

— JOHN FIRE LAME DEER, *Lame Deer, Seeker of Visions*

I was born in 1953 on April Fool's Day, and from my earliest years dreamt of becoming a teacher. In grammar school, my younger sister, Susan, and I arranged a corner of our shared bedroom where we placed a blackboard with colored chalk and a small wooden table with two blue plastic chairs. After "real" school ended, Susan's friend came over and we all "played" school. As the teacher, I creatively expanded upon whatever I'd learned that day and even designed tests, which my two willing students took (and I loved grading with my red, felt-tipped marker.) In tenth grade, I began writing short stories and decided that when I grew up, I was going to become a high school English teacher and writer.

We were a middle-class family, and while Susan and I always had our basic needs met, neither of our parents seemed to care who we were or what we might be interested in. Their focus was control and making sure that anything we did appeared to others the way they thought it should. My father traveled for his job, and when at home, deferred to my mother. A strange energy circulated in the house. It was our norm, so I was used to it, yet whenever I spent time with my friends and their families—in the flow of love and safety—a deep sadness would arise. Why couldn't I have that?

My parents and extended family are Jewish, but nobody taught Susan and me anything about Judaism. When I was ten years old, I wanted to experience Temple and asked a friend if I might join her family. I dressed up in my favorite clothes—a multi-colored flowered skirt, velvety blue top, and matching blue tights. (That was the style back then.) She and I sat in the back seat of her family's brown station wagon, and once we arrived, everyone—her mother, father, brother, and us—walked into the

Temple together. This simple, normal experience of healthy belonging had me on the brink of tears.

The building was large (to my ten-year-old perspective), and while the wooden benches were uncomfortable, we were in one of the first rows facing a wide stage filled with colorful, ornate objects. Even as a child, I knew they were sacred. I felt like I was in the audience of a play that was unfolding, as the Rabbi—his voice deep and forceful—spoke aloud to us, read from a book, and silently prayed. When the cantor sang ancient songs in a haunting, unknown language, I closed my eyes and felt the rhythmic intonations move into my soul. The reverence in the room was tangible. I loved the experience—the feeling of community, the presence of spirit I had no name for, and most of all, being part of a family who cared about me, at least for a few hours.

On Jewish holidays, my sister and I were allowed to stay home from school—but there was a catch—if we went outside, where someone might see us, we had to wear skirts. Even as kids, we understood this had nothing to do with being Jewish and everything to do with looking and playing the part. Inside, we celebrated Christmas with a tree and presents. My big lessons about religion began in ninth grade. Not only did I have a blond-haired, blue-eyed, non-Jewish boyfriend, but to make matters worse, he was from

The reverence in the room was tangible. I loved the experience— the feeling of community, the presence of spirit I had no name for, and most of all, being part of a family who cared about me, at least for a few hours.

the "other side" of town. This inspired my normally detached father to bring me into his home office and, with a depth of seriousness I rarely witnessed, pontificate about the immorality of mixing religions. Christmas died in our house that year, and we celebrated Hannukah instead, although no one taught Susan and me what the ritual meant.

My father's parents—Grandma May and Grandpa Fred—were culturally Jewish, but they lived in another state and didn't have much influence on me. My mother's parents—Grandma Tillie and Grandpa Louis—lived closer. They were my special elders. I loved going to their house and eating homemade Jewish pastries and chicken soup with matzo balls.

I was a non-rebellious daughter, more conservative than most of my classmates, but not as perfect as my mother expected, so during my senior year of high school, she stopped speaking to me. I don't recall why but do remember that her silence lasted the entire year. This was in 1970/1971 when I was eighteen years old. Back then, I wanted to attend the local community college and begin realizing my teaching dream, but living in that house was a dysfunctional nightmare and I had to get out. Since my mother was wedded to her shut-down mode, I asked my father for help. His reply, "Either live here or don't go to college," was devastating.

I knew if I stayed in my parents' home, I would never survive emotionally, so in June, after my high school graduation ceremony—which no one in my family attended (including me)—I found an old suitcase in the basement and packed some clothes. My mother stopped by my room, eyed me coldly, and said, "Whatever you don't take, I'm throwing away," and promptly turned her back and walked out the door. I had a much-loved childhood doll, "Betsy Wetsy," and even though I was well past the age for dolls, I packed her safely among my clothes.

On moving day, before getting into a friend's car, I turned around for one last look at the childhood and family I was leaving behind. My mother had already gone to work. My father silently peered at me through his upstairs office window. And Susan, with whom I'd shared little since our days of playing school, wasn't there either. Our sisterhood was complicated, and once I was gone, our minimal communication ended.

I adopted a new sister—survival.

Searching for Meaning

Who are we? Why are we here? I've sought answers to these elusive existential questions for as long as I can remember. Since life couldn't only be about what I'd learned from my parents, I continued the spiritual quest I'd begun as a ten-year-old. At nineteen, I was living in Boston, where friends and I ventured to the local Krishna temple. If you arrived early and participated in the devotional chanting, which we did, they let you stay for a free dinner. I loved the food; basmati rice dishes laden with spicy, coconut-milk curries are still one of my favorite meals.

We went again the following week, which was when I had an unexpected experience in the prayer room. Amid the overpowering scent of incense, an abundance of statues of sacred deities, and devotees rhythmically chanting, "Hare Krishna. Hare Krishna. Krishna. Hare," my body spontaneously tensed, adrenaline surged, and I became flooded with a feeling that I was doing something wrong. The anxiety grew, and as it peaked, a strong inner knowing erupted: worshiping any*thing* or *one* was not for me. So even though the aroma of the evening's curry permeated the room and enticed my tastebuds, integrity did not allow me to stay for dinner.

My pull toward spirituality continued. For a short while I explored Sufism, the Islamic belief of seeking knowledge of God through direct experience, and while this included dancing, which I liked, Sufism didn't offer satisfying answers to my countless questions. I traversed books and paths—the writings of P.D. Ouspensky, Ram Dass, and Carlos Castaneda, as well as works on Buddhism, Tarot, and Theosophy—searching for the central teachings I believed the others must spring from. Why didn't one religion explain it all? I wanted the ocean, not the rivers or tributaries flowing into it.

When I was twenty-two and out one night with a friend, I overheard a conversation that piqued my curiosity. It was about Eckankar, a spiritual teaching that offered tools to explore and develop one's own relationship with the Divine. Had I found the ocean?

Eckankar, which means "co-worker with God," was the first path that both satiated my metaphysical quandaries and expanded my awareness about the mystical aspects of existence. I walked upon it for a few years and even received a second-level initiation, but eventually became disenchanted. Devotion to the Living Eck Master, a tenet of Eckankar, was a practice I couldn't embrace, and although my involvement phased out, invaluable teachings about karma, reincarnation, the expansion of consciousness, and spiritual Light and Sound, remained.

Marriage, Motherhood, and Midwifery

It took too many years for me to recognize the long-lasting emotional harm my upbringing caused. I became pregnant at twenty-six and married my baby's father, a man with combined qualities (unfortunately, not the good ones) of both my parents. Being pregnant was a blessing, but my marriage was not. Nevertheless, I had an empowered homebirth, a rite of passage that unearthed my innate perseverance and strength and transformed me into a more vibrant and awake version of myself.

I loved being a mother and tried hard to create a healthy home for my son, but it takes two committed parents for this, and the dynamic between my husband and me made it impossible. I left the marriage shortly after turning thirty, an act that initiated a ceaseless phase of dealing with the constant ramifications of my ex's need for power, something he appeared to desire more than the welfare of our son whose custody we shared.

Then, on my thirty-fifth birthday, instead of receiving a celebratory card from my parents (we had reconciled for a while), I opened a brief, typewritten letter that began by stating what a bad person I was and always had been, and ended with, "Therefore, we are disowning you." That was their word: disowning. My ex-husband happily entered their family, and the daily difficulties I faced raising my son increased exponentially.

Throughout it all, I found myself magnetized to everything childbirth-related and participated in a local "labor coach" (now called "doula") training and began supporting pregnant women and couples at their births. The work was rewarding, but it soon became difficult to be immersed in the emotional lives and hopes of my clients only to arrive at the hospital and defer to decisions made by the medical staff. Pulled by a strong desire to safeguard the sanctity of childbirth, I joined a midwifery class taught by Elizabeth Davis, a local homebirth midwife who'd recently written *Heart & Hands: A Midwife's Guide to Pregnancy and Birth*. I was living in Berkeley, California, at the time, and it was an easy drive (on trafficless days) over the Bay Bridge to San Francisco, where she taught and practiced. Before the course was over, Elizabeth offered me an apprenticeship—a phenomenal opportunity that led to my primary-care midwifery practice. In tandem, Suzanne—a woman I'd met at the labor coach workshop the previous year—and I created Full Circle Childbirth Services, through which we designed and implemented diverse birth-related classes and workshops in the Bay Area. I'd finally become a teacher!

Spiritual Awakening

At thirty-eight, I found true love, married again, and believed it would last forever. But love *is* blind. At least it was for me. My remarkable, open-hearted husband was an addict who was unwilling to get help, and my forever lasted only nine months. Shortly after our separation—which would become a prolonged heartache—during the summer of 1992, my twelve-year-old son and I went camping at Yosemite National Park. We spent our time hiking, swimming, cooking on the outdoor fire, and ending each fulfilling day with s'mores. At night, after we got into our tent and he fell asleep, I snuggled in my sleeping bag, turned on the flashlight, and read two books my ex had left at the house: *The Way of the Shaman* by Michael Harner and *Black Elk Speaks* by John G. Neihardt. It was new material for me, and the teachings and stories reached inside my soul and brought me to what felt like a precipice over a limitless expanse. Upon returning home, I enrolled in a shamanic journeying workshop and was then embraced by a

perfect full circle—the director of the local Native American Health Center asked if I'd be interested in teaching labor support and childbirth education to her staff. There was only one answer: *Yes.*

She invited me to a Yuwipi ceremony, a traditional healing ritual led by a Medicine Man from the Lakota Nation of South Dakota. It was a special, one-time event. I didn't know anything about it or realize how much honor her invitation bestowed, but I absolutely wanted to go and asked my friend Lisa, always up for a new experience, to venture into the unknown with me. The ceremony took place in Oakland, California, at the Native American Meeting House—which, if memory serves, was the size of an exceptionally large living room with an industrial-type kitchen off to the side.

Lisa and I were the only non-Natives present, and since everyone seemed to know what was going on but us, we leaned shyly against the wall and watched the organizers prepare the space for about sixty people. First, they created a small, central circle made up of the Medicine Man, drummers, and singers. A larger circle formed around them for people seeking healing, and an even larger outer circle, where Lisa and I sat, surrounded everyone. The ceremony needed to take place in complete darkness, and black plastic bags were tacked over every window to assure not even a glimmer of light could shine through.

When the electric lights were suddenly turned off, a mysterious fear of blindness emerged and settled in my stomach. I was in knots. Afraid. In my mind's eye, I saw myself frantically running from the room into the safety of a lighted area, but I knew if I did, I'd miss out on everything. My physical eyes desperately searched for any remaining traces of light—there had to be one—and I found it. The sliver coming in through a window across the room was enough to assure me I wasn't blind. I relaxed, the pit in my stomach digested, and I settled into the moment.

While the drummers rhythmically played two large ceremonial drums and the singers vocalized ancient Lakota healing songs, a deep, masculine voice suddenly interrupted my serenity. "Robert" (the Medicine Man's name), the voice said. "There's light coming in through that window over there." Everything stopped. The room fell silent, and all the electric lights suddenly turned on. It was so bright I thought the sun was shining in the center of the room. There went my lifeline. I breathed deeply, reoriented, and while the helpers patched the window, I took Lisa's hand, squeezed it, and held on tight.

The next time darkness descended I knew I was okay.

The Medicine Man said, "The healing spirits will manifest as sparkling lights." And specified,

When the electric lights were suddenly turned off, a mysterious fear of blindness emerged and settled in my stomach. I was in knots. Afraid. In my mind's eye, I saw myself frantically running from the room into the safety of a lighted area, but I knew if I did, I'd miss out on everything.

"It's important to refrain from touching them." The reverberating drums, combined with what sounded like ancient vocal intonations—from low to high and high to low—transported me into an intoxicating, otherworldly expansion. I had no idea what the Medicine Man was doing, but in the darkness, I began seeing what looked like hundreds of twinkling stars and hearing rattles being shaken so close, I thought physical people were encircling me. We were truly in the presence of healing spirits. At one point, Lisa released my hand, and when a breeze touched my skin, I realized she was waving her arms in a state of ecstasy. I had no idea she had accidentally touched a light.

A discombobulated and fearful Lisa arrived at my house early the next morning. "A spirit from the ceremony contacted me in the night," she said. "I can still feel his presence." We didn't know what to do, but were clear about one thing—we needed to ground. Using our imaginations, we each visualized a cord of energy within the center of our bodies that we breathed down, out, and as far into the Earth as possible. Once we felt solid and connected, we lay on the floor and held hands. My job was to stay grounded and trusting. Lisa was feeling the spirit's presence and had the task of giving voice to the message, and even though she was trembling, she was able to receive our very first teaching from the Spirit Realm: *You must grow your respect for men.* We were not surprised to hear this.

I had read about channeling, a dynamic dialogue where a person becomes the voice for unembodied beings and acts as a bridge between the spirit world and this one. Some people enter a trance state to accomplish this. Others, like Lisa, remain present, and spontaneously speak the spirit's words or use their own to describe images they're being shown or the instant awareness they're having.

Communicating with spirits was a new experience for Lisa and me, and little did we know our first encounter was the beginning of weekly sessions, a commitment that lasted two years. Initially, we responded intuitively to our unusual challenges, but over time, Lisa evolved into a proficient channeler, while I remained the inquisitive questioner. We received diverse teachings from Chief Flying Eagle, the spirit from the Yuwipi ceremony who first visited Lisa, but it didn't take long until other members of his community stepped in: Latunda, the chief's wife; Sitting Bear, midwife and healer; and Diningneedle, mentor for young women. Like the Medicine Man, our new friends were of the Lakota nation. They called themselves the Milky Way Village spirits.

Our spirit teachers encouraged Lisa and me not to place them on a pedestal. We were just like them, they said—although at the moment, we were embodied, and they weren't. They taught us there's a purpose for everything that occurs, a spiritual overview we only needed to look for. The Milky Way Village spirits were essential healers and teachers for me during the initial years of separation from my husband. They opened my eyes to new angles of vision that allowed me to heal and move on in ways I might never have managed on my own.

As my suffering over the sudden end of my marriage finally receded, I became ready to explore something else. I was still working in childbirth at the time—teaching classes for aspiring professionals and attending homebirths as a midwife—and wanted to know, "Within the Spirit Realm overview, what is happening from conception through postpartum?" Each week, I brought a new topic to our meetings. I asked the questions, and Lisa channeled the answers, which often led me to ask more questions. We recorded everything, and once I transcribed the tapes (it was in the early 1990s), I shared the information with students, clients, and friends. The teachings we received changed lives.

CHANNELING

Amid all this, I decided I wanted to learn how to channel, and after multiple rocky starts—becoming disoriented, not being grounded enough, letting my mind interfere—I finally became as skilled as Lisa.

Today, whenever I want to learn about something, I bring together open, like-minded people for a channeling session. Our first task is to decide on our questions. Once we're satisfied, we ground ourselves, open a ceremony, and invite the most evolved spirit teacher from the Light to speak with us. There are limitless disincarnate beings, so it's vital to be specific and engage only with the most advanced. This is where energetic discernment, which comes with experience, is invaluable.

I close my eyes and focus on my heart/soul space, the area in the center of my chest, and create a grounded connection with the Earth. Once I sense an energetic presence, I breathe and notice. If it's a being whom I'm already familiar with—like my Teacher or Ezekiel, two outstanding spirits you'll soon meet—I might begin speaking their message to the group immediately. (Once invited in, the spirits are ready.) If it's someone new, I make sure the energy is refined, loving, and safe before engaging. There have been a few times when I've felt uncomfortable, and instantly said, "No." Afterward, I re-grounded, even deeper, and began again. This rarely happens, but it's important for you to know it's possible.

If the new energy feels right, I silently ask the spirit to identify itself and continue in the ways I described—by spontaneously speaking its words or using my own to illustrate images I'm being shown or the instant awareness I'm having. Most of the time, the spirit begins with a message, and when that's complete, the designated questioner asks questions.

An entire session lasts about two hours (I channel for an hour), and we close each one by offering gratitude. I like to re-ground before opening my eyes, which is when I have the honor of beholding the beautiful, friendly faces of the people who have been sitting across from me. We gaze at one another in awe, and then—almost without fail—spontaneously burst out laughing. The entire process and experience are boundless and otherworldly. Everyone loves it.

Channeling an evolved spiritual being is amazing. The teachings tend to arrive through our linear minds, but since reality is far more expansive than anyone's mind can grasp, the guides offer information that meets our level of consciousness, then stretches us out so we can open further. I don't know how they do this. It's fascinating to listen to a session months and even years after the teachings were given and notice information I initially missed. The dimensionality is mind-blowing.

I'll always be grateful for my partnership with Lisa. Our fearless commitment to growth birthed profound spiritual insights that continue to evolve and influence me and many others.

Hands-on Healing

During that same period, the early nineties, I wanted to learn how to become a vehicle for Light. It's one thing to channel the wisdom of an evolved, disincarnate being, but another altogether to access cosmic energy or spiritual Light for the purpose of healing. I traveled to San Diego and attended a four-day, hands-on healing workshop taught by Barbara Brennan, Spiritual Healer and author of the breakthrough book, *Hands of Light, A Guide to Healing*

Through the Human Energy Field. When I returned home, I wondered if I should enroll in her school. There was no doubt that becoming a healer was my destiny, but the school was on the East Coast (I was still in California) and expensive for my budget. I asked Sitting Bear, through Lisa, about this, and she said: *You can go to the school and learn how to heal like them, or you can just heal.* I chose the latter. And, via the template we were taught at the workshop of combining specific hand placement with a conscious intent to become a channel for healing Light, I opened to spirit teachers and began practicing on students and friends.

Hands-on healing, not unlike channeling spiritual wisdom, is a multi-dimensional undertaking that demands absolute integrity. From those "newbie" days to this present moment, it continues to be an honor to put my invisible "healer hat" on my head, place my hands upon someone, and become a conduit for Light. Like participating in the miracle of childbirth—it never grows old.

Only a year after learning hands-on healing, the next step in my evolution as a healer surprised me—teach it. I was still offering childbirth-related classes and had begun teaching shamanic journeying workshops, but hands-on healing was a relatively recent skill, and I was a little insecure about what to do. I decided if I worked solely with students who already knew me, they could support my evolving process, so I created an invitation-only series. The response was humbling. On the first evening of a six-month commitment, twelve eager participants, eleven women and one man, sat in my physical living room (unlike the mystical living room you're sitting in) ready to explore. These gracious students allowed me to expand, gain my footing, and become the healer I am today. Yes, I was the official teacher, but we were immersed in this new aspect of my education together.

MEMORIES

Healers can't focus only on helping others; we must attend to our own healing as well. I call this "the two-footed walk." I see one foot as my healer foot, and the other as my personal foot. Occasionally, when I'm enjoying a long healer-foot phase, I hear my personal foot calling, "Hey! You've gotten too far ahead. Pay attention to me." It might not be the best timing (Is there ever a "best" timing?), but I recognize this voice as an aspect of my soul, and I stop, listen, and give it the respect it deserves. Every time I do this, energy frees up, and not only does my personal foot take a big step forward, my healer foot does as well. Ideally, both walk together (or sometimes run!) in a balanced, grounded symmetry, navigating diverse terrain.

During the time I was teaching the first hands-on healing series, I began feeling there was more to heal from my childhood—I suppose my "personal" foot was ready to lead—so I consulted an energy healer. At our third session, I naively stated, "I want to shed whatever is keeping me from my personal power."

I lay on the healing table in relaxed surrender and trust, and the instant she placed her hands on my feet and the energy began flowing, something extraordinary happened. My system was inundated with previously unknown memories of childhood sexual abuse accompanied by newly unearthed body sensations and profuse emotional anguish. I'd had inklings…*Did something happen to me as a child?…*, yet the distinct remembrance of this truth lay hidden until that moment.

Sexual abuse creates an exceptionally painful experience of disunity. How is it possible to believe that the people who are supposed to love, protect, and care for us can be the most hurtful? How did I live through it? Why did it take me forty-two years to remember? And how did my body store all the energy?

I wanted to heal as thoroughly as possible and began seeing an insightful, fearless, nontraditional therapist. The work was predominately experiential and intensely challenging. Breathing. Yelling. Anger. Tears. It was scary to release emotions far beyond anything I ever imagined possible, but it was also liberating—for as I surrendered, the details of what I'd felt was "off" in my family, including the oddly distant relationship with my sister, Susan, gradually clarified.

I was sexually abused by my father from age three until about nine. First, it was only me, then he alternated between me and Susan. When it became only Susan, any sense of respite automatically merged with guilt over what was happening to my sister in the next bed. Our mother knew. We were living in a one-bedroom apartment at the time, and my parents slept on a sofa bed in the hallway just outside our room. This is where she would lie, waiting for him to finish.

Since regaining these memories, I've thought about my mother's childhood. Why hadn't she protected her little girls? Her father, Grandpa Louis, was always good to Susan and me, but had he molested her? Did this explain why any time I developed a close relationship with an elder—the dance teacher, a neighbor I loved babysitting for, my aunt, the family who took me to Temple—my mother made sure to put an end to it? Was she afraid I'd tell? As my gifted therapist guided me into and through these torturous memories, I wondered if my mother's harsh, detached ways were related to guilt, fear, or even jealousy. I suppose she had to be controlling if she wanted to protect the secret. And as far as my father…I'll never understand why he found it perfectly normal to violate his young daughters.

Sexual abuse engenders separation. Not only within the self—for our very survival necessitates not only detaching from the event as it occurs, but also participating in crazy-making relationships with

Healers can't focus only on helping others; we must attend to our own healing as well. I call this "the two-footed walk." I see one foot as my healer foot, and the other as my personal foot.

our abusers, many of whom are family members. As I said earlier, I wasn't allowed to spend alone time with any adult either inside or outside of my family. Susan and I lived this separation, even with each other. And while therapy and Spiritual Healing have helped me reunify the formerly scattered puzzle pieces of my life, my sister was not so lucky.

It's difficult to find a correct statistic for childhood sexual abuse because most of it, like Susan's and mine, is unreported. Many say it happens to one out of four boys and one out of three girls. *That's a lot of people.* If this was part of your childhood, or you have an inkling like I did, seek support. Talk therapy can be helpful for a while, but survival lives within our cells, and the decisions we make about life are based on experiences. Work with a trustworthy person who has delved into the abyss of their emotional past and emerged with personal and professional roots as deep as an oak tree. That's the "midwife" you want by your side.

PHUTU CUSI

While I was walking the two-footed walk—concurrently attending weekly therapy appointments and teaching the Spiritual Healing class—I became drawn to the Andes Mountains of Peru. That September of 1996, John, my friend and a class participant, and I joined a group of seven others traveling there to participate in an initiation that facilitates movement out of the third level of human consciousness and into the fourth. Our leader was Juan Nuñez del Prado, anthropologist, Andean mystic, and keeper of an ancient Inka prophecy that speaks about the unfolding of twelve levels. The trip was called "The Hatun Karpay" or "Great Initiation."

Juan's father, anthropologist Oscar Nuñez del Prado, is credited with "discovering" the Q'ero in 1955, and when Juan was ten, he met these "masters of the living energy," as author Jane Parisi Wilcox later called them in her book of the same name. Juan followed in his father's footsteps and became an anthropologist, but his life took an unexpected turn. While he was doing academic research on Andean spirituality, Juan met Don Benito Q'oriwaman, a famous healer living in a valley near Cusco. "After that," Juan said, as quoted in Wilcox's book, "my intellectual paradigm was blown." He studied with Don Benito for ten years as well as with four other fourth- or fifth-level Q'ero paqos (shamans) during and after that time. Since then, Juan has become an expert on the Andean mystical traditions and shares these sacred teachings around the world.

According to this nameless, difficult-to-summarize prophecy, most of humanity is living in the third level of consciousness—which is dominated by fear and separation—yet when we reach the fourth level, we choose love over fear and Unity over separation. This was the purpose of our ten remarkable days—to participate in ceremonies and teachings that Juan had received over the course of a decade, so we had the tools and preparation to evolve into the fourth level.

Then, when enough people worldwide are living love and Unity, collective consciousness will heighten the opportunity for six women and six men to rise to the fifth level, where each of them will have the ability to heal all illnesses with a single touch. The sixth level involves the emergence of enlightened leaders who literally shine, and the seventh, as Parisi writes, is the level of "Supreme Creative Principle," which is "not achieved by humans alone, but through our collective, collaborative interchanges with nature."

During the Hatun Karpay, we spent three glorious days visiting Machu Picchu, the fifteenth-century Inka citadel. During our first bus ride up the steep, switch-backed road to the ruins, where we were surrounded by the majestic Andes at every turn, I found myself wildly magnetized to one mountain in particular. It looked like a giant crystal with two peaks, one rounded and the other smaller and pointier. Although it wasn't as tall as the others, this lush, forest-green being (as I would come to know her) emanated Mount Everest-like power, and each time the bus wound around the road and it came into view, I exclaimed, "John, look at that mountain!"

I was entranced.

Juan told us, "Her name is Phutu Cusi, which means Flowering Joy, and she's the only female Apu (mountain spirit) at Machu Picchu." As I spent more time at the ruins, I discovered Phutu Cusi wasn't powerful to me alone; the Inka placed almost every stone window in view of her.

Yes, I had fallen in love with a mountain, an Apu who, I believed, had summoned me to Peru. My heart nearly broke when it was time to say goodbye. I had no idea that even though I was leaving Phutu Cusi, she wasn't leaving me.

A few days before Christmas that same year, I was sitting under the "Spirit Tree," a large grandmother acacia growing at the far end of my backyard in Piedmont, California. Countless ceremonies had taken place under her embracing foliage and watchful gaze, and a naturally formed bowl in the heart of her branches held years of offerings from clients and students. The birds were singing their evening songs, and as I leaned against her trunk and immersed myself in their harmonies, a surprise visitor entered my consciousness. Phutu Cusi!

Once I attuned myself to her energy (in the same way as during a channeling session), she informed me (I was channeling Phutu Cusi!) that two thousand years ago, tyrannical magicians had placed an invisible seal at her base to block the dynamic power of Pachamama from flowing up through her body and into the atmosphere.

The world needed this divine feminine energy now, she said, and she wanted me to remove the seal. I had no idea how to accomplish such a thing, and although Phutu Cusi was unwilling to tell me, I eagerly agreed to her wishes.

Shamanic Initiation: Part One

At certain stages of the journey your faith is strong, but then sometimes it quivers a little bit. So, you have to find ways to explore your doubts.

—Ram Dass, "Methods for Strengthening Our Faith"

Before I share this story, I'd like to make a few disclaimers. The first is a reminder about my spiritual upbringing. While Judaism was my family's religion, there were no Temple visits, religious instruction, or holiday celebrations. Compared with how my friend Naomi was raised—in a family very active in the Jewish faith—I grew up with a lack of religious teachings and had little to no Jewish identification instilled in me. As Naomi and I grew older and began wondering about the purpose of life, I was virtually a blank slate, with no ideologies or doctrines to compare my thoughts and experiences to. This absence of spiritual identity made my search a little easier than Naomi's, who had to sift through multiple layers of instilled beliefs before discovering her own, which ended up being more mystically oriented than she had been taught.

Next…in 1973, when I was twenty years old, my boyfriend and I were visiting his family's house during Easter, and one lazy afternoon we were watching *The King of Kings*, a movie about the life of Jesus. At one point during the film, I became overwhelmed by what felt like a never-ending déjà vu,

a palpable memory wave that transported me into a clear awakening—I had lived during those times. That experience opened a doorway into a surprising, yet somehow familiar past that consistently shows up as I walk my spiritual path.

Throughout this book, you'll recognize several names of my spirit helpers. If any remind you of childhood religious instruction you might have received or been force-fed, I ask you to please take a leap. Be like Naomi and sift through your layers of instilled beliefs so you might discover those that have been *yours* all along. I hope you can see these beings not just as spiritual icons but also as evolved people, like I do.

Now it's story time.

My visitation from Phutu Cusi occurred at a time when I was channeling Mother Mary for the hands-on healing class. To some, she is the mother of Jesus, and to others, one of many diverse aspects of the Divine Mother. Mary was offering the group guidance on how to become powerful healers. When a student asked, "What do we need to learn next?" she responded:

The miraculous healings you wish to accomplish are not difficult, yet they take Faith and Trust. When there is Faith, Trust, and acknowledgment of oneself as Divine, healings are simple, for they follow the knowing. But the knowing must be accomplished first. I will help you develop Faith and Trust, but you must first explore your doubts. As doubt fades, Faith materializes. Call unto me. I will help you release your doubts. I wish for you to be prepared. It is a misconception that you are less capable healers than I am.

I wanted to accomplish the miraculous healings Mary spoke about and so I prayed daily, asking her to help me release fears or doubts I had about anything—the existence and presence of spiritual realms, the Unity of all beings, and whatever else. My prayer was as passionate as when I saw the energy healer and asked to shed whatever was keeping me from my personal power. Because I hadn't yet understood the potency of shedding and releasing whatever was "in my way," I had no idea about the depth of chaos and dysfunction that could arise. Too shortsighted (and maybe doubtful) to consider that anything might manifest on this physical plane, after a month, I was unexpectedly propelled into a dramatic encounter with my most ingrained and unconscious fears and doubts.

It happened on January 21, 1997, when I was forty-four years old. I had completed a healing for a client, when Michon, a close friend and integral member of the healing group, joined me on some errands. We were at the copy shop, attending to a perfectly mundane task, when without warning, a sense of otherworldliness began overlaying my present-moment reality. It reminded me of how I'd felt at the Yuwipi ceremony. I assumed it was a result of the refined energy I'd recently channeled for my client, until...*WHOOSH!* A sleeper wave of energy rushed through me. *WHOOSH.* Then another. *WHOOSH.* Time appeared to stop, and I felt detached, as if I were an actor in a movie. I didn't understand what was happening, but one thing became clear: I had to get home.

I drove carefully (it was only a few minutes), parked the car, and with a concerned Michon on my heels, rushed up the stairs in a state of intense urgency. As soon as I unlocked the door, I understood: *I was going to die.* "Michon, we have to go to the Spirit Tree right now!" I frantically poured myself some water, pulled pictures of my seventeen-year-old son off the wall, cradled them in my arms, and raced outside to the tree. Thus began my initiation—not into death, as I'd originally believed—but rebirth.

During childbirth when a woman is in labor, she frequently feels as if she's dying, and she is—an old life is ending, and she's being reborn into a new one: motherhood. When she enters the intensive transition phase, she needs to be reminded of what's happening—that each rigorous and challenging contraction is normal—and opens her cervix the final bit so she can push her baby out.

I'd been thrust into the transition phase of an energetic labor, but unlike my clients, I hadn't known I was pregnant!

In most labors, a transition contraction arrives every couple of minutes and lasts ninety seconds, each becoming more acute than the previous. I imagine my tsunami-like contractions lasted about the same amount of time, yet instead of opening my physical body so I could push a baby out, they were expanding my energetic body and pushing *me* out.

Caught in a continuous series of energetic waves that I believed were intent on taking me away from everything I knew and loved, I did what women in labor do—surfed the contractions with my breath. This helped for a while, until I realized I was moving toward what I intuitively knew was the Death Gateway, a place I'd never heard of until that moment. That's when paralyzing fear and instantaneous knowing overtook me.

I discovered that upon death, when a spirit leaves the body, it moves through a long, grayish, energetic tunnel known (to me) as the Death Gateway. This tunnel eventually merges with a tunnel of Light, which expands into pure Light where there are no more tunnels, only unlimited, boundary-less Light.

Caught in a continuous series of energetic waves that I believed were intent on taking me away from everything I knew and loved, I did what women in labor do—surfed the contractions with my breath.

With each relentless wave, the Spirit Realm began feeling more tangible than the physical. "I'm not leaving. I'm not leaving!" I screamed, using all my will to keep from being swept away in the current. With barely time to breathe, I knew that if I became the least bit distracted, or my will wavered *for even one second*, I would slide through the tunnels and into the Light. "Michon, help keep me here. Don't let me go."

I became too big for my physical body to contain, and the further I expanded beyond it, the more I felt its insignificance. I was simultaneously in multiple dimensions and levels of awareness. Human me tried to submerge myself into the cool, moist dirt at the base of the Spirit Tree, while at the same time, my energy body peeled, like cling wrap, from my physical body as I felt and watched myself move through the gateway.

How do you fight against a river's current as it surges into the open mouth of the ocean? I needed a foothold in the present if I was going to move against the flow. It wasn't my time to die! I had a son I loved beyond measure. I would not die.

"Annie," said Michon, midwife extraordinaire who miraculously understood and continuously reminded me of what was happening. "You're in a massive expansion. Panic creates constriction. Embrace the expansion and know that you're safe."

This multi-faceted, hellish exposure and immersion into my fears and doubts flashed through myriad phases. I felt alone. Terrified. In panic-stricken primal survival. I experienced neither Oneness nor Unity with anything. The thought of calling to Mother Mary never occurred to me. At one point, I believed evil forces were pushing me out of my body and into the Death Gateway.

I doubted everything I'd learned from my loving, benevolent spirit friends and related to only one thing—Michon—whose devoted support fed my will.

The intensity, which must have lasted four or five hours, felt endless, yet the waves finally calmed, and I no longer felt like I was dying. As I became more present and coherent, Midwife Michon suggested that I go inside the house. I concurred.

But first I leaned against the Spirit Tree, placed my forehead solidly against her bark, and kissed her. "Thank you," I whispered. Then I turned my back and walked away. Michon followed. Once inside, she recognized how ungrounded I was and asked, "Are you ready to come back into your body?"

"Yes."

And then, "How do you want to call yourself in?"

"I want to drum."

She instructed me to get the hoop drum I use for ceremonies, sat me in front of a mirror, and told me to drum myself in. And I did, while calling to my spirit guides who I *finally* knew were with me. *Boom. Boom. Boom. Boom!* I stared into the mirror, rhythmically beat the drum, breathed into my body, and grew a new grounding cord. The instant it entered Earth, I wept.

That was my pushing stage, and I was the newborn.

SHAMANIC INITIATION: PART TWO

Ask, and it will be given to you; seek and you will find;
knock, and it will be opened to you.

— MATTHEW 7:7

THE WAVES RETURNED THREE DAYS LATER. I'd been out hiking with my friend Elizabeth, and raced home, fear exploding through my veins. It was clear I didn't have the strength or will to birth myself a second time, and I asked Elizabeth to call other friends to help me. When shamanic healer Jane and hands-on healers Nicole and Dawn finally arrived, they found me walking around the house manically, clutching my medicine bundle to my chest. In labor once again.

Jane took over. The women grounded, opened a ceremony, and purified with sage. Then they drummed, rattled, and asked the most powerful spiritual beings for their assistance. I was possessed by the need to move around, and when Jane told me to lie down on the floor next to her, I thought she was crazy. I couldn't imagine being still. She asked if I wanted to return to my body and live. *Absolutely—yes!* I wanted to be my son's mother. I promised Phutu Cusi I would help. I had an entire life to live.

Jane lay down on one side of me, Dawn on the other, and both held my hands. I stared at the ceiling while Nicole drummed, and Jane journeyed on my behalf. At one point, I sensed she was struggling, and fear moved through my blood and saturated my body. What if she couldn't help? Jane finally sat up, blew formerly scattered soul-parts into my heart and the crown of my head, and then picked up her rattle and shook it all around me, sealing everything in. She placed a copper ring on my finger and said, "All of your bodies are wedded to your physical body," and then, "You are wedded to yourself and to the Earth." We embraced amid a river of flowing tears and mutual relief.

Unfortunately, I was still feeling energy waves, and yes, fear. It was amazing how much I had. My friends decided we should go for a walk. It was a moonless night, and the neighborhood streets were empty, so we had the world to ourselves. The crisp air invigorated me, and the trees—a different species from the Spirit Tree—were soothing. Overhead, hundreds of bright, twinkling stars connected me

I was possessed by the need to move around, and when Jane told me to lie down on the floor next to her, I thought she was crazy. I couldn't imagine being still.

to something far outside of myself. *I liked having a body.*

When we returned to the house, Nicole ran a warm, lavender-scented bath, which I soaked in for hours. Jane did a final journey, and once she was confident that everything was complete, went home. Later, when Dawn was leaving, she hugged me and said, "Annie, I see the eyes of a newborn infant in your adult eyes."

Nicole stayed, and the next morning, she and I went out to the Spirit Tree. It had only been four days since I'd labored there with Michon, but a lifetime had passed. I took off my clothes and sent energetic roots deep into the Earth, envisioning them intermingling with the physical roots of the tree. My body was enlivened by the cold, damp, foggy air. Nicole poured a bucketful of water on the dirt at the base of the tree and created a four-foot circle of mud. I stepped into the thick, clay-like puddle and raised my arms as she finger-painted my naked, newborn body.

Standing tall, dressed in Pachamama's thick, brown skin, and rooted to the Spirit Tree, I repeated what I'd said to Jane the night before, "I want to be my son's mother. I promised Phutu Cusi I would help. I have an entire life to live"—but this time added, "I want to facilitate the miracle healings Mary spoke of." Nicole drizzled warm water over my head and whispered in my ear, "Welcome back, Annie," baptizing me into my new life. As the liquid trickled down my mud-encrusted body, the clouds spontaneously parted, and Grandfather Sun emerged just in time to warm my newborn self.

Even with all these wondrous blessings, I yearned for greater context, so John contacted Juan, who was teaching in the United States, and arranged a visit. He arrived on Valentine's Day, three weeks after my initiations. Juan told us that when he was young, he'd experienced the waves as I did and had been afraid as well. He described them as "waves of living energy," natural cosmic forces. Upon learning this, I remembered another thing Nicole had said, "First there were waves of energy pushing you out of your body. Then there were waves of Earth, pulling you in. They felt similar, which is what made it so frightening and confusing."

Juan said my initiation was a result of my participation in the Hatun Karpay four months before, a manifestation of my movement out of the third level of consciousness—fear and separation—and into the fourth—love and Unity. During his visit, whenever I felt waves of living energy, Juan knelt before me and lowered his head so I could transfer them to him through my hands. His wisdom was the final blessing I needed to help me understand my initiatory experiences and feel solid enough to integrate them.

FAITH AND TRUST

The Hatun Karpay and my prayers regarding Mother Mary's directive were two forms of the same edict—if I wanted to grow into the healer I came to Earth to be, I had to release fear and doubt. This resulted in an impromptu dive into my murky, unconscious "ocean of fear and doubt," which was so deep and tumultuous I almost drowned! Wouldn't it have been wonderful if I had remembered Mary's words?

Call unto me. I will help you release your doubts. I wish for you to be prepared.

As I write this over twenty-five years later, I know my guides were with me the entire time and, along with Michon, helped me ride waves, tread water, and eventually step onto the shore. I was never meant to drown (though I certainly didn't know it then) but rather to become aware of my third-level disunities, leave the separation myth behind, and land in the fourth level.

Living Unity and assisting others to do the same are at the core of my purpose. Teachings have been fierce, beginning with a childhood based in separation, fear, and lies; to the fourth-level initiation, which nearly did me in; to all that's come after; to this present moment. When people ask, "What is your spiritual path?" I reply, "Faith and Trust." It's not a straight path. Nor is it flat. And it's certainly not simple.

On a good day, when life flows and the ground under my feet is soft, velvety green moss, it's an easy choice. But when an earthquake occurs, and the path becomes strewn with rocks, Faith and Trust

When people ask, "What is your spiritual path?" I reply, "Faith and Trust." It's not a straight path. Nor is it flat. And it's certainly not simple.

take a multi-dimensional turn. Are they present only on a good day? No, it doesn't work that way. But even on challenging, rock-strewn days, I still choose them. And while the path of Faith and Trust consistently offers me opportunities to walk it with renewed commitment, I love how profound and forgiving it is.

Before Juan left my house, he made plans with John and me for another trip, one that included responding to Phutu Cusi's request. That September, the three of us, along with Nicole, Jane, and a few others, spent a month together in Bolivia and Peru. We stayed an extra day in Aguas Calientes, the foothill town below Machu Picchu where the base of Phutu Cusi is located. And under a clear blue sky and radiant sun, we stood across from my favorite Apu as each of us in our own ways energetically removed the limiting seal.

The shift was tangible. So was her remarkable Ayni.

Everyone was in a deeply altered state, but when Juan took one look at Nicole's flushed face and energetic disarray, he immediately recognized that something sensational was happening—Phutu Cusi was inside Nicole! He kneeled before her in the same way he had done with me, lowered his head, and received the Phutu Cusi *karpay*—energy transmission—through Nicole's quivering hands.

We each took a turn.

A Prayer

In 2001, four years after receiving that fateful teaching from Mother Mary, I was channeling her for another healing class when someone asked, "Can you give us a prayer?"

The Light of Love is All flowed from my mouth.

Ever since then, this prayer has become my mantra.

The Light of Love is All.

This sacred prayer is alive.
I repeat it at every Healing Ceremony.
When I channel Light.
When I pray.
If I feel scared, in despair, or unable to sleep.
I've shared it with hundreds of students and clients, many of whom reported immediate relief and healing while repeating it.
I offer it to you, but please, receive it from Mother Mary.

The Light of Love is All.

CHAPTER TWO

The Four-Petaled Flower

Every human being is a precious Four-Petaled Flower of Wholeness.

— SARAYNA, Spirit Teacher from Teotihuacan

I hope you're still feeling embraced by the essence of the prayer you received—*The Light of Love is All.* Continue receiving its warmth and healing medicine while you read about how I was led to the Four-Petaled Flower.

I was fifty-three years old and in a phase of personal and professional stability. On the other side of a tumultuous year that included a relationship breakup, as well as a move, I was finally feeling settled. I liked my new home, a double-wide trailer on a grassy hillside with a view of the local mountain, my healing practice was thriving, and friendships were strong. It was a typical day. I was relaxing into the soft velour of my cozy orange chair, basking in the brilliant summer sun shining through the open window while hearing the familiar sounds of Apu's predecessor, Amigo—my large, black Labrador mix—barking at low-flying turkey vultures. I closed my eyes.

Then something atypical happened. A mysterious heat filled my already warm, sun-drenched body. I opened my eyes and looked outside. The green-brown earth and multicolored oak leaves looked fuzzy. Not blurry, just more dimensional than usual. After taking a few deep breaths, I understood—an unconditionally loving presence had entered me. *Ahhh.* I was receiving a blessing from the Divine Mother. But this wasn't Mary, with whom I was familiar. I inhaled deeply and caught a faint scent of roses. It was Guadalupe, Mother of Mexico.

I'd never thought much about Guadalupe, yet her story is significant.

The Spanish invaders landed in Anahuac (what came to be called Mexico) in 1519 and tried for over a decade to convert the Indigenous population to Catholicism, but the deeply spiritual Aztecs remained true to their cosmovision. Then, in December 1531, in what was originally called Tenochtitlan and is now known as Mexico City, a mystical woman appeared to Juan Diego, a humble native and one of the few converted community members. Juan, or Cuauhtlatoatzin—which in Nahuatl, the native language, means "One Who Speaks Like an Eagle"—was on his way to church early one morning when he heard singing atop Tepeyac Hill, an ancient temple shrine to the Aztec Earth goddess, Tonantzin, or "Sacred Mother." He stopped to listen. When the heavenly music ended and Juan heard someone call his name, he decided to climb the hill.

That's when he saw her. The beautiful, brown-skinned, glowing apparition was dressed in a long, blue-green, hooded cape scattered with golden flowers, bright stars, and an array of symbolic imagery. Under her cape, she wore an even longer dress that extended below her feet. It, too, was covered with golden symbols. A black sash wrapped high around her torso displayed a blossoming belly.

There are many versions of this story, and the following words spoken by Guadalupe to Juan Diego are based on multiple oral accounts of her appearance. They can be found in the book *Nican Mopohua*, translated as *Here It Is Recounted*, which was written by Antonio Valeriano in Nahuatl, the Aztec language, in 1543. His original work has never been found, yet a copy was first published in 1649 by Luis Lasso de la Vega.

One of my favorite books about Guadalupe is *The Aztec Virgin: The Secret Mystical Tradition of Our Lady of Guadalupe*, by John Mini. He goes into great detail about her extraordinary visitation, including its symbolism, repercussions, and the sociology of the times.

This is what Guadalupe said (in part):

Know, my youngest child, I am the Forever Whole and Perfect Maiden Saint Mary. Honorable Mother of the True God, Honorable Mother of the Giver of Life, Honorable Mother of the Creator of Men and Women, Honorable Mother of the One who is Far and Close, Honorable Mother of the One who Makes the Heavens and the Earth. My wish is for them to build my Temple here, where I will give people all my love, compassion, assistance, and protection. I am the Compassionate Mother of you and your people here in this land, and of all the other people who love me, call to me, search for me, and confide in me. I will listen to their pain, suffering, and crying and heal them from their misery. And so that desire may come into being, go to the bishop in his palace in Mexico. Tell him that I'm having you go to explain to him how I want a temple built for me here. Tell him every detail of what you've seen, heard and experienced here with me.

Juan immediately set out on his task, but Bishop Zumarraga didn't believe him and demanded proof. The next day on Juan's way to church, the mystical woman appeared again and made the same request. He complied, yet, still lacking proof, Juan's pleas to the bishop were rejected a second time. On her third visit with Juan, the magical, persistent woman asked him to climb the hill where she was standing, collect the Castilian roses growing there and bring them to the bishop. They would be the proof he needed, she said.

It was winter, and even so, these roses did not grow in Mexico—so imagine Juan's delight when he reached the top and discovered a blossoming field. He picked the red, velvet-petaled, perfumed flowers, carefully placed them in his cactus-fiber poncho, known as a *tilma*, and ran to the church where he waited all day. When Juan was finally received, he offered the tilma bouquet to Bishop Zumarraga, but it fell to the ground, unfolded, and the roses scattered everywhere.

Juan and the bishop looked down at the open tilma, and were astonished to see an image of the Forever Whole and Perfect Maiden staring up at them!

Bishop Zumarraga finally had his proof and ordered that a small temple be built on Tepayac Hill above Tonanzin's cave. Juan's simple tilma, now mystically inscribed with the image of Guadalupe, was displayed at the front.

Tecuauhtlacuepeuh—Guadalupe's original name—is translated as "She Who Comes Flying from the Regions of Light like an Eagle of Fire." After Juan shared this translation, Bishop Zumarraga decided the image was too powerful for the Catholic Church and instead declared that it sounded like "Guadalupe." According to the Church, Guadalupe was (and is) a manifestation of the Virgin Mary, but to this day the non-converted Indigenous population consider her their sacred goddess, Tonantzin. And since both groups entered the same building to pay homage to their chosen deity, it's said that Guadalupe unified the Aztecs with their conquerors.

Over five hundred years later, while sitting in my sun-warmed chair, I couldn't deny what had happened. Was I supposed to go to Mexico? Even though I was an avid traveler, I wasn't feeling a need to leave home, although I did begin reading travel books and mentally exploring…in case I changed my mind.

During the same time, I developed a cavity and made an appointment with a recommended dentist to have it filled. After the initial shot of Novocain, without any warning or explanation, he placed a dental dam—a thin, six-inch square latex sheet some dentists use to isolate the area they're working on—in my mouth. Instinct took over, and I screamed, "Get that thing out!" Frightened by my severe reaction, the dentist immediately removed the dam and jumped back. I flew off the chair, ran out the door, fumbled with my car keys, and sat in the driver's seat for a long time, trying to discern what happened. It had been fourteen years since I first remembered my childhood abuse, but in all the healing I'd done, this experience was new. The sensation of the dental dam in my mouth was like an exploding stick of dynamite that exposed a world of stored emotions. The depth of my anguish astounded me. I cried for days.

Was Guadalupe's impromptu appearance her way of inviting me to receive a healing I was unaware I needed? I decided to go to Mexico after all. Emily had recently moved there to paint a mural of Guadalupe at a retreat center, so I got in touch, and we created a plan.

A few weeks later, Emily and I met in Mexico City and joined thousands of spiritual pilgrims at the Basilica—a 1,000-acre shrine devoted to Guadalupe. While the original temple remains at the top of the hill, a large, central cathedral was constructed in 1976 where Juan Diego's tilma, still intact after more than five hundred years, hangs encased in bullet-proof glass and framed in gold. It hasn't deteriorated, the colors remain crisp, and as documented in John Mini's book, since 1665 continuing to 1981, *not one* scientist has been able to disprove its authenticity. (As of this writing in 2022, I was unable to find anything to the contrary.)

While Guadalupe's love was a balm to my soul, I continued feeling the disunification and weight of the emotional reaction that ambushed me in the dentist's office. However, I was in luck. It turned out that Emily's new home was about thirty miles northeast of Mexico City in a small village across the road from the ruins of Teotihuacan. I knew Emily had participated in several Toltec-inspired spiritual journeys there with students of Don Miguel Ruiz, Toltec shaman, and author of *The Four Agreements*,

While Guadalupe's love was a balm to my soul, I continued feeling the disunification and weight of the emotional reaction that ambushed me in the dentist's office.

so I asked her to guide me. Would the ancient energies of the ruins heal my terror and unify my soul?

According to archaeologists, the city of Teotihuacan, established as early as 400 BCE, was once inhabited by immigrants from various parts of Mexico and had served as a vibrant cosmopolitan center. It's been said that the community was united by a spiritual practice that brought people's hearts and minds into balance, and this awareness was a foundational thread woven into the fabric of the city's architecture. Here's an example: When the Teotihuacanos noticed a natural tunnel that led to a cave, they hollowed out the walls, carved it into their sacred Four-Petaled Flower symbol, and used the cave for ceremonial purposes. They then (no one agrees on how many years later) constructed the now-2,000-year-old Pyramid of the Sun, the tallest structure at Teotihuacan and third-largest pyramid in the world, directly on top of the cave.

There's no consensus as to why this exceptional city was abandoned, but some say the most likely causes include its unsustainable population growth, combined with mismanagement of natural resources and insufficient food production. When the Aztecs discovered the ruins in the 1400s, it had been deserted for centuries, and mounds of dirt and grass camouflaged sacred structures and objects.

They called their discovery Teotihuacan—which, roughly translated from Nahuatl, means, "The place where man becomes God."

The first Four-Petaled Flower I ever saw was in that very place on the first day of my fateful journey, as Emily and I walked through a mystical, dimly lit, underground portal leading into the Temple of the Feathered Conches. We were greeted by a vertical, two-sided stone column with five carved and red-painted Four-Petaled Flowers on each side. Around the corner is the main altar area, which is about four feet deep, equally wide, and framed on both sides by columns of rock-carved feathered conches. These are surrounded by more Four-Petaled Flowers. The entire temple, which includes a few energetically potent rooms off to the sides, eclipses all identification with the mundane world and is a sacred universe unto itself.

Emily and I ceremonially moved throughout the ruins for five full days, during which I felt enveloped within ancient energies supporting me to release what seemed like a lifetime of suffering. Then, after two weeks of healing and deepening friendship, I traveled alone to the magical mountain town of Tepoztlán, an area known as a healing vortex, and completed my healing mission by climbing the famous Tepozteco mountain.

I stopped on each step of the precipitous stones and man-made ladders of that sacred mountain and consciously released the remaining imprints of my emotional heaviness. When I reached the top, I understood that the sudden, unexpected dental experience had exposed repressed emotions from my traumatic childhood, the depth of which had overtaken the adult me. Emily's guidance, combined with Guadalupe's love, the dynamic healing energy of the Four-Petaled Flower, the ruins of Teotihuacan, and the Tepozteco mountain provided countless opportunities to let go of burdens I'd unknowingly carried my entire life. When I returned home, it was with a lighter heart and stronger sense of inner Unity.

Traveling to sacred sites is an intuitive, age-old healing modality, and my trip had been so empowering that Emily and I decided to use it as a guide for helping others. That began a five-year period in which we brought groups to the Basilica, Teotihuacan, and Tepoztlán for healing and awakening. During one of those journeys, we decided it was time to immerse ourselves as directly as possible in Teotihuacan, free of all interpretations offered by modern archaeologists, and learn directly from the ancestor spirits.

With that in mind, our group climbed the steep, vertical steps to the top of the Pyramid of the Sun and sat in the center, directly over the cave of the Four-Petaled Flower. I inhaled rays of warm sunlight through the top of my head and exhaled them down my entire body to the cave beneath us. Once I felt centered and grounded, I asked my loving Teotihuacana spirit teacher, Sarayna, who had come to me during my initial healing journey, for wisdom regarding the Flower. I spoke her words out loud, sharing her description (as I've written in A Letter to You), and then:

My people loved and revered the Four-Petaled Flower. Every home had a specific shrine where it resided and radiated. Sometimes, during ceremonies and festivals, we became the flower and would dance, sing, and integrate the cherished symbol inside of ourselves.

Every human being is a precious Four-Petaled Flower of Wholeness, and each day is an opportunity to live as one. Receive its energy, become the energy, and feed it to all humanity.

Ever since I entered the Temple of the Feathered Conches, the Four-Petaled Flower has become a fixture in my life. A framed photograph of the first one I ever saw graces the wall of my healing room. Emily painted a distinct flower—all four petals are yellow and surrounded by blue, with a red center that's also surrounded by blue—on the hide of my ceremonial hoop drum. It activates with each beat, so much so you can feel the energy of the flower come alive. In my backyard, large rocks outline a giant Four-Petaled Flower, the outer edge of each petal full of blossoming, multi-colored plants. I've filled the center with sand, and Apu loves digging, rolling, and nesting in it. (Bird-chasing, loyal Amigo has passed.) A fire pit sits in the center.

Now that I'm awake to the Four-Petaled Flower, I'm amazed at how frequently I see it. It shows up in paintings and tiles throughout Peru, Greece, Mexico, and the Southwestern United States. I've found it painted on Italian pottery, engraved as part of metal Hungarian latticework, and even in garden decoration design. But most amazing of all, this ancient symbol is in the center of Guadalupe's dress, just below the sash that displays her pregnant womb!

I'm grateful to the dentist who—by being his professional, technical self—revealed a profoundly wounded and disunified layer of my soul. I wonder if Guadalupe would have appeared without that experience? Would I have gone to Mexico and entered what's become a daily relationship with her? If my childhood wounds hadn't spontaneously emerged, would I have visited Teotihuacan and discovered the Four-Petaled Flower?

I never considered that the Four-Petaled Flower would become such an important "character" in this book, but the more I wrote, the more it demanded my attention. I trust that I've finally satiated its needs, which I believe are to enter our consciousness, awaken our petals, and assist us with our inner unification process. I love the Four-Petaled Flower. It's like a person to me, as real and solid as the original stone-carved images.

BECOME A FOUR-PETALED FLOWER

Look in the mirror and say, "I am a Four-Petaled Flower of Wholeness."

Breathe into the middle of your chest— the center of your remarkable bud— and as you exhale, envision the petals unfolding.

Imagine your unique flower come alive with color, scent, passion, and creativity.

Become what you are—an exquisite Four-Petaled Flower.

And remember what Saranya suggested...

Every day is an opportunity to live as a Four-Petaled Flower.

Receive its energy, become the energy, and then feed it to all humanity.

Welcome to the EAST

THE PETAL OF BEGINNINGS

You're preparing for the voyage from Spirit Realm Unity into Earthly duality.
Once you depart, you'll travel through a wave-filled gateway to your destination
Where you'll immediately begin growing a physical body.
Here's a heads-up…
A part of you is going to fall asleep. Forget who you are and where you came from.
But don't worry. This spiritual slumber won't last forever.
Even if it takes an entire lifetime (or more) to awaken,
You will.
Enter this petal with an open heart.
Infuse its fragrance through your newborn cells,
And allow the nourishing perfume to
Fertilize and grow your seeds of spiritual awareness.
Welcome to the world, young one.
It's Spring.
The early morning, yellow glow of Grandfather Sun is peaking over the horizon.
Eagle lives here. Jump on his back,
And discover life from a heightened overview.

CHAPTER THREE

Foundations

We are here to awaken from the illusion of our separateness.

—Thich Nhat Hanh, *How to Connect*

Eagles are high-flying birds of prey known for their superb eyesight. While humans have 20/20 vision, if that, an eagle has 20/5—which means the eagle can see at twenty feet what isn't clear to us until we're standing five feet away. So, make yourself comfortable on Eagle's strong, feathery back and get ready for expansive sight. Hold on tight. He's going to soar above all things familiar and show you life from his vantage point.

This chapter contains what I consider foundational spiritual principles, the bedrock of what I've experienced, explored, and come to believe as true. Since all chapters within each medicine-wheeled petal emerge from the ones before it, consider these teachings the ovary at the very base of the pistil in the center of all flowers.

My Truth

My truth has arisen from the story of my life. I've shared how I began spiritually seeking as a child, and that once I entered my forties, I participated in workshops led by outstanding teachers. And while spirit guides have taught me more than I can say, I've learned an equal amount from clients, friends, and family. For me, human heartache and spiritual awakening have walked side by side, and even as an elder, childhood wounds never fail to emerge and offer healing and learning opportunities. I'm continuously humbled by how my fieldmouse perspective can rise to the heights of an eagle's flight.

All of which brings me to my dear friend, Lucy, who often asks, "What is the point of this life exercise?" This chapter is my attempt to answer her question. Of course, how can I know…? It's absurd to think there's an absolute to anything. But I have come to a few understandings that appease my questioning mind (and occasionally hers), enhance my spiritual perspective, and feel right. I encourage you to receive what you need and let the rest go.

Who Are We?

We are spirit. Sparks of Loving Consciousness merged as one luminous, pulsating Light. Part of the Mystery, as I call it—maybe even the Mystery itself. I believe our collective voice might sound like a glorious, celestial chant, "Love, love, love."

How were we created?

This is easy; I don't know.

Why are we here?

I'm not going to address anything scientific, because however true those theories might be, they don't speak to the spiritual, so I'll say this: every culture on the planet has a unique creation story. There's also Darwin's theory of evolution; the story of Adam and Eve; and the belief in extraterrestrial seeding. (And while it's my experience that we're not the only life form in the universe, here I mostly address human life.) I can't claim to know how, when, or why we began, but I do know this: regardless of the mysterious specifics, most theories and stories agree we started out as spirit in the Spirit Realm and then became embodied spirit / human beings in this one.

Like Lucy, you're probably still wondering, "What is the point?"

This is what I believe: We are spiritual beings who have incarnated on Earth to remember our unified identity, while at the same time, living as individuated human beings. I'm going to put it in the context of a Four-Petaled Flower. In your mind's eye, imagine a giant one. Now inhale. Do you recognize the aroma? It's the universal flower essence of Love.

Take a magical magnifying glass and look closely at the flower. Can you see that it's made up of an unlimited number of smaller flowers?

This is Oneness. An infinite number of flowers creating the whole.

Focus even more closely and look at the smaller flowers individually. Notice the variety of color and how the unique energies of each petal merge within the centers.

Inhale. Isn't the perfume intoxicating?

This is Individuation.

See the entirety once again, this time with all the distinct colors and scents unified. Inhale again. Do you recognize the scent? The convergence of individual Four-Petaled Flowers ignites the Love essence of the giant flower.

This is Oneness again. The whole as the sum of its parts.

ENERGY

I know you're still relishing the euphoric Love essence, but do you think you can continue reading at the same time? I hope so, because I'd like to talk about energy. Don't worry. I'm not going to bore you with a diatribe on quantum physics, but since the word shows up throughout this book, it's important I share my definition: *Energy is the transcendent manifestation of the Divine, the universal Source of life.*

All matter, whatever the form may be, is made up of Divine frequencies. This includes animals, rocks, trees, the wind, sun, and water. Even cars, buildings, and lightbulbs—because *all things* are composed of the same cosmic substance. The way

I see it, everything is a living, conscious aspect of spirit. Now, you might not believe your car has a consciousness, but as you continue reading this book and decide to experiment with communicating with what the culture has determined are inanimate objects, you might become surprised when the battery, something you rarely think about, has a message.

Sometimes we can see energy in action—like during a tornado, earthquake, or lightning storm—but most of the time, it's subjective. We feel or sense it. Like when you walk into a room and somehow know that a person is angry, even if they deny it. That's sensing energy. Or when you're planting tomatoes in your garden, your hands covered with moist, rich soil (if you're like me and aren't wearing gloves) and you suddenly feel at peace. That's feeling Pachamama's energy.

Through the lens of the Q'ero, everything is living, interconnected energy, classified in two specific ways: refined/*sami* and heavy/*hucha*. Ideally, our bodies are full of sami, which makes us feel vibrant and energetic. Hucha, on the other hand, is uncomfortable and manifests as unhappiness or illness. There is no moral judgment about these energetic states—sami is not "good," nor is hucha "bad." That's a Western construct. As human beings, we have a multitude of emotions throughout the day, so creating hucha is normal. What's important is recognizing when we have too much. Later in this book, I'll share how you can easily release hucha and fill with sami—but first, the basics.

Through the lens of the Q'ero, everything is living, interconnected energy, classified in two specific ways: refined/sami and heavy/hucha. Ideally, our bodies are full of sami, which makes us feel vibrant and energetic. Hucha, on the other hand, is uncomfortable and manifests as unhappiness or illness.

HEALTH AND HEALING ESSENTIALS

Most of us have become so consumed with "getting through and surviving life" (think about that for a moment…) that we've not only lost our inner compass, but our awareness of the very foundation beneath our feet—the Earth—has lapsed. Even more important, too many people have forgotten that they live inside a body. We wake up to a blaring alarm and immediately get ready for the day: make coffee or tea, shower, brush our teeth, get dressed. We leave time to eat…maybe. No wonder we're frazzled by noon. Hungry. And dis-unified.

I find that taking time to center within myself, ground, and offer gratitude are essential not only to my health and healing, but to my mood and consciousness. I do a centering and grounding exercise each morning; before beginning a healing; at the start of a class, workshop, or talk; or whenever I feel unsettled.

These actions are restorative any time of the

CENTERING, GROUNDING, AND GRATITUDE

Experiment for a week. Center and ground at the beginning of each day, then notice how you feel at noon. This practice precedes all other experiential opportunities throughout the book.

- Find a place where you won't be disturbed. It can be your bedroom floor, living room couch, patio chair, a patch of dirt in your yard, or even the bathroom. It might be on your morning walk.

- Breathe.

- Put both palms flat on your heart/soul space. Take a few deep breaths, and with each inhalation, say: "I am centered in my body."

- If you had a restless or dream-filled night, say: "I call myself back." And breathe in any parts that might have scattered.

- Once you feel centered, it's time to ground.

- Imagine a cord of energy beginning at your heart/soul space and moving down the middle of your body. Take a deep breath in and then exhale this cord down and out through your first (root) chakra, the energy center between your legs, at the bottom of the bowl of your pelvis. See this grounding cord enter Earth.

Grounding looks and feels differently each time we do it. How far did your cord go today? Did it grow roots? Land in water? Reach the glowing, red-orange magma at our planet's center? If you're unable to visualize, what do you sense or feel?

Conversely, was your grounding cord unable to leave your body? Is it stuck? If so, look at what might be in the way. Can you see, feel, or sense something? Is the blockage a color? Energy? Person? Energetic obstructions can be surprising. Are you holding on to anger? Is someone in your space you hadn't realized was there? Are you afraid, for any reason, to claim your body?

- Breathe into your heart/soul space once again, exhale down and out your cord, and say: "I am centered and grounded."

Now, it's gratitude time. What are you grateful for today? A person? Event? Your health? Being alive? The green grass and the blue sky? Noticing previously unknown stuck energy? Even if your life is in shambles, finding something to be grateful for can shift your mood and elevate your consciousness. It's difficult for me to be sad when I'm thinking about the goodness in my life. Gratitude adds the final touch. It consistently expands my awareness, lightens my load (if I have one that day), and anchors me in ways that centering and grounding might not.

day. Once I'm solidly in my body, I add gratitude. I speak out loud to the Mystery and verbalize what I'm thankful for, beginning with my spiritual creation, and continuing to my life, health, abundance, privilege, family, and friends. The amount of time I spend expressing gratitude varies, as does the length of time it takes me to ground. I do all this when I'm out with Apu for his morning walk. If you saw us on the trail, you might notice the smelling-everything dog and the breathing-deeply-and-talking-to-herself crazy lady.

The illusion of separation from Source—the Mystery of all life—is our core human wound.

THE CORE HUMAN WOUND

Now that we're solidly in our bodies, we're ready to explore the invisible factor which I believe is at the center of suffering—the collective spiritual amnesia that took hold as evolution unfolded and the outer physical world became more alluring and demanding than the inner.

The way I see it, the illusion of separation from Source—the Mystery of all life—is our core human wound.

It's a catch-22: First, we incarnate and remember Unity. Then, as life intensifies, our survival demands that we refocus, so we forget about our spiritual identity and live within the paradigm of what's in front of us. That's when we start believing ourselves to be separate from one another, a doctrine that leads to fear, which then heightens our individual survival actions. And, if we're all living this way, our experiences not only validate outer separation, but cause us to separate, or disunify, within ourselves. The loss of solace inherent in belonging is a devastating wound within the psyche of most human beings.

Spiritual amnesia is most prevalent in the Western world, where money, power, and technology have replaced Unity. It's not as common in countries such as India and Tibet, where a more intact spiritual context exists. In less enlightened cultures, we have become seekers desperately trying to find our original connection with spirit, one another, and even ourselves, but the paradox is—we've forgotten there's no place to go. The Light, love, and connection we're looking for all live within.

Longing for Oneness can create a void that informs a person's entire existence. "Why do I feel so empty?" some wonder, "I have everything." They might try filling the vacancy with alcohol, drugs, cigarettes, sex, or food. Work. Power over others has become a rampant default, and depression is way too commonplace. And, while some of us find solace in religious institutions, it's worth asking, "Do they foster Oneness or separation?"

REINCARNATION

As spirits living a human existence, tasked with remembering Oneness while at the same time individuating, we need multiple opportunities to actualize this goal. Reincarnation, the philosophy that our spirit is continuously reborn, offers us all the time we need to fall into and then arouse from the spiritual slumber that goes hand in hand with human beingness.

The belief in former lives is a foundational tenet of Hinduism, Jainism, Buddhism, and Sikhism, but most people in the Western world believe the present is all there is, and any ideas of past and future existences are foolish. I believe our paths of self-discovery and service began in spirit innocence and mature through wisdom gained from lifetimes of experience. Reincarnation is a gift that supports us as we take as long as we need to remember Unity.

Karma

Do you ever wonder, "Why is life saturated with strife and grief? Do we need to suffer to spiritually awaken?"

To answer this, it helps to have a general understanding of karma, a Sanskrit word meaning "action" and a concept that originated in ancient India. According to Hinduism, Buddhism, Sikhism, and other Asian religions and philosophies, karma—often referred to as "the law of cause and effect"—is a spiritual law of nature and the means through which humans evolve. Each action we take brings to us a reaction of similar frequency, the past affects the present, and present choices affect our future.

One night during the first Spiritual Healing class, I channeled spirit teachers Alura and Athena, beings who've evolved past the need for physical embodiment. This is their view on karma:

The purpose of karma is to learn about love, for love is the true nature of the universe. Everything that exists is love, Light, and spirit. Each one chooses to learn this through their unique process, and while lessons and teachings vary, all experiences contain opportunities. The strength of any teaching depends upon what the individual has chosen for itself, as well as what its guides deemed important for that spirit to learn. While everything created must be put into balance, love is the goal of all karma.

Everyone forms karmic attachments throughout their incarnations. Some are life-enhancing, and others so binding they feel like inescapable prisons. Have you ever met a person and immediately felt you've known them forever? Perhaps you've thought, "I know I have karma with him" or "I'm sure I was your mother in a former life." Karma can be an experience that offers us a sense of otherworldly connectivity, and when we become aware of it playing out in our lives, we feel less separate. More connected. Most of us have wondered at times, "Why is this relationship so complicated?" or "I can't believe how deep this love feels; it's as if we've been together before." Unexplained kinship might even allow some people to acknowledge a spirituality they thought hadn't existed.

A spirit teacher said: *Karma can be changed in an instant.* I struggle with this.

For example, if a loved one is experiencing a life replete with suffering, is that a manifestation of their karma? Or are they simply unwilling to transform or heal? Can we *really* change karma in an instant? If so, is it because it's *part* of our karma? I like what the Dalai Lama says about karma in his book *1400 Lessons from the Fourteenth Dalai Lama*: "Irrespective of whether we are believers or agnostics, whether we believe in God or karma, moral ethics is a code which everyone is able to pursue."

Spiritual Parents

The profound human hunger for unconditional love is central to separation. Many of us expected our parents to fill this internal emptiness, yet as we grew older, had to accept that this was not possible. A human being cannot satiate a spiritual need, and even the most spectacular parents are human. If yours made you feel unconditionally loved and spiritually connected, consider yourself blessed. For the rest of us, we can ask: What happened in our parents' lives that created unhealthy beliefs and distorted manifestations of love? What caused them to become so internally disunified they took their disconnection and suffering out on us?

Adopting spiritual parents can offer opportunities to accept the faults and frailties of our human parents, while at the same time quench the craving within our souls that yearns for unconditional love. A spiritual parent can manifest in various forms and limitless orientations and contexts. A mother might be Isis, Spider-Woman, Pachamama, Quan Yin, the ocean, Phutu Cusi. Ever since Guadalupe called me to Mexico, leading me to the Four-Petaled Flower, I've considered myself a *Guadalupana*, a daughter of Guadalupe, and have embraced her as my spiritual mother.

A spiritual father can be Christ. Buddha. The sky. Krishna. Mohammad. Mount Everest. Mine is Ezekiel, another teacher I was able to receive due to my lack of formal religious education. Born sometime in the sixth century BCE, Ezekiel was a Jewish temple priest who became a visionary and prophet. He initially showed up as a brilliant spokesperson who sat in the center of a spiritual council I was channeling. The crazy thing was, he looked like a giant frog—yes, you read that correctly—and told me to call him "The Frog-like One." It was easy to let go of his appearance because his wisdom, guidance, and prophecies were flawless.

One evening during a sleepless night in 2007, The Frog-like One visited me as an elder with long grey hair and a matching beard. He held a staff. "My name is Ezekiel," he said. When I asked him why he was part of my life, he told me I had been his daughter (even though there is no Biblical mention of Ezekiel having offspring), and ever since that lifetime, he'd vowed to protect me. I doubt this book would have been written without him.

The best way for me to complete this chapter of spiritual foundations is to ask you from the bottom of my heart...

If you haven't considered that the illusion of separation from the Source of all life is real, please do so. Even a simple mental exploration can be the fairy dust that inspires awakening.

I'll conclude with this:

The Brotherhood of the Light, evolved masters who spoke through me only once said:

We are all love. Love binds the Universe.

Don't you know that?

The music of love is the foundation of all existence, and as it eternally plays, devoted partners karma and reincarnation will dance until separation loses its power, and Unity is remembered and lived by all.

CLAIM YOUR SPIRITUAL PARENTS

While you might choose to have multiple spiritual parents, as I did, all you really need is one. Do any come to mind? If not, what about your favorite mountain, or the giant willow tree you played under as a kid? Your childhood dog. Don't forget about Mother Earth and Father Sky. The moon and sun.

Make it official.

Create an altar and place a picture or statue of the parent(s) you've chosen. During one of my many visits to the Basilica, Guadalupe told me that not only is she alive on the original tilma, but in all her images. I've adorned my home with pictures and statues of her. It's harder to find a likeness of Ezekiel, but I searched online and printed and framed one that feels right to me. He (as well as a large frog in honor of his original persona) and Guadalupe sit side by side on the mantle of my red-brick fireplace.

Whoever your parents might be, honor them. Include them in your centering, grounding, and gratitude practice. Talk to them. Ask for guidance. And most important, receive their unconditional love daily. After all, that's what they want us to do.

CHAPTER FOUR
Spirit Chooses Form

Things that are separate shall be united and acquire such virtue that they will restore to man his lost memory.

— LEONARDO DA VINCI, *Notebooks*

In the early 1990s, while Lisa and I were meeting with the Milky Way Village spirits, I was a midwife with relentless questions about all things birth-related, and through Lisa's excellent channeling abilities, our friends offered us answers. We recorded each session and once I transcribed it (a perfect way to integrate the information), I shared the teachings with students and clients, who, in turn, shared them with their students and clients. Much of the information in this chapter was received and experienced during that time, and I'm grateful to every person (and spirit teacher) for their intimate stories and wise contributions.

CHOOSING TO INCARNATE

As spirit, Sparks of Loving Consciousness, we all share the same destiny, yet there is one huge variable: we each have a distinct level of consciousness. I know this is a tricky statement. If everyone is spirit, then aren't we the same? Yes, of course. But does each person remember this? In macrocosmic

unified consciousness—the entirety of the Four-Petaled Flower—yes; in microcosmic, individuated awareness, where limitless flowers exist and make up the whole, no. That's why between lives, when we're learning and growing in the Spirit Realm, the assistance of our guides and teachers is paramount.

Who are these guides and teachers? Alura and Athena said:

As one moves through and completes its cycle of human evolution, one becomes a co-worker within the spiritual realms and can assist others in the awakening of consciousness.

These "evolved co-workers," then, are our guides and teachers. Some people might know one or more of theirs, many are unaware, and most don't believe they exist at all. Ultimately, it doesn't matter. What's important is that loving beings of higher consciousness support us, not only when we're in spirit form, but as embodied humans—whether we sense, see, hear, communicate, or know their names.

Spirit teachers consider innumerable learning

possibilities as they assist us in the creation of new lives. What do we need to resolve from the past so we might expand into the future? Perhaps the completion of specific karma, distinct lessons and teachings, the healing of recurring issues, or a movement into unprecedented experiences. What type of body will serve our goals? Gender orientation? And then there's our family... I imagine there might be infinite situations and conditions we and our teachers consider during life preparation.

Earth is a place of free will, and since incarnation is not a programming of any kind, no one is bound to live under a single life plan. Predestination—the belief that life has been designed, set in stone by a higher power, and once we become human, we have no control—seems a view too narrow for the Mystery. Divine creativity is limitless, beyond our wildest imaginings. One day we might walk the direct path of our spiritual intentions, while on another we might move in an unexpected trajectory that *appears* to take us off our path, but that's impossible. There is no single path. The entirety of life is a path.

A spirit can travel on the freeway, drive down the side streets, or engage in a scenic-route tour. All roads lead home—to remembering Unity— and, since free will exists in every moment, no one is ever on a time clock. Every experience is a

A spirit can travel on the freeway, drive down the side streets, or engage in a scenic-route tour. All roads lead home—to remembering Unity—and, since free will exists in every moment, no one is ever on a time clock.

valuable opportunity to become more self-aware and consciously unify what might have separated over time. Imagine the collective laugh resounding throughout the universe when we grasp that the illusion of separation has been our biggest teacher all along.

What looks easy to accomplish from the panoramic perspective of the Spirit Realm can be challenging within the energetically dense nature of Earth, where there are spirits that have taken on too much. I've known several people whose lives have been filled with tremendous hardships, and through dreams, healing ceremonies, therapy, or hypnosis, realized that their altruistic spirit-self intended to ease the suffering of humanity. The problem was, once they incarnated, the reality and scope of their plans became overwhelming.

It's easy for me to personally explore this concept. A few years after my sister died, I had an awakening. One of the reasons her life was so difficult was because she absorbed some of my heavy energy from childhood. Susan was born with a big-picture awareness of my destiny and knew I had to survive to achieve it, so part of her life plan was helping me stay alive and sane. I believe she had a karmic debt to me and am both sad and grateful for her payment.

Then there's the collective. For example, what about the people in Tibet and other parts of the world who are experiencing ethnic cleansing? Or the victims of the September 11 disaster? Was it *spiritual* altruism that led them to *humanly* participate in what might be a massive collective karmic cleanse? Are they somehow easing the suffering of humanity by taking it on themselves? We can ask these questions about any person or group that suffers, and while I don't have the answers, I do raise questions and explore our often extremely confusing spirit/human partnership later in the book.

Back to the personal... If you wonder about your spiritual purposes and goals, take some time and examine your life. Has anything been a struggle? Do themes or patterns repeat? If you have a physical ailment, have you considered that your illness might be a teacher? What qualities are unique to *you*? As we recognize what we, as spirits, are trying to teach and remember, we can begin to heal, unify, and absorb this reawakened knowledge into our consciousness. Patterns end when their necessity in our journey becomes obsolete.

Gateway and Guardians

When the time arrives for a spirit to journey from the Spirit Realm into the womb of its future mother, it travels through a tunnel of wave-like living energy called the Birth Gateway. Each distinct journey is determined by karma, purpose, and intention, yet one aspect remains the same—we are never alone.

Every spirit has a Birth Guardian, a loving spiritual midwife who not only escorts us through the Birth Gateway passage but remains close throughout our gestation, birth, and newborn lives for as long as they determine we need them. Birth Guardians are readily accessible throughout our entire lifetime, which is why I've included an opportunity at the end of this chapter to assist you with contacting yours.

Here's something intriguing about the Birth Guardian—when our lives are complete and it becomes time to return to the Spirit Realm, she (in my experience, the Birth Guardian is energetically female) becomes our Death Guardian and devotedly guides us through the energetic waves of the Death Gateway, the complement of the Birth Gateway. This was one of the reasons the second part of my initiation was so confusing and scary. The waves of both gateways felt the same. It's important that I emphasize—*we are never alone*—even if it feels that way, which it did for me under the Spirit Tree, where my excessive fears and doubts separated me from any awareness of spiritual companionship and support.

At times I've led a visualization for students to help them remember their Birth Gateway experiences. During one, Lisa, my channeling partner, shared, "I felt the energy of my mother calling, 'Come, my love. Come,' which made it easy to surrender to the waves and land into a glorious, love-cushioned conception." Lisa learned that with help from her guides, she had consciously chosen her mother, and since their karma and energies were aligned, was treated to a wondrous gateway experience.

It's not that way for everyone. Some spirits, propelled solely by their will to incarnate, dive into the energetic waters of the Birth Gateway knowing little about their destination. They might ride the waves with ease…until they sense their future life. If those energies feel disharmonious, the spirit must discern whether to stay its course. Others continue and unite with their future mother, while still others re-choose, which is when their Birth Guardian escorts them back to the Spirit Realm to receive further teachings before another incarnation.

During Lisa and my conversations with the Milky Way Village spirits, I remembered a few things about my journey through the Birth Gateway. I had been clear about my incarnational purposes—to work through a massive amount of karma, become a mother to the being who became my son, and evolve into a healer, teacher, and author—yet, in the final third of the gateway, when I began feeling the energy of my mother, I resisted. My commitment to incarnate had been so consuming I hadn't even considered her! (Or if I had, I'd forgotten.) You might wonder why my guides didn't prepare me. Well, you know how teachers are…they see further down the path than we do, and while they point us in the right direction, empirical learning solidifies teachings.

I now understand that my mother was part of a package deal, you might say, and came with my father, who, for karmic reasons, I did select. Looking back, I see what an important part of the "package" she was, for if she had been empowered instead of deeply wounded, my entire life would have unfolded in a different direction. I suppose my guides chose her for me. During my gateway dilemma, my Birth Guardian showed me two paths—return to the Spirit Realm where I could re-choose a less intensive life or be conceived into a family where my basic nature and gifts would be invisible. "Was I willing to live that reality?" she asked.

After my initiation, my healer friend Nicole pointed out that I'd "created a hard path by incarnating into a modern culture where there is no tribal community for us, no elders. This was a big choice, to leave or stay, and you needed to be given it." That choice began in the Birth Gateway, where I placed my spiritual goals above my human needs and united with my mother. This awareness continues to broaden the context of my life.

Although spiritual strength comes from resting between lifetimes, the magnetic pull of the gateway can be stronger than the need to pause. I learned from the Milky Way Village spirits that my sister, Susan, had spent little time in the Spirit Realm between her most recent, former incarnation and moving into the Birth Gateway for this one. I can't say I know why or understand this, but I do trust it. Like me, Susan was willful, determined, and purposeful (and as I said earlier, I was a small part of her purpose), but unlike me, after forty-six years of alienation and suffering, she completed her intentions and passed on in her sleep. I believe she achieved her goals and is now in the Spirit Realm, taking time (for once) to rest and assimilate before her next adventure.

Conception

Before any of us can begin our next adventure on Earth, a few things need to be in place for conception to occur. A spirit must be willing to leave the vast, formless knowledge available in the Spirit Realm and embark upon a pilgrimage into form. Its future mother must consciously (as in a planned pregnancy) or unconsciously (as in an unplanned pregnancy, where consent exists on a spiritual level) agree to allow its growth inside her body. And of course, there must be willing sperm and eggs.

Even though we live in a time of technological advancements and breakthroughs regarding conception, it can still be difficult to become pregnant. Why? A scientist might state several physiological reasons, but since this is a place of spiritual overview, my answer is simple: conception isn't possible without a willing spirit. It's the same with all fertilizations: unassisted and spontaneous, in-vitro, donor eggs or sperm, or any other method. A healthy embryo, once implanted in a woman's womb, will only grow if a spirit claims the developing body. Nothing can live without spirit. It must be present at conception as well as the birth of its human self. If it isn't, no matter how normal and healthy the baby might look, it will not be alive.

The Body

Every childbirth is different. Some newborns emerge from the sanctity of the womb bombarded with bright lights, loud sounds, and insensitive handling. Others arrive in pools of warm water and breathe air for the first time while nestled in their mother's loving arms. Whatever the individual experience may be, we've all been transformed from disembodied spirits into embodied spirit/human beings.

It's a gift to have a body, although finding balance can be difficult. Skin, bones, muscles, blood, cells, and physiological systems are universes unto their own, and when a spirit chooses to inhabit this corporeal realm, it might need time to adjust. My client Roger told me he was able to feel his expansiveness of spirit self while at the same time his "condensation into form." This made him uncomfortable, and although he tried for years to embrace his body, he was unsuccessful. It was only when he took the phrase "all you need is love" to heart and began loving his human form that he began to feel embodied comfort.

We can follow Roger's lead. Choose to see oneself as a unified being in a harmonious, spirit/human partnership and love our miraculous form. Look in the mirror. Can you imagine the Light of Love radiating out of your heart? In our modernized culture, we tend to focus on physical "imperfections" and dislike our bodies. "My thighs are pudgy," someone says. "I like my face, but my nose is too big," criticizes another. "I'm too short." "I'm too tall." "I'm bald." "I'm fat." "My ears stick out."

If we can expand our minds and look at our bodies through spirit eyes, imperfections don't exist. Even when a person is born without a limb, while challenging on a human level, their body was perfectly designed by the spirit who chose to reside in it. There are no accidents, because from the perspective of spirit, all choices intend karmic resolution and expansion of consciousness. And while it can be challenging to really *get* that everything is purposeful, we must remember: our bodies are custom-designed garments. We put them on for our travels into form and remove them when we return to the Spirit Realm. It's a little like Halloween, except we've identified with the costume.

Let's stand in front of the mirror together and take a good look at the reflecting costume. See it for what it is. I'll do it if you will. Body image, certainly for women (and some men as well), can be difficult to come to terms with. When I was younger, my body looked fantastic from a cultural perspective. Did those reflections reach my mind and enhance my self-love? No, they did not. Now, as an elder, there are days I love my aging body. But there are other days when I'm still affected by spiritual amnesia and deny my body costume—and myself— the love we deserve. Think about me the next time you're in front of the mirror. Smile. Remember. And choose self-love.

Let's stand in front of the mirror together and take a good look at the reflecting costume.

Spiritual Dilemma

Disunity between our spirit and human selves creates what I call a "spiritual dilemma." This happened for Roger, who felt his "condensation into form," and for me in the Birth Gateway, where I had to decide whether to unify and become human or return to the Spirit Realm. It unfolded differently for Elise.

While I was doing a healing for Elise, it became apparent that she wasn't fully embodied, and when I innocently asked if she was willing to rejoin herself, her vehement response surprised me. "*No!* I don't want to be on Earth. I never wanted to. I want to be with my people. They're not here, so I can't be. Even if I wanted to be in my body, I can't, because then I'll lose touch with my people. Let me go back where I belong! I hate Earth; it's too heavy and dense."

Elise had forgotten that no one forces a spirit to incarnate, so I used a simple form of hypnosis to guide her inward and ask specific questions to see what she might recall. Through the process, she remembered that she'd spent many lifetimes incarnating upon energetically refined planets, not dense ones like Earth, and because of this pattern, decided it was time to come here. No one had forced her. Spirit Elise was aware that she had karma to resolve and needed to experience the profound healing and awakening opportunities Earth provides.

When she left the Spirit Realm, Spirit Elise moved freely within the Birth Gateway currents until the energy shifted and began thickening. That's when she froze, made decisions about human life, and refused to fully incarnate. I supported Elise as she re-experienced the incapacitating fears of losing contact with "her people" and ending up alone in what she considered a foreign place.

Spiritual Dilemma is the result of separation and disunity. For Elise, being human meant separation from her spiritual family, yet her task—perhaps an aspect of her karma—was to trust that she could have both. I encouraged her to breathe deeply, expand her inner senses, and connect with her gateway counterpart. Elise's newly awakened perspective prepared her, and she willingly opened her heart and united with her formerly frozen self.

After the healing, even though Elise felt new aches and pains (a result of her enhanced embodied state), nothing kept her from showing Spirit Elise the beauty of Earth. "They" went hiking, ate healthy food, and spent time with friends. As she became more grounded, Elise gained insights regarding the necessity of her incarnation and was thrilled to experience how the relationships with her guides did not end, as she feared, but improved.

Elise finally gained a sense of peace and purpose in her life.

QUESTIONS FOR REFLECTION

It can be helpful to have some knowledge about your spirit journey into form. Memories of incarnational choices, Birth Gateway experiences, conception, and birth all offer vantage points from which to view our lives. Even a small amount of perspective can nourish our awareness, self-compassion, and forgiveness. Elise's story is a prime example of this. To assist you in awakening your memories, ask yourself:

- Am I aware of my spiritual guides or teachers? If so, am I open to their influence?

- Do I have memories of making plans for this life?

- How did "spirit me" feel about coming or returning to Earth?

- What lessons did my guides and I decide were important?

- Is there specific karma I committed to complete?

- How does my choice of culture or location serve my spiritual intent? Gender? Body type? Family?

- Do I remember anything about my conception? If so, what was it like? Has the experience affected me in any way?

- Where was I born? Was my birth loving or traumatic? Was I separated from my mother or family? Left alone in a nursery? Did I need medical care? Was I adopted?

- Am I able to claim my physical body? Do I like it? Can I live happily within it, or do I feel trapped, impatiently waiting for the time I can take it off and become spirit again?

- Do I feel emotionally wounded by any of these experiences? If so, how does that manifest?

If you don't know or remember much, that's okay. Maybe having answers isn't necessary for your growth. If you do want to learn more about your spirit journey into form, try this:

Once you complete your centering, grounding, and gratitude practice and have some extra time, ask one of the above questions. And then just sit. Notice what, if anything, arises—a feeling, sense, story— and if it does, explore your experience.

While we all have the same destiny—to remember Unity—each of us has our own timing and creative pathways. Trust yours.

Connect with the Birth Guardian

Begin this way:

- Find a place where you won't be disturbed and sit quietly. Have a pen and paper nearby.

- Breathe deeply. Center and ground.

- Is your mind active? Breathe the linear energy down and let it fill your heart.

- When you feel centered, grounded, and present, breathe deeply once again.

- Call to your Birth Guardian. Ask her to visit you.

- Notice the subtle or dramatic energy shift as she makes her presence known.

- When the time feels right, speak with her. She might arrive with a specific message.

- Ask questions. Be interactive, even if you think you're making it all up.

- Trust and enjoy your experience.

- When your visit is complete, give thanks, and center and ground once again.

Pregnant Women and Their Partners:

- Once you've centered and grounded, call to your baby's Birth Guardian, and proceed in the same way as previously written.

Healers and Childbirth Support People:

- Before you do anything, consult with the baby's Birth Guardian, and create an exchange that enables you to work cooperatively with her during the session. She knows the unborn one and its family well and will guide and teach you. Oftentimes, she has specific information about the healing and/or birthing process. Ask questions and be open to hearing (sensing) her responses.

- When the exchange is complete, share your experience with the family.

- If you attend the labor and birth, remember, the Birth Guardian is there. These beings are known to take active roles and become accessible to both you and the parents. Call to her if you have concerns about anything, especially as it directly pertains to the baby. She won't "release" the unborn one to its mother until she feels the time is right.

CHAPTER FIVE
Soul:
Bridge Between Spirit and Human

The first peace, which is the most important, is that which comes within the souls of men when they realize their relationship, their oneness with the universe and all its Powers, and when they realize that at the center of the universe dwells Wakan-Tanka [the Great Spirit], and that this center is really everywhere, it is within each of us.

— BLACK ELK, *The Sacred Pipe*

We've reached the final chapter of the East petal. You've been soaring on Eagle's feathery back for a while. Has your vision expanded? Did you experience newly awakened memories? Continue to hold on as Eagle stretches his wings wide and glides with ease through thermal currents. His deliberately slow descent will give you plenty of time to integrate as you learn about some of the essential distinctions that, from now on, will be integral to this book. And since the words spirit and soul are often interchanged, I'll begin with them.

A spirit is a spark of Loving Consciousness, part of the Mystery of life.

A human is a spirit in a body, thus, a spirit/ human being.

Now here's something that might be new:

A soul is a bridge that unites the partnership of a spirit and a human.

The goal of an embodied spirit is to remember its unified spiritual identity, while at the same time, experiencing individuated human uniqueness.

We are spirit within soul within body.

THE HUMAN SOUL

Soul is where spirit accomplishes its goals. Located at and radiating from the center of our chest, the heart/soul space, our soul is a circular, multi-layered expanse of living energy that surrounds us. Some people call it "the human energy field." To the Q'ero, it's an energy "bubble," a term I like.

Between lives, a soul inhabits its spirit, like a wildflower seed living inside the Earth during winter. For a wildflower to germinate, sprout, grow, and express its one-of-a-kind self, it needs the correct soil and weather conditions. What a soul needs is a new incarnation of its spirit.

When the time is right, a spirit, pregnant with its soul, moves from Spirit Realm Oneness into the energetic waves of the Birth Gateway and travels toward conception. It ebbs and flows within the unpredictable tides until the sperm and egg, specifically chosen for its future body, unite. At that instant, the spirit exits the gateway, joins them, and completes their union. This miraculous meeting of the worlds creates cellular division, the fertilizer that sparks the germination of both the human and its soul seed. Blastocyst becomes embryo, embryo becomes fetus, and the baby and its soul grow in tandem.

The Inner Soul Skin

The human soul has two skins. The inner skin develops first, grows with the fetus, and becomes a protective energetic coating that closely surrounds its physical body. This skin doesn't become "solid" until the baby leaves the watery womb and is born into the air of the Earth Realm.

The inner soul skin can be likened to the foundation of a house. A shattered house with a strong

Between lives, a soul inhabits its spirit, like a wildflower seed living inside the Earth during winter.

foundation can usually be rebuilt. Our inner skins are similar. They're like breathable, impenetrable layers of fiberglass that take the brunt of an ordeal yet remain intact. During traumatic experiences, heavy energy can penetrate the soul and unleash a tidal wave of reverberations, which result in fragmentation. If the inner skin didn't exist, the damaging energy might enter with lightning bolt precision and move directly into the physical body.

Trauma can be so intense that the inner skin, strengthened by whatever medical and spiritual treatments are administered, is the invisible factor keeping a person alive. If it tears, the body is no longer protected, and healing can be difficult. Fifty percent of trees die when struck by lightning. The rest become weakened and, like us, can revive if their "foundations" are strong enough. There's an ancient redwood tree in Northern California that was struck by lightning. When the electrical current met the tree, it hollowed out the center but somehow enhanced the overall health of the tree, which continues to grow thicker and taller. When Juan was visiting, we sat inside its darkened womb-like center and prayed.

The Outer Soul Skin

By the time we're about seven years old, in addition to the inner soul skin, a separate, energetically solid outer skin has formed. This expands our energy bubble, like a balloon filled with air. Close your eyes. Breathe into your center, and as you exhale, imagine yourself inside a fully inflated balloon. Can you envision the border? That's the edge of your outer soul skin. The soul can expand three to four feet from the body, although in energetically refined circumstances, like when we're in nature or deep meditation, it enlarges further.

Our outer soul skin defines our personal space. Do you have difficulty creating boundaries? Merge with people and lose yourself in their energy? Absorb the feelings of others? If you answered yes to any of these questions, your outer skin might be diffused. Perhaps the way you survived your childhood was by blending with others; maybe having a sense of what they were feeling helped you know the safest way to respond. Close your eyes and visualize your outer skin becoming more solid.

Conversely, do you feel separate, like there's a barrier between you and others? If so, your outer skin might be thick. Many of us who were violated as children developed walls of energetic protection. (The expression "thick-skinned" might have more meaning now.) Close your eyes and explore the dimensionality of your outer soul skin. If it feels too dense, imagine it at a consistency that helps you feel safe within your personal space.

Our souls breathe and expand and contract throughout the day, depending upon our moods and situations. Look at your energy bubble again. Is the outer skin close to your body or far away?

Imagine something frightening or sad. Did it change in any way? Fear and turmoil can contract a soul as tightly as a rosebud and bring the outer skin so close that we become tense. Breathe into your center and visualize a pristine place in nature. Did your soul respond? When we feel joy and safety, our souls are akin to blossoming lotus flowers. And when hearts come together during lovemaking, they can nearly dissolve.

HUCHA WITHIN THE SOUL

Our emotional terrain comprises the landscape of our souls. Trauma and unhealthy beliefs collect as heavy energy, or hucha, which can rise to peripheral areas and thicken like cream. Too much energetic accumulation in the outer soul skin creates a thickness, which, in addition to generating a feeling of separation, limits the amount of space available for the Universal Energy Field to enter and feed the body. If the outer skin is dense, the rest of the soul and body can be depleted. And, because the soul is mirror-like—meaning everything in the outer areas reflects to the inner and eventually to the body—the quality of this skin affects our spiritual, mental, emotional, and physical health.

Some of us try to dissipate the hucha of a loved one by taking it on ourselves. Children are experts at this. When their parents argue, many try to resolve the situation by absorbing the heavy energy into their souls. This might make their parents feel better for a few minutes, but the child is now coated with their hucha and must relieve themselves of this uncomfortable feeling. A tantrum is a perfect way to release what isn't theirs. Has this ever happened to you? Instead of having an emotional outburst, try shaking your arms, legs, and entire body. I call this the "crazy dance." It's a fun way to resolve the problem.

When we first began our incarnational journeys, we were like lamps with the Light/spirit on and the shade/soul clear. Rays of Light emanating from translucent souls. Throughout copious lifetimes of identity amnesia, cultural conditioning, trauma, karma, and survival, the fabric of our souls is not as clear as it was. Formerly transparent areas have become coated with hucha, making our "lampshades" dusty. While spirit remains bright eternally, dust on the soul decreases its outward radiance. Have you ever met a person whose energy feels dull, or so heavy you could almost see it? Their soul is filled with hucha, and the Light of who they are is blocked by all the dust.

Notice your soul throughout the day. What are you doing when you feel contracted? Who are you spending time with? What activities or people create joyous expansion? If you're ever in a situation where you feel too expansive, breathe into your center, exhale, and pull your outer skin closer in. When your soul feels tight or cramped, breathe in and exhale expansion.

CHAKRAS

The word "chakra" is derived from a Sanskrit word meaning "wheel." Chakras are energy centers within the soul that unite the soul with the body. Some traditions say we have one hundred and fourteen of these wheel-like centers, but all agree there are seven major chakras, each with a front and rear counterpart that meets in the central vertical energy column parallel to the spine. Chakras look like spinning wheels of multi-colored lights with outward-facing, funnel-shaped vortexes. They receive energy from the Universal Energy Field, metabolize it, and move it through the soul to "feed" our bodies. All one hundred and fourteen chakras support energy, health, and well-being, yet the seven major ones have ongoing relationships with specific organs, emotions, glands, and more.

I've purposely decided not to write about chakra colors. Before I went to Peru and met Juan, I thought there were *official* colors. But when I learned an ancient Inka ceremony that works with the energy centers, I discovered something interesting—the locations are the same, but the colors are not. Volumes have been written about the chakra system, and I leave you to your exploration. Here is basic information about the seven:

The first chakra, called the root chakra, is located between the legs, at the pelvic floor. The large, circular part of the funnel is on the outer, downward side and the smaller funnel opening faces in and up. When we receive energy from the Earth, it moves directly upward into our central energetic column. And when we ground, it's where our cords travel from our bodies into the Earth. Survival issues are related to this center.

To locate your second chakra, place one hand just below your belly button and the other on your lower back. This center has a relationship with sexuality and creative flow.

The spinning wheels of the third chakra, also known as the solar plexus, are found in the center of the front of the body and the middle of the back. This is the place of personal power, as well as digestion. Do you have digestive issues? Feel into this center. Like the soul, individual chakras breathe. Is it open or closed? Is it spinning freely or is it congested? We take enzymes to help with physical digestion, but what are we doing about the energy that created the problems in the first place? Rest both hands on your third chakra, channel Light, and intend it to "digest" whatever excess energies it might be storing. Feed any heaviness to Pachamama.

The fourth chakra is the heart, which is located at the center of the chest. Inhale energy through the front of your heart and exhale out the back. Now inhale through the back and exhale out the front. Imagine a figure eight with each breath, the tips of the inner funnels meeting and kissing in the center. This chakra is about love, but not only of another. Do you have back pain in this area? Often the front

Before I went to Peru and met Juan, I thought there were official colors.

of a center is open, but the back can be an entirely different story. I once had a client with a thick, energetic wall covering the rear aspects of her chakras. Giving love was easy for her, but receiving it was another matter. Both are important.

The fifth chakra is located at the front of the throat and the back of the neck. This center is all about speaking our truths. Do you have recurring laryngitis or sore throats? I'm one of too many women with thyroid issues. As an abused child whose voice was silenced, this center became a storage locker for my unspoken words.

To find your sixth chakra, also known as the third eye, place one hand on the front of your forehead and the other on the back of your head. This center, where we also find the mind, is a place of intuition and visualization. My Teacher said: **The mind is an instrument of the soul**. The problem is—it wants to be the conductor. Our minds love being right, do *not* like change, and have the overwhelming power to either anchor us to the density and repetition of suffering or support us in breaking free. I've met brilliant linear thinkers who have a difficult time with inner sight, so I ask them to breathe into this center and exhale the energy of their mind down and feed it to their heart/soul space. (Try this when you have a headache.)

The seventh major energy center, the crown chakra, is at the top of the head. Its counterpart is the first or root chakra. As with the others, the wheel of this center faces out and the smaller end faces in. When energy flows into and through this center, it moves down the central energetic column.

Many see the crown as our spiritual center; however, I'd like to share something I learned about the crown/root relationship. There's an erroneous belief that we must consciously open our crown chakras so we can connect with the spiritual realms, but doesn't this mean that spirituality lives outside of us? I used to do this myself, until my initiations taught me that not only is it a bad idea, it's also unnecessary. Continuously opening this center results in well-traveled, out-of-body pathways, which some people use too frequently or forget to return on. Common repercussions include headaches, spaciness, and exhaustion. Seizures are also possible, as I'll show you later.

Here's something important I share with clients and students: *Forget about the crown!* If you're like them, you find this surprising and might laugh. I say, "Focus on the root. Practice centering and grounding and the crown will take care of itself." Try this for a month and see what happens.

Yes, we are spirits, Lights of Love living within the center of our heart/soul spaces—yet if we want to remain healthy humans, we also must live within our bodies.

There's an erroneous belief that we must consciously open our crown chakras so we can connect with the spiritual realms, but doesn't this mean that spirituality lives outside of us?

LIVING LIBRARY

Our souls have been storing memories for our spirit consciousness ever since we began our incarnational cycles. Each one is a lushly woven tapestry made up of gifts, talents, difficulties, and unresolved events from any point in time—past lives or a minute ago.

I liken these distinctions to books, which is why I call the multi-layered fabric of the soul a "Living Library."

When the time becomes right (most likely determined by our soul's path), we notice specific books. Or a book we've already read piques our interest. Have you ever felt that an aspect of your past was behind you, the wound and repercussions healed, only to become triggered or fascinated when you least expected?

I was in the process of completing this book when the book of little Annie—the abused, neglected girl who was found in the cloakroom closet during my first soul retrieval (a story I'll share in the next chapter)—fell off a shelf of my Living Library and landed in my lap, screaming, "Read me again!" So I complied and focused my attention on little Annie. She was scared and needed someone to love and support her as only a mother could, and since I am her mother, I gave her what she (I) never received as a child. My sixty-nine-year-old response to little me awakened new awareness and paved another pathway for my inner unification. Healing is a lifelong opportunity.

When a library book falls off a shelf as if out of the blue and demands to be read, it means we've entered the layer of our Living Library where the original wound is located. (Or at least we're getting close.) It's rarely convenient timing, but a part of us is suffering, and if we want to heal and become empowered, we must take the time to reread the book. The good news is: the layer is often more energetically refined than in the past, and since we're familiar with the book, it's possible we need only another brief "read" to gain new perspective and then return to the present moment. This is all part of life as a Four-Petaled Flower of Wholeness.

SOUL TYPES

Are you a twin, triplet, or multiple? If so, you're living a dual soulular experience. You each have your unique soul with its inner and outer skins and Living Library, yet when you were in the womb, an oversoul with a protective layer grew around you and your sibling(s). This facilitates an understanding of Unity most of us don't have and is a phenomenon you'll both/all share your entire lives.

Souls or energy bubbles aren't limited to individuals. There's the family soul. Community soul. The soul of a city. Are you in a committed relationship? Then you're a part of what Linda Jean, my healer friend who's been with her partner since they were sixteen and are now in their late sixties, calls a we-soul. These energy bubbles are like having an oversoul that encompasses two or more individual souls. The most obvious are twins (and multiples of any number), people in committed relationships, and children and their parents. But belonging to one doesn't mean you're not part of others. I imagine there are a limitless number of unique soul expressions, all of which unify everyone.

THE COLLECTIVE HUMAN SOUL

Ezekiel told me:

Each individuated human soul has a unique imprint, energetic signature, and vibrational current, and all combine to create the dynamic of the collective human soul. Everything individual affects the collective.

This is not unlike the Four-Petaled Flower, where each petal combines in the center to create the energy of the entire flower.

In 1999, I was the leader of a planetary mission to release a wellspring of love energy in western Tibet, an undertaking that was similar to, but more intensive than, what John, Juan, and our group did for Phutu Cusi. The Tibet trip not only became a hallmark of my life, it's also where I gained an understanding of the collective human soul and was primed for another initiation, which I'll share later.

This part began after my friends and I had completed a six-week purification journey throughout northern India and Nepal and were finally ready to fly to Lhasa, Tibet. I'll never forget stepping off the plane. The sky was bluer than I'd ever seen, the air crystalline, and the sun so bright and powerful that when it hit the windows of the airport building, the glaring reflection caused me to squint, despite my sunglasses.

I got sick the next morning. We thought it was the altitude, which likely played into it, but it seemed like something else was going on. I was weak, had no appetite, and my heart physically hurt. I spent three days bedridden with an undiagnosed ailment before my three traveling companions gathered around me and asked, "Annie, what is your heart trying to tell you?"

I closed my eyes and immediately became bombarded with images of past and present human atrocities. My inner sight was overwhelmed, and I began to name aloud what I was seeing: gaunt, wide-eyed, starving children in India; ethnic cleansing and genocide in Guatemala and Rwanda; Native American children stolen from their families and abused at boarding schools; men with heavy artillery forcing thousands of families from their homes and herding them along dirt roads like cattle. To this day, I still see images of women, unable to stop walking in fear of being shot, leaving their dead infants by the side of the road. As these visions emerged one by one, I felt them all and wailed at life's violent inequity. Then, as unexpectedly as they began, the pictures stopped. So did my words. After a period of silence, Jeanie asked, "How is your heart feeling now?"

I took a long, deep, emotionally exhausted breath. *The pain was gone.*

My soul had been acting as a container for those (and perhaps other) circumstances of collective human suffering, and by speaking each, the energy within me released, which discharged the pain in my heart. This is a perfect example of the power of emotional release and how it moves hucha and restores health. (There are times I think naming our truths might heal anything.) I had no idea I'd been collecting the world's agony. If I had continued, would a heart attack have been in my future?

Ezekiel said it best:

Some spirits have elected to carry soulular themes of the merged collective. While this is a creative way to take on healing and awakening for the entirety of the human soul, it is a difficult task for the human who is that spirit.

Pachamama

Let's take things one step further. Earth is a living being known by many names: Mother, Gaia, Terra. The Hopi call her Tapuat, meaning "mother and child." The Q'ero call her Pachamama, the name I use. Pacha can mean universe, world, or Earth; Mama means mother. Like all embodied beings, Pachamama is surrounded by a soul, a giant energy bubble that all beings upon her glorious body live within and are affected by.

Originally, Unity was Pachamama's dominant energy and expressed itself in her outer skin. And, like all outer skins, this mirrored the entirety of life within her bubble and upon her body. During human evolution when the outer physical world became more tangible and alluring than the inner, and the illusion of separation from Source took hold, a depth of heavy energy was created, which our guardian, Pachamama, began absorbing into her soul. This is akin to children taking on their parent's hucha, although this time our Earth Mother was taking on ours. Eventually, this hucha became part of her outer soul skin, which shifted the template of Oneness into a template of duality.

In 2011, Ezekiel shared:

The template of Earth must shift. It is time for separation to end and a restoration of Unity to begin. Although there is paradox, because for unification to occur, there must be a separation of sorts.

How prominent are the energies and forces of separation upon your planet? Many developed ancient cultures did not last because of their need for power, control, and destruction.

Separation can be a means to bring about Unity. Look amongst the leaders. If you have rulers abusing power and a country full of people who disagree with their ways...if the people within the country unite—there is Unity. Yet they are uniting to rid the country of the rulers—which is separation.

Unity and separation walk hand in hand, side by side.

All life forms go through an evolution of consciousness and Pachamama is no exception. It's become time for her outer soul skin to return to its original Oneness template, and she's entered a healing vortex to accomplish this unprecedented feat.

Ezekiel continued:

The changes you feel within yourself and see outside yourself are occurring for Earth. Everything is interconnected.

Do you feel yourself swirling around the healing vortex with Pachamama? Duality and separation are fighting for their lives so fiercely that there are days I can barely cope. But there *is* a way for us to help. Since Pachamama has taken on our heavy energy, the more refined energy we create will help accelerate her healing goal.

Let's look at our personal wounds and suffering and do what it takes to heal. Choose to live in Oneness *now*, as if the template were already restored. The more of us who view life in these ways, the faster Pachamama's healing transition will be, and the sooner her outer soul skin of Unity and Oneness will revive and flourish.

A Divine Partnership

Soul lives in two worlds—spirit and human—and serves as a bridge connecting and supporting both. It stabilizes us in our bodies, is a Living Library of our incarnational history, and as the sovereign arena for healing, acts as a sieve for our pain and suffering.

The elements of our individual souls are uniquely ours and a part of our spirit beingness from lifetime to lifetime. As lessons are learned and karma is completed, knowledge passes through soul's sheath and is absorbed into spirit as pure consciousness.

Then, when our physical lives are over and our soul no longer has a body to protect, it closes, becomes seed once again, and unites with its spirit until another incarnation stimulates its rebirth.

Every individual spirit/soul partnership affects the collective human soul, and the entirety of the collective makes up the soul of Pachamama. And that's just the beginning.

All are One.

Maintain the Energy of Your Soul

Sit or lie on the Earth. Is the sun out? If it is, feel the warm rays enter and move through your body. Is the wind whirling? Spread your arms, call it to you, and ask it to free the hucha from your soul. Is it raining? Absorb the heavenly waters. Breathe the healing moonlight into your cells. Linger in the twinkle of stars. Are birds, frogs, or crickets singing?

Bring Pachamama into your body.

Close your eyes and center and ground. When you're ready, imagine being in the middle of a large bubble (or balloon). Inhale through your heart/soul space and exhale out your entire body.

In and out...

Fill your body and soul with your fullness of self.

State an intention to release your heavy energy. You don't have to know where it's located, just breathe into your center and exhale hucha down and out.

Offer it to Pachamama. She loves eating, digesting, and transmuting it into sami and then offering it to the beings in the lower worlds.

Take your time. Let it all go.

When you feel complete, breathe Pachamama's empowered sami up through your cord, let it permeate your body, then exhale it through your center and fill your bubble to its outer edges. You'll have lots of room.

Enjoy the feeling of being centered, grounded, and replete with refined energy.

Welcome to the SOUTH

THE PETAL OF ADOLESCENCE

You've grown, not only in height (look how tall you've become!), but in knowledge.
Are you ready to continue your education?
Trickster Coyote makes her home in this petal
And will be your partner as you explore the awesome human soul.
But try not to become too serious,
Because if you do,
Your new pal might mess with your youthful mind.
Whenever that arises,
(And it will; she likes to take every opportunity she sees),
Recognize what's happening, and LAUGH.
Go for a swim. Have a picnic.
Turn the music on LOUD and dance!
The long, hot Summer days will shed plenty of Light on any confusion.
Nurture your knowings as they awaken.
And enjoy discovering that
You were born with greater wisdom than you ever imagined.

CHAPTER SIX

My Spiritual Healing Essentials

Although the world is full of suffering, it is full also of the overcoming of it.

— HELEN KELLER, *Optimism*

In the Sioux tradition, Coyote is considered a "Heyokah," a respected empath who sees life differently than most, and through humor and surprise, jars us out of conditioned ways of thinking into entirely new points of view. Let the fragrant scent of this South petal be your Heyokah. Stretch your mind and allow any lenses that might be limiting your vision to dissolve as you learn about essential elements of my Spiritual Healing practice.

The *Oxford English Dictionary* defines healing as "the process of making or becoming sound or healthy again." I'd like to add: Healing is awakening. And since this book is replete with remarkable healing and awakening stories, let me acquaint you with some of my helpers and my style of working. I've already introduced you to Mother Mary, Guadalupe, Sarayna, and Ezekiel. Now it's time to tell you about the rest of the crew. I'll begin with my Teacher, a being that showed up at the shamanic journeying workshop I attended in the early 1990s as a long-white-haired, cape-wearing wizard holding a tall staff.

THE WIZARD

The Wizard, as I called him at first, a being of unsurpassed wisdom and miraculous abilities, soon became my Teacher in all healing modalities. Then, in late 1996, five years into our relationship, he offered me a tremendous challenge.

I was washing dishes—something I enjoy—my hands warm and nurtured in the soapy water. A breeze floated through the open window, and I inhaled the fragrance of blossoming yellow roses growing outside. Amid this delightful trance, I heard a voice: *I want you to know that I am Jesus.* It was so clear. I could have sworn someone was there, on my right, the place I normally felt The Wizard's presence. I stopped what I was doing to better listen but heard nothing. I continued dishwashing.

I want you to know that I am Jesus, the voice repeated. I decided it couldn't be happening, so I ignored the voice and went into the bedroom to make the bed. *I want you to know that I am Jesus*—a third time. No longer able to deny my experience, I called Nicole, my devoted healer friend and traveling companion, and asked if she would meet me at the local brewpub. Two dark, malty beers later, I shared my story. Nicole smiled, looked directly into my eyes, and said, "Of course. That makes a lot of sense."

After that, The Wizard, now known to me as Jesus, wanted me to channel him in his new identity. I was intimidated and put it off. Until...guess who unexpectedly showed up while I was doing a channeling for a Spiritual Healing class? He apologized for the surprise, saying he'd taken that opportunity because I hadn't provided another. (This was true. I was still in denial and had no plans to provide one.) The first thing he wanted us to know was that he was *a shepherd of humble origin, an ordinary man among men. Yes, he was born bearing gifts, the abundance of the Father* (as he called the Divine), *yet he sprang from the loins of everyday people.* At the end of the communication, he asked if we would accept him as a healing teacher.

When the channeling was complete and I opened my eyes, not only was I energetically hyper-expanded, but my students were drastically triggered. A long and passionate discussion arose regarding their experiences with what they called "Christian dogma," which had plagued them in

My Teacher is a presence who is always available and on my right. He accompanies me at every Healing Ceremony and moment of life, and his brilliant wisdom and potent medicine are infused throughout this book. Whenever you see the word "Teacher" with a capital "T," you'll know who I mean.

their childhoods and subsequently turned them off to spirituality. (This is why I made my spiritual disclaimer earlier in the book.) Their palpable anger helped me once again understand the value and importance of my non-religious upbringing, which had led me to the moment when, without any associations, I could meet my Teacher and allow him to be.

If you have similar reactions to the name Jesus, I encourage you to experience him not as a person, but as a level of consciousness—the Christ consciousness—which I see as our awakened selves. Or perhaps a fifth-level healer, as in the Inka prophecy. You can even view him as an ordinary man, as he said to me—a humble shepherd. If these don't work, imagine him as the long-white-haired, cape-wearing wizard I originally met.

My Teacher is a presence who is always available and on my right. He accompanies me at every Healing Ceremony and moment of life, and his brilliant wisdom and potent medicine are infused throughout this book. Whenever you see the word "Teacher" with a capital "T," you'll know who I mean.

You might be wondering why Ezekiel and Jesus initially came to me in random forms. I believe it was a teaching that shows how the form a spirit takes doesn't matter. What's most important is the energy and wisdom that emanate from the form. A being can look like a spiritual icon, but if love, Light, and wisdom aren't present, I suggest you don't engage. (Said by one who's received blessings and healings from a Wizard and a Frog.)

CHANNELING LIGHT

I've mentioned that I participated in a hands-on healing workshop in the mid-1990s with Barbara Brennan, and upon my return home, practiced what I'd learned. I'd center, ground, place my hands on a person's feet, and breathe the Universal Energy Field or UEF, which Brennan says (in part),"…permeates all space, animate and inanimate objects, and connects all objects to each other…" in through my crown, to my center, and exhale it down my arms and out my hands into their body and soul.

One day, I tried something new. I breathed Earth energy up through my root and then followed the same routine. Earth is a different quality of energy than the UEF, and I worked with it if a client was excessively ungrounded. Over the years, when different spirit teachers showed up and taught about diverse universal energies, lights, and rays, I experimented with each one. Until Mother Mary gave us the prayer, *The Light of Love is All*. She taught that the most potent healing energy comes from within—the Light of Spirit residing in the center of our chest—and that very Light, she said, is the Light of Love. Ever since then, that's all I work with.

I can channel Light anytime. If I feel physical pain, or sad or afraid, I place my hands on my body and repeat, *The Light of Love is All*. If I'm in a store and a mother is yelling at her child or a person in the checkout line ahead of me appears ill, I inwardly chant and trust that Light is moving out my center toward the people who need it, as well as into the entire environment. For me, the Light of Love is an integral aspect of Spiritual Healing. It purifies, heals, and unifies. At the end of this chapter, I'll teach you how to work with our Divine birthright.

CEREMONY AND THE MESA

A ceremony is a mystical unfolding. It creates an expanded yet contained and protected space where we can feel Unity with the Divine. It's a place to pray, offer gratitude, ask for help, and even sense a spiritual connection one might not otherwise feel. I open a ceremony for all significant experiences, including the day I became serious about writing this book. There's no single correct way to do this—there's only *your* way. Here's mine:

Whether alone or with a client, the very first thing I do is sit with my *mesa*, a medicine bundle of the Q'ero tradition. Mesas hold sacred objects—stones, crystals, feathers, pictures, gifts from teachers, and whatever might be of significance to the holder—all wrapped together in a special (to the user) cloth. Each object within this portable altar carries the energy and spirit of its representation. For example, I have a stone in my mesa from Apu Ausangate, a significant mountain to the Q'ero, given to me at the base of the mountain by an esteemed medicine person. It holds the energy of the Apu, as well as the man who gave it to me. The small picture of Guadalupe contains the energy of her mystical, loving manifestation. When I activate my mesa, each being emerges, which means Apu Ausangate, Guadalupe, and all the other "mesa people," as I call them, are with me. Juan taught that mesas are an extension of our personal power. They remind me of the Four-Petaled Flower, where each object (or petal) is a unique, singular energetic being, yet the collective grouping within the cloth (or center of the flower) creates a unified, distinct energy.

With my mesa on my lap, I close my eyes, center, ground, and intend to become the "hollow bone" of which Lakota Medicine Man, Frank Fools Crow, spoke. As empty of mind and body as possible, I pick up the mesa and, as I've watched Juan do many times, place it on my forehead, where I honor it, and then bring it to my lips, where I blow in my living energy.

After that, I place it on my solar plexus, where, with three deep breaths, I push/feed my hucha into it. I don't necessarily know its location; I just breathe and pull it up from my feet and down from my head and push it out. A mesa "eats" hucha, digests it, and transmutes it into sami. The more it consumes, the more powerful the mesa becomes. Once mine completes this task, I ask it to infuse me with its newly enhanced sami and inhale deeply, filling my body and soul. I'm then ready to open a ceremony.

That's when I take the mesa in both hands, honor and blow my living energy into it once again, and raise it up and call, "Spirits of the mesa, come, come," inviting all the mesa people to join us. I place it on my forehead and pray, "Spirits, Masters, Healers, Teachers, Shamans of the Light, help me facilitate a miracle healing." Once everything feels complete, I offer my breath / living energy to my mesa one more time and place it on an altar. I have absolute Faith and Trust in whatever occurs next.

Once the healing, talk, class (even a colonoscopy or dental procedure!) is complete, I close the ceremony with prayers of gratitude. It might have been open for a few hours, a day, a weekend, or, regarding this book, years. I take my mesa in both hands, blow into it, raise it, and call the spirits back. I honor it at my forehead one more time, thank all the beings for their loving assistance, blow my living energy in again, and put it down. These ways are not necessarily traditional and have evolved over time. As you explore creating ceremonies, your ways will evolve as well.

INTENTION

I assist all healing clients in creating an intention, a concise affirmation that names the state of being they're aspiring to. "What does your miracle look like?" I ask. If someone struggles with depression and says, "I don't want to be depressed anymore," I might push back and say, "No. There's not enough power in that. Can you imagine how you would feel if you weren't depressed?" Creative thinking helps us realize our desires. In this case, when the person says, "I'm joyful," the difference in perspective is evident, and transformation has already occurred. An intention is a dynamic assertion, a prayer that affects a person's entire self. Once named, it becomes a focused energetic, a key unlocking the layers of the soul that need attending so the intention can manifest.

The Healing Table

When clients lie on my healing table, they have one assignment: *receive*. I put my mesa somewhere on their body, sit at their feet, and with palms up, place my hands on the soles of their feet. Then I repeat to myself, *The Light of Love is All*, as healing Light flows through me into their body and soul and flushes out embedded stagnancies and blockages. I call this "the purification of the soul" phase. Invisible helpers, invited during opening prayers, receive and transmute the heavy energy.

I tend to channel Light at a person's feet for a long while, although I never know the amount of time because there are no clocks in the healing room. And while there are energy healing practices that teach specific hand placement, experience has taught me that believing there's a "right" location and routine is limited thinking. Light goes wherever it's needed. I'll show you how this works.

Lucy had abnormal pap screens, a test detecting precancerous and cancerous cells in the cervix, for two years. She was unwilling to participate in invasive procedures and tried every alternative healing treatment possible, but in the end, her test results remained the same. Lucy's intention was: "Optimum Health." During her healing, I wasn't aware of any helpers, didn't receive any specific messages, and did nothing unusual or special regarding her cervix. I just sat at her feet, channeled Light, stood up, continued along her torso to the top of her head, and completed the healing at her shoulders. And guess what? Lucy's next pap was normal.

Sonja was an active woman in her late thirties with two young children. She'd been in a jet ski accident during the summer and had undergone several surgeries, including one in which a rod had been placed in her left knee. Sonja now walked with a cane and was suicidally depressed. She agreed to see me weekly for six consecutive weeks.

We participated in the same routine each time—opened a ceremony, spoke briefly, and then Sonja lay on my table and received. All intentions were focused on her emotional state.

During the fourth healing, I became acutely aware of Sonya's knee, which I'd completely forgotten about. Cells were growing around the rod, and I thought this might create potential problems. Did the rod need to be removed? Sonya had been told it would be permanent, but I encouraged her to speak with her doctors anyway.

New MRI pictures revealed that the rod *did* need to be removed. Seemingly unrelated, Sonya was a cigarette smoker, and it had been noted in her medical charts that her lungs were partially deadened, yet her new X-ray showed perfectly healthy lungs. After the rod was removed, Sonya fully recovered the use of her left leg, and her depression lifted.

It didn't matter what Lucy, Sonya, or I thought the outcome of their healings was supposed to be. Light has its own ideas. Invisible healers show up. And while our intentions might be expansive, Divine creativity is limitless.

PLEIADEAN HEALERS

This brings me to the Pleiadeans. When I offered the first Spiritual Healing class, I wasn't sure what I was going to do, but believed if I organized a few meetings, something amazing would happen. One afternoon while preparing for the fourth class, I felt the presence of refined energy. I checked in and discovered it was a Pleiadean healer who called herself Energeesa, the first of many spirit teachers to join us and bring themes and insights for class.

There are seven stars called "The Seven Sisters" within the Pleiadean system, and that night, Energeesa took the class on a guided visualization to one of them. My Teacher said: *Imagination is the bridge to the spirit realms.* And following his advice, each class participant arrived at a vast, bottomless pool surrounded by thick, marble-like columns. Energeesa invited us to get in and merge with the velvety waters. Near the pool stood the Hall of Energies, a large structure filled with healing tables, chambers, and seamless, open-to-the-cosmos windows. Energeesa instructed us to lay on one of the tables and receive the unique energy she called "Pleiadean Love Light" through the hands of one of the healers.

Once we "returned" from our Pleiadean escapade, everyone in the class said they felt euphoric and aware that a deep energetic purification had taken place within them. We were all a little spacy and ready for food to help us re-ground our bodies (I've discovered that burgers are a fantastic remedy for this). I still spiritually travel to these power spots for myself and on behalf of others.

Energeesa and my "Pleiadean family," as I call them, often assist at healing ceremonies. The surgeons are miracle workers—tall, etheric beings with long arms and fingers and a soft masculine energy. (Do you remember *Close Encounters of the Third Kind?* That's how they appear to me.) They arrive, immediately get to work, and leave as soon as the spiritual surgery is complete. I've never seen their faces. My job is to keep the vibration high by channeling Light.

I've had incredible experiences with these doctors, like when I worked with charismatic, thirty-five-year-old Franklyn, who was riding his motorcycle one day when he collided with a truck. He broke both knees, shins, wrists, and his upper right arm, and had metal rods holding his left leg together. It was a miracle he survived. But something was going on with Franklyn's right knee—every time he tried to bend it, he was overwhelmed by excruciating pain, a phenomenon three surgeries had been unable to remedy. Franklyn was exceedingly skeptical about my work, but one of his good friends convinced him to have a healing. His intention was: "I am pain-free."

While Franklyn lay in bed, I placed my hands on his feet and channeled Light. It wasn't long before the Pleiadean surgeons appeared and showed me the source of his pain—an area on his knee where a nerve had been stripped and left bare. They numbed the region, encased it in what I've wished many times I had in this reality—their miraculous green/ gold healing salve—coated and realigned the nerve, and left as quickly as they'd arrived. I continued channeling Light until the healing was complete. My Teacher offered this message: *Tell Franklyn to see himself as he was and wants to be again. Active. Riding. Moving. His mind must cooperate with the future shape of his form. This is his task.*

He also wanted me to tell Franklyn that his pain would be gone within three days, something always difficult to relay because it involves a specific time period. But how can I work if I don't fully trust my Teacher? Three days later, as foretold, suffering non-believer Franklyn became a pain-free believer.

Then there's Elizabeth. One morning, she woke

Energeesa and my "Pleiadean family," as I call them, often assist at healing ceremonies. The surgeons are miracle workers—tall, etheric beings with long arms and fingers and a soft masculine energy.

up with a limp left arm and throbbing pain in her neck, and after four months of unsuccessful traditional healing, came to see me. While she was on the healing table, the Pleiadean surgeons arrived, and I was privileged to observe them remove spinal bone spurs, something I'd never heard of. When the surgery was complete, they salved the area and left. My Teacher said to tell Elizabeth that for the next two days she'd feel as if her spine had been cut in two, and on the third day, it would be healed. That's exactly what happened. On day three, Elizabeth woke up and excitedly waved two strong arms over her head. The pain was gone.

And Miklos… I was in Hungary with my apprentice, and interpreter, Csilla. We went to Miklos's house, where we were greeted by his daughter and her husband. About seventy years old, Miklos appeared to be in decent health, but he was dying of lung cancer. To my surprise, healing this wasn't his focus. Miklos had accepted his eventual demise and happily shared stories about his exciting and joyous life. The problem was, ever since his lung surgery a year and a half ago, he'd been suffering from relentless back pain. Miklos and his family asked, "Can you help?"

Miklos lay relaxed and open on the living room couch. I sat at his feet, positioned Csilla with her hands on his solar plexus, and we both channeled

Light. At some point, I became aware of the Pleiadean surgeons, who pointed to an unnecessary stitch the human surgeons had taken, which bound together tissue that was never meant to be connected. They numbed the area, relieved the tension by cutting the connection, put their green/gold healing salve on it, and left. As far as they were concerned, everything was complete. Again, my Teacher declared the pain would resolve in three days.

Once Miklos sat up, Csilla, who had also been aware of the surgeons, and I shared our experiences. The family listened intently, expressed gratitude from the bottom of their hearts, and in what felt like the same breath, offered each of us a beer. For many Hungarians, Spiritual Healing is an ancient, respected part of their culture—not like in the Western world, where it's considered a strange, "New Age" anomaly. Csilla and I loved how Miklos and his family completely accepted the normalcy of an extraordinary situation. Three days later, we received an elated phone call from his daughter—Miklos's pain was gone.

The Natural World

How can I talk about awakening and becoming whole or healthy again without paying homage to the natural world? Everything has a spirit, a conscious awareness, and lives within an interconnected lifestream. Have you been to the ocean lately? When was the last time you dangled your feet in the cold, pristine water of a mountain lake? Hugged a tree? Listened to the early morning songbird chorales? Have you gone out at night and basked in the glory of the stars? Merged with the energy of the moon?

Like the "people" in my mesa, Pachamama is alive and conscious. If you choose to believe what the Milky Way Village spirits taught—that each life event has purpose—then the gray-and-white cooing dove that lands in your bird feeder in the instant you look out the window has a message for you. Do you need an assurance of grace? When I notice a turkey vulture, one of my favorite messengers, soaring high above my head on invisible wind currents, I stop, watch, and receive the offering. Oftentimes, it's about trusting the flow. If there's a flock, I'm reminded of community support within that flow. Even a dead deer on the side of the road can impart a teaching, perhaps a reminder of a recent loss of innocence and how you survived the trauma.

You can believe the multi-colored dragonfly landed on your head for no reason, but what fun is that? And while no one would dispute that it's normal for frogs to congregate around water, I prefer to believe their *ribbit, ribbit, ribbit* is Ezekiel reminding me he's there. And then there's the student who told me you can talk to anyone, anywhere, through the moon. I love that insight. The natural world consistently shows us how we're part of, not separate from, Nature.

It's our job to believe it.

SELF-LOVE

Love is the soul's path. The awakener. The unifier. The power that melts defenses and frees essential memories that support us to remember inner and outer Unity. And since nobody can make us heal but ourselves, we must begin with self-love. Even in the healing room, when spirit helpers work their magic, a person must get themself there. You might be thinking, "Self-love…how trite. I've been hearing this forever." One of my clients felt the same and became furious when I shared a message from a spirit teacher *specifically for her* about self-love. Another looked me directly in the eyes one day and said, "I don't do self-love."

How deep are your wounds? Are you living in Oneness or separation? Do you love yourself enough to commit to a healing path? To take the time to seek out and participate in the most effective practices and helpers for you? To explore what may be a concealed reservoir of emotions? How passionately do you want internal freedom?

Healing not only requires commitment; it can be uncomfortable. We've built our entire lives upon our wounds and the beliefs that arose from them. The shift out of the familiar and into new intentions and goals often requires a middle ground, one where we're no longer in the past, but not yet firmly in the future. This leaves us, for a time, in an identity crisis—an experience no one likes—and is a reason

Love is the soul's path. The awakener. The unifier.

many people either do not walk a healing path or begin one and then stop, turn around, and revert to old ways.

Ask yourself: Am I willing to move out of cultural and personal stereotypes of my suffering/ailment/diagnosis into the not-knowing? Can I lose "control" of my predictable life for a period? Can I trust being in unfamiliar emotional terrain? When I asked a client—a devoted, practicing Catholic—if he deserved a miracle, he replied, "No. That's for others, not me." I disagreed.

Do *you* deserve a miracle?

My Teacher shared this prayer for practicing self-love:

The heart is the core of the entire universe, and in the center of the heart is Unity.

The task of human beings is to live in conscious Unity.

Breathe to your heart. Feel your heart. And begin with self-love.

Is there anything keeping you from loving yourself today?

Can you have compassion for yourself?

Can you forgive yourself?

Place your hands upon your heart and ask yourself these questions. When you feel complete, chant the prayer, *The Light of Love is All,* and allow its healing essence to infuse your heart.

THE EMOTIONAL COMPONENT

Most of us try to skip the emotional aspect of healing. I understand. It's rarely fun and can be frightening. Plus, our culture offers little space or validity for it. For whatever reasons—a relationship break-up, disturbing childhood memories surfacing, the death of a loved one—when anything arises that takes our carefully constructed life and throws it up in the air, we're expected to catch the pieces as they fall, reconstruct them, and move on. When Humpty Dumpty fell off the wall, all the king's horses and all the king's men were unable to put him back together again. What happens when we "fall off the wall?" Do we allow ourselves time to put ourselves back together? After all, we have responsibilities—jobs, children, relationships, and more. "Cowgirl up," a rancher friend says. What if it takes too long (according to others) for us to "come back together?" Does that mean we're unstable or overly emotional?

Emotions are energy that our bodies create, absorb, and compile. The longer the heavier emotions remain, the greater the likelihood they'll form a density that will end up manifesting on the physical plane as illness. As abused children, my sister and I weren't allowed to express our feelings, but we certainly *had* them. Where did they go? My screams of, "No! Stop!" had no outlet, so they lived inside my throat and created thyroid disease. Susan's suffering drastically affected her mental health. Stored emotions can ruin our lives. Admitting we have them, and then honoring and releasing them, frees the energy and creates space for health.

When I was in counseling for my childhood traumas, I was afraid to dredge up old emotions. I believed if I let myself feel, I'd become lost in the past and unable to return to my present-time self. It took several visits before my desire to heal overcame this fear. I'll never forget that session—I released so much rage that by the end, my body felt like a limp rag doll. How was it possible to store all that? Re-experiencing invisible, pent-up childhood feelings took me to the edge of myself, and yet...I returned.

Something similar happened with Ally. Ally was in her early fifties, in a happy marriage, and enjoyed her work. She appeared cheery, but immediately after we opened the ceremony, her face morphed from joy into terror. Ally spoke about growing up in an abusive household and said that ever since childhood, she'd had a deep, gnawing fear of everything. Up until that point, she'd been able to manage it, she said, but it had begun threatening her marital intimacy and keeping her from enjoying life. Her intention was: "I am safe, and I love myself."

Ally lay upon my healing table, breathed deeply, and received the flow of Light. After a long period of silence, I engaged in what I call an "inner dialogue"—a process during which I become a spiritual midwife and guide clients into the depths of their souls so they might birth clarity and empowerment. It's what I did with Elise and her spiritual dilemma. Midwifery is never solely about childbirth.

Women instinctively know how to give birth. A midwife is there to hold a space of normalcy, attend to complications, and offer guidance if they become lost or afraid. It's the same with healing.

I asked Ally if she was able to locate the center of her fear, and as she gazed inward, she discovered there was no center but instead saw her fear as a thick blanket swaddling her entire body. Ally realized this blanket had been her constant companion since she was young, numbing her sorrow and keeping her from feeling alone. She knew it no longer served her, but how could she let go of such a long-cherished, protective friend? Wouldn't she be alone again? And exposed?

Ally was quiet...the calm before the storm... until a volcanic eruption of old grief and torment engulfed her. She wailed, holding nothing back. When her anguish shifted into anger, Ally directed loud, forceful daggers of rage toward her parents. Finally, her emotions spent, she spoke to her friend, "fear," and thanked it for keeping her company for so long. She then lovingly unwrapped the blanket (which only she could see), offered it into the arms of spirit helpers, and embraced her newborn self.

The Brotherhood of the Light offered this wisdom about fear:

Fear is a friend and teacher, not an enemy. When one begins to see fear as such, one can better acknowledge, honor, and work with it. Go to your fear with the respect one would go to a loving teacher. Converse with it.

Listen as it speaks to you of the reasons for its existence. Fear is deadly, for it can become more palpable than love. Love your fear, for in loving your fear, you love yourself.

This is exactly what Ally did. She needed little help from me, just the right guiding words here and there. And her face! It morphed again—this time out of terror and into the most exquisite expression of self-love I'd ever witnessed. Ally's courage to get down and dirty and allow her emotional truths to emerge changed her entire life. She experienced a true rebirth and possibly kept herself from becoming ill.

THE HEART

Everyone is born with an unguarded heart and a conscious memory of spiritual Unity and Oneness. But life changes us, and for those who've experienced disturbing or dangerous events, safety becomes a central concern. That's when the will to live kicks in and motivates us to create diverse survival techniques, one of which is the energetic placement of barricades, walls, and fences around or within our hearts. Unfortunately, these enclosures, which once made us feel safe, like Ally's blanket, end up creating separation, like my experience at the river.

A withdrawn, fearful woman named Laura came to see me. She spoke little and offered nothing about her past. When Laura lay on my healing table, I placed my hands on her feet and breathed as Light streamed through and purified her soul. I infused each energy center, connecting one to the next, and when my hands rested on her crown, my Teacher said: *It is time* and took me on a journey on her behalf.

I found myself standing in front of a jail cell. An aspect of adult Laura was there, wearing a crisp, green, prison-guard uniform and fiercely protecting something inside the cell. I looked through the metal bars and saw a pale, sickly-looking heart on a metal bench. "Why does this heart need to be imprisoned?" I asked. "Did it do something wrong?"

Prison guard Laura was silent.

"Are you willing to unlock the cell?"

"No," she staunchly replied, "the heart must be in jail forever."

I looked to my Teacher who said: *Allow the Light of Love to melt the guard's heart.*

I gently positioned my hands on Laura's heart center and intended that the Light melt the heart of the non-physical prison guard. After what might have been ten minutes, the jailer became willing to open the cell and allowed me to pick up the fragile, barely beating heart. I held it tenderly next to my own.

My spirit helpers brought us to a pristine lake for healing. While I sat on the grassy shoreline, Laura was escorted in gradually, until she was completely immersed. I waited. When she emerged from the water, it was evident a transformation had occurred. Her green prison uniform had been replaced by a

The human heart is an aspect of the Cosmic Heart and as such, is in perpetual union with the Divine. This makes our potential for loving limitless.

white, flowing caftan that her now serene body relaxed and expanded into.

My Teacher infused the rejuvenated blood-red, beating heart into Laura's heart center and whispered something in her ear that I couldn't hear. He said to me: *Tell Laura her mantra is, 'My heart is home, and I am safe.'* I restored healed Laura into her physical counterpart and shared the story. Again, we didn't speak much, but her bright eyes and knowing smile showed me she understood.

Laura had placed her heart behind bars, not because it had committed a crime, but for safety. Do you feel safe? What is the state of your heart? Are there fences or bars constricting it? If so, ask yourself, "What have I been protecting myself from? Is it a past or present situation?" And "Is the protection still necessary?"

"Love is the bridge between you and everything," said Rumi. Let's recycle the wood from our heart barriers (or the metal from the bars of our jail cells) and use it to build a vulnerability bridge—from our hearts to *all* hearts. This type of retrofitting takes courage, but what else can we do? Our suffering doesn't only affect us; it lives in every communication we have. We might not be able to change the entire world, but we can change ourselves. Enhanced happiness and personal power await when we express our emotions and uncage our hearts.

The human heart is an aspect of the Cosmic Heart and as such, is in perpetual union with the Divine. This makes our potential for loving limitless. Imagine a world where individual wounds are healed. Where heart fencing no longer has a purpose. And each human being knows that All are One. Even one person's self-love, vulnerability, and courage contribute to the collective memory of Unity.

Healing is a choice. Once you decide it's time, surround yourself with helpers who feel right to you. Pray for a miracle. Spend as much time in the natural world as possible. And remember—*this is important*—feeling old emotions doesn't mean you'll get lost or stuck in the past. It's possible to fall apart and come back together again.

In my version of Humpty Dumpty, when he came back together again (with the help of skilled and compassionate healers), he no longer looked like an egg but had transformed into a Four-Petaled Flower! We can do the same.

Loving oneself enough to walk a healing path doesn't mean we'll never stop smiling, our physical illnesses and disharmonies magically disappear, or old wounds won't resurface and catch us unaware. It does mean, however, that we can awaken from imprisoned dreams and begin creating new, free ones.

And that's when life becomes an adventure.

CHANNEL THE LIGHT OF LOVE

Let's take the prayer—*The Light of Love is All*—to the next level.

Place your hands on your heart/soul space, close your eyes, and imagine a Light there. This is the Light of Source living within us. The Light of Love.

Envision it as a candle flame.

Breathe in, and then exhale. Focus each inhalation on the Light and imagine your breath further igniting it.

Say the prayer, *The Light of Love is All*, with each inhalation and exhalation.

With your hands remaining on your center, breathe in and exhale the Light from there, but this time, move it down your arms, and out your hands. There's no need to push.

Allow the Light to flow naturally as it nourishes the center of your being.

Now that you're in a rhythm, try one more thing.

Place your hands somewhere else on your body. Are you prone to headaches? Put them on your head. Is your neck tight? Put them there. Does your stomach hurt? Let them rest on your belly.

Breathe to your center.

Exhale Light down your arms and out your hands while repeating *The Light of Love is All*.

Are your hands tingly? Hot? How does your body feel? Everyone likes validation, but it's important for me to say, "Sensations and experiences are irrelevant." What is relevant is trusting that you are the Divine Light residing within you, as well as a human conduit for it.

Everyone can channel the Light of Love, which I believe is the most potent healing Light that exists.

CHAPTER SEVEN

Shamanism and Spiritual Healing

*The reason why the world lacks unity, and lies broken
and in heaps, is, because man is disunited with himself.*

— RALPH WALDO EMERSON, *Nature*

This is the final chapter in the South petal. Ahhh, my friends, you've grown up so fast. How's your relationship with Coyote been going? Have you been chuckling together? Enjoy her company for a little while longer while you explore shamanism—a vital aspect of my work as a Spiritual Healer.

Shamanism is a timeless, and often considered the oldest, cross-cultural spiritual path that can be dated back 100,000 years. It is experientially based, which takes it out of the categories of faith-based religions or belief systems. This is because the direct revelations each person undergoes color the unique lens through which they see the world and become teachings for their lives. Shamanism is practiced throughout the world, and every culture has its distinctive shamanic cosmology, symbols, initiatory events, practices, and beliefs.

I've decided that the best way to help you gain an understanding of shamanism is to defer to the words of Michael Harner, my workshop teacher and founder of the Foundation for Shamanic Studies,

who is acknowledged as the world's foremost authority. In an interview in *Shamanism*, Spring/Summer 1997, Vol. 10, No. 1, he defines the word shaman as being from the original Tungus language, referring "to a person who makes journeys to nonordinary reality in an altered state of consciousness." He calls shamans "see-ers" (seers), or "people who know" in their tribal languages, because they are involved in a system of knowledge based on firsthand experience.

To describe shamanism a bit more, I include Michael's reference to a book written by Mircea Eliade, *Shamanism: Archaic Techniques of Ecstasy*, in which the author "concluded that shamanism underlays all the other spiritual traditions on the planet, and that the most distinctive feature of shamanism—but by no means the only one—was the journey to other worlds in an altered state of consciousness."

SHAMANS

A shaman is a healer who receives a spiritual calling. This can come at any age and might be as simple as a community-recognized innate ability, a profound connection with the Earth, an inherited family lineage, or a strong inner awareness that this is their path. Some are directed through dreams and visions by the spirits themselves.

All shamans go through some type of initiatory event: a near-death experience, being struck by lightning, or even a mental breakdown—which, as Malidoma Patrice Somé, West African shaman said, "signals the birth of a healer." Malidoma has stated that what Western cultures deem as mental illness, his culture, the Dagura, sees as "good news from the other world." They believe these people have been chosen to relay a message from the spirit realm and so do whatever it takes to support them. We think they belong in hospitals, where the main support is often medication.

Every shamanic initiation is deeply personal, and in its way, a form of dis-memberment. The coming back together or re-memberment is what begins the new lifestyle. There are as many callings and initiations as there are shamans, from Indigenous and traditional to Western and modern.

Just as soul is a bridge that connects spirit with human, a shaman is a bridge that connects the spiritual realms with this one. To do this, they attain an altered state of consciousness through culture-specific as well as empirically learned techniques.

Just as soul is a bridge that connects spirit within human, a shaman is a bridge that connects the spiritual realms with this one.

They might listen to a drumbeat or the drone of a didgeridoo, shake a rattle, or dance. (Or a combination.) Some work with plant medicines. Ayahuasca, a vine that grows in the Amazon rainforest, when cooked in combination with the leaves of the charuna plant, results in a dynamic brew that creates psychedelic effects that allow the shaman to diagnose and heal their clients.

Every action a shaman takes is unique to themselves and the purpose of the healing. They journey with intent and receive assistance from compassionate spirits of various shapes, sizes, forms, and energies. Once their task is complete, they return to what Michael Harner calls "ordinary reality" with the necessary information to resolve whatever the physical, emotional, mental, or spiritual problem might be.

Most shamanic traditions have three significant worlds—the middle, upper, and lower—each containing an infinite number of realms. Since shamanism is experiential with varying energetics, visions, and insights, these can be difficult to describe. My experience is: the middle world refers to our earthly reality in the past, present, or future. You might find yourself in the house you grew up in or, as I did in one of my early journeys for a friend, in her father's study furnished with brown leather chairs, tall bookcases, and a huge desk. The lower world often appears like this one, although without the same rules—gravity doesn't exist, horses fly, unicorns roam the land and sky, and we can breathe under water. The upper world can be more etheric. Colors are heightened, and while feeling grounded may be difficult, standing on a cloud is natural. To me, whether up, down, or middle, some realms are personally relatable and others exceedingly strange. Some are energetically dense, and others refined. A realm might be filled with people or have none. Each has remarkable qualities, and through intention, we reach the appropriate one(s) via a "shamanic journey," something most people can learn to do. (Although having the skill does not make one a shaman.)

Shamans often travel with power animals, unique spirits that escort them to their destinations and help navigate spiritual terrain. A power animal lives within the soul and provides support, guidance, and protection. Their gifts are as distinctive as an elephant is from a cougar, snake, or raccoon. Shamanically speaking, everyone has a power animal, but sometimes, for unknown reasons, it might leave and not immediately be replaced. This loss generates an energetic void, and the first action a shaman might take on their client's behalf is a power animal retrieval. If you ever learn the shamanic journey, your power animal will become your ally and friend within the spiritual realms.

Shamanism Enters My Life

In late 1992, a few months after I returned from the trip to Yosemite, I participated in a weekend shamanic journeying workshop led by Michael Harner. He taught us "core shamanism"—which, as defined by the Foundation for Shamanic Studies, "consists of the universal, near-universal, and common features of shamanism, together with journeys to other worlds, a distinguishing feature of shamanism. As originated, researched, and developed by Michael Harner, the principles of core shamanism are not bound to any specific cultural group or perspective." It was challenging, humbling, and exhilarating, and in two brief days, I went from believing I was unable to do it to retrieving my workshop partner's power animal. He retrieved mine as well, and Horse has been my solid companion in every journey I've taken since.

During the weekend, I noticed a flyer for a soul retrieval workshop scheduled to take place a few months later. I didn't have any idea what it was all about, but a strong inner knowing arose, signaling that I needed to attend, so I registered immediately.

Soul Retrieval

Before I define soul retrieval, I must first speak about trauma. The American Psychological Association defines it as "an emotional response to a terrible event like an accident, rape, or natural disaster. Immediately after the event, shock and denial are typical. Longer-term reactions include unpredictable emotions, flashbacks, strained relationships, and even physical symptoms like headaches or nausea." These "longer-term reactions" can be attributed to dissociation, a state that has been named "post-traumatic stress disorder" or PTSD for short.

What is dissociation? What dissociates? Does the dissociated "thing" go someplace? If so, where? Can we get it back? Is it possible to heal from PTSD? To "reassociate?"

Shamanism enhances the psychological view of dissociation. Remember, during traumatic incidents, heavy energy penetrates the outer soul skin and creates space for parts to dissociate or split off. This can be seen as a bad thing, but there's another way of looking at it. It often is what allows us to survive.

There are people who've experienced traumatic events who find talk therapy a helpful healing technique. Some rely on EMDR—Eye Movement Desensitization and Reprocessing—which they say can be a lifesaver for releasing stored emotions. Others attest to the ability of pharmaceutical medications to mask or calm their inner suffering. I received help from a somatic therapist and discovered that using breath, voice, body, and ceremony worked powerfully for me. But despite all these modalities and more, too many people spend years within the traditional mental health system unable to break free from damaging childhood conditioning and traumatic experiences.

Trauma, as defined above, is "an emotional response to a terrible event," an experience so dreadful or frightening it can change our lives forever. Is there an event in your life you've been unable to get over? Are you taking medications to ease the emotional pain? Have you been hospitalized because of it?

When a part of the soul dissociates, it remains stuck in the time when the trauma occurred. Some parts are aware of their dissociated state and others are not, but all live as if the original experience, no matter how much time has elapsed since it occurred, is happening in the present moment. This fragmentation causes us to straddle two simultaneous realities: the tangible present, and the traumatic past. Aristotle, the Greek philosopher from 300 BCE, coined the phrase, "nature abhors a vacuum." I've discovered this to be true with the soul. When a part leaves, hucha fills the space, which not only affects that specific area of the soul but our entire soulular makeup.

Soul loss can manifest as depression, what appear to be irrational fears, anxiety, insomnia, repetitive patterns, addiction, suicidal thoughts, spaciness, memory gaps, immune-deficient illness such as chronic fatigue, coma, and a myriad of other human conditions. The longer the loss, the more likely our suffering is prolonged and the potential for illness increases.

Most of us are not conscious of soul loss in our day-to-day lives—until we hear a siren and run for cover because we're catapulted back into war. Or we're afraid to drive past the scene of an accident that happened thirty years ago. It's not uncommon for windy days and the smell of smoke to provoke anxiety for survivors of wildfires or 9/11. When something happens in our present that triggers a past trauma—like my dental dam experience—PTSD or soul loss activates. This resonance exists because, as multi-dimensional beings, we *are* our soul-parts, and until we recognize, heal, restore, and lovingly integrate them, we're affected by their state of being. And even then, like little Annie, they might need attention from time to time.

There are limitless places where a soul-part can end up, from personal realms based on the unique make-up of an individual to untold dimensions of the collective, like heaven or hell, the Cave of the Lost Children, or the Land of the Dead.

Steve Beyer, author of *Singing to the Plants*, writes, "It is soul, not spirit, that is the true landscape of shamanism. Shamans deal with sickness, envy, malice, betrayal, loss, conflict, failure, bad luck, hatred, despair, and death—including their own. The purpose of the shaman is to dwell in the valley of the soul—to heal what has been broken in the body and the community."

Shamanic soul retrieval is an ancient, multi-cultural ceremony where, through a process unique to the shaman's environment, traditions, helping spirits, personal experiences, and ingenuity, lost parts are found, offered healing, and returned. As you might imagine, soul retrieval can enhance traditional therapy and even save lives.

As you might imagine, soul retrieval can enhance traditional therapy and even save lives.

PARTICIPATING IN SOUL RETRIEVALS

As is characteristic of how I learn, before I went to the workshop, I wanted to experience my own soul retrieval and was referred to a practitioner by the Foundation for Shamanic Studies. A casually dressed woman who might have been around forty, my age at the time, greeted me at the door. She led me into a small room where a lit candle, a rattle, and feathers were placed on a circular, wooden altar. There was a round hoop drum leaning against the wall where an open window overlooked a flower garden. It smelled like sage.

We sat on the floor on an earth-toned area rug and faced one another. After speaking briefly, she closed her eyes and began softly singing and gently rattling, her way of calling in the spirits. We lay down together on the rug with the sides of our bodies touching, and when she turned on a drumming tape, the entire room filled with dynamic, rhythmic beats. After what might have been ten minutes, she sat up, reached her hands out in front of her, received something I couldn't see, and brought it to her heart. Then she blew it into my heart/soul space and my crown and rattled around me.

She told me she'd found a six-year-old part of my soul hiding in the cloakroom closet of my kindergarten room. (Little Annie.) I remembered that closet.

I was away from my parents for the first time and recall feeling different from my classmates. *I was keeping a secret, remember?* Metaphorically, I was hiding in the closet. She was kind and skilled, but I left without any idea of what to do.

In early 1993, I flew to New Mexico to attend the workshop, which was taught by Sandra Ingerman, respected shamanic healer, teacher, and author of *Soul Retrieval: Mending the Fragmented Self.* When I returned home, I practiced as much as possible by offering soul retrieval healings to friends. Now, almost thirty years later, I can wholeheartedly say— shamanic soul retrieval is a direct and powerful pathway to inner Unity. To paraphrase Sandra, people spend years in traditional therapy trying to heal from a traumatic event, which can be likened to playing a game of cards without having the full deck. Soul retrieval finds, heals, and restores the dissociated parts, and once the deck is complete, a rapid (at times, amazingly so), healing process unfolds.

In the beginning, I facilitated soul retrievals separately from my other healing work. Clients and their friends and family would come to my house, and while the actual journey took under fifteen minutes, the three-hour ceremonial evening was an opportunity for teaching, group participation, and celebration. I loved working that way.

After a few years, I noticed that a hands-on

Almost thirty years later, I can wholeheartedly say— shamanic soul retrieval is a direct and powerful pathway to inner Unity.

healing session one week before a soul retrieval both energetically refined the soul and enhanced the client's readiness to receive returning parts. I practiced like that until discovering I could journey without the use of a drum. That's when soul retrieval, if necessary, merged with hands-on healing, and became Spiritual Healing Ceremonies. Regardless of the process, it's a privilege to participate in soulular unification.

I do, however, have a dogma: *a healing must be done for each part before it is returned.* This is obvious if it's sad or afraid, but not so if the soul-part is in a joyful state. For example, if a child's home life is unsafe, their survival will likely require adaptation, so the young one must relinquish their childhood and adjust. They do this by dissociating. But what happens to their innate youthful innocence? The soul-part expresses it in another realm, which is why it appears joyful when found. Dissociation always equals trauma. Soul loss might be the result of one specific event, such as a car accident, or several thematic ones, like the example above, which at their tipping point catalyze the dissociation.

Unless my Teacher shows or tells me something different, we bring all parts to my magical healing spot in the lower world, a place where it's consistently daylight with a bright blue sky, shining sun, and puffy, cotton-ball clouds. The healing alchemy takes place in a pristine lake surrounded by old-growth trees, and each part is brought into the inviting water by either me, my Teacher, or spirit helpers. A magnificent boulder, guardian to all activity, sits on the grassy shoreline.

I included soul retrieval stories in previous chapters before explaining the nuances, and now that you have a more in-depth understanding, I hope you'll return to them. Here are more, all showing their healing and unification potential.

Post-Traumatic Stress

I met Marc on a quiet beach in Mexico. He was visiting a mutual friend and shared his story as we strolled together on the sand. Marc had been a Green Beret during the Vietnam War and returned home with a severe case of medically diagnosed PTSD. He spent years seeing countless doctors and ingesting an assortment of prescription medications, but never received relief. It didn't matter where he was—in bed, on a park bench, at the mall—Marc was unable to escape the war. At his final psychiatric appointment, his doctor said, "You have the worst case of PTSD I've ever seen. There's nothing we can do for you."

We set up a healing for the next day. Marc's intention was: "I am home."

My Teacher and power animal brought me to a battlefield where an adrenaline-pumping, hyper-alert part of Marc ran around trying to seek cover amid dozens of other scattered parts. Overwhelmed,

I asked my Teacher, "What should we do?" He replied: *Gather all the pieces and place them in this basket.*

I looked down to see a large woven basket at my feet. I picked it up, raised my arms, and called, "Marc! Come. Come." Parts of Marc not only from the battlefield but from all stages of his life appeared, floated around me, and dropped into the basket. Once it became filled, we took it to my healing spot, where I immersed both the basket and all its contents into the sacred water.

It didn't take long before a vibrant, present, twenty-year-old Marc emerged and was joined by Cougar, his new power animal. Marc climbed on Cougar's back and yelled, "I'm ready. Let's go!" I raised my arms and brought them to my heart/ soul space. Then I sat up and transferred them from the Spirit Realm into this one by blowing them into Marc's heart and crown. I rattled around him four times, as I had been taught at the workshop, and encased them into his soul.

This is an example of the spirits using the intention of a healing, one Marc and I thought was solely about his war experience, as an opportunity for what could have been lifetimes of dissociation. Instead of one soul-part returning—Marc during the war— parts with a relationship to his intention that had dissociated over time entered the basket as well.

A few days later, Marc said he'd slept better than he had in years. I never saw him again, although our mutual friend told me he remained calm and present and believed he had finally left the war behind.

FEAR

Betty's childhood had been difficult, and at forty years old, she spoke in such a low voice I could barely hear her. Her intention was: "It is safe to speak."

Betty lay peacefully on my healing table as I channeled Light, and when my hands were resting on her fifth chakra, my Teacher and Horse took me on a journey. Down we went, deep under the ocean, until we reached the very bottom. I dismounted from Horse, looked around, and saw iridescent fish encircling a small area. I was instructed to dig. A shovel appeared, and I soon uncovered a large, heavy, old-fashioned treasure chest. Spirit helpers picked it up and placed it on the ground. It was unlocked.

I opened the curved top and was dazzled by the sparkle of brilliant jewels. Rubies. Emeralds. Diamonds. Sapphires. My Teacher said they were a manifestation of Betty's voice and had been hidden ever since she was five years old. He picked each one up, held it tenderly, and purified it with golden Light emerging from his hands. When he was finished, I transferred the precious jeweled bounty of Betty's voice from the spiritual realms into the physical and blew it directly into her throat.

Betty's childhood trauma and subsequent soul loss had depleted her throat so significantly that as an adult, she could barely speak. Three days after the healing, a worried Betty called to say she'd been talking non-stop in a childlike voice. I suggested it might be her five-year-old self and encouraged her to check in with her soul-part, as well as to allow a few more days for the energy of her voice to harmonize within her throat. A week later, Betty joyfully reported that she had her adult voice back. And was using it!

Soul retrieval isn't just necessary for our emotional health. Sometimes a body part needs one. After a client's heart attack, during her healing, I was brought to another realm to retrieve and restore the energetic template of her healthy heart. I was told her physical heart needed to be reminded of its well-being. Consider soul retrieval whenever you have a specific body or organ disharmony.

ABUSE

Millie was twenty-seven years old. From ages six through twelve, she'd endured such radical physical and emotional abuse that it left her physical and emotional bodies literally numb. Her intention was: "I am safe."

I was taken to a realm where a seven-year-old part of Millie's soul was frozen inside a thick encasement of ice. Even I was cold. My Teacher instructed: *We will melt the ice enough for you to converse with her.* I held my hands up in front of what looked like a three-story, six-foot-thick block, and as they began radiating heat, the ice started dripping. I continued until only a thin sheet remained. Little Millie, still inside, stared at me. I said, "My name is Annie, and I'm here on behalf of adult Millie. She loves you and wants you to return to her. She's all grown up, married, and has a daughter you can play with." Little Millie replied immediately, "I want to play with her," and when the ice completely melted, she fell into my arms.

My Teacher said: *We will take little Millie to a natural hot spring for healing.* We traveled to a nearby area and placed her in the revitalizing water. After a while, little Millie felt so invigorated that she began singing and dancing. "Are you ready to go home and have fun with your new sister?" I asked. "Yes!" she sang. I returned little Millie, accompanied by her power animal, a brown bear who showed up while she was soaking, to adult Millie's soul.

Becoming numb had saved Millie from a traumatic childhood yet was impeding her life as an adult. Over the next few weeks, as her soul-part energetically integrated (and played with Millie's daughter), Millie's physical body enlivened and formally frozen emotions began to surface. Once she felt grounded enough, Millie found a supportive therapist to help her heal her childhood traumas.

STUCK

Olivia was confused. Even though she had a healthy daughter, a comfortable home, loving friendships, and enjoyed her job, she felt stuck. Her intention was: "I'm happily walking my highest path."

My Teacher and Horse brought me to a realm where a lifeless shell of adult Olivia's body was encased with dozens of energetic cords attached all over and trailing out. My Teacher told me: *We will bring her for cleansing and rejuvenation.* He placed the limp "shell" on Horse, and we flew to my healing spot, where spirit healers immediately attended to it. Then, still riding on Horse, my Teacher escorted me to another realm, where an adult aspect of Olivia was sinking in a large pond of quicksand. An assortment of concerned animals—giraffes, deer, squirrels, polar bears—sat on the shoreline but didn't help because they were afraid of falling into the quicksand themselves.

Olivia called, "Annie! Can you get me out of here?" (Sometimes a soul-part recognizes me.) I looked at my Teacher but was suddenly distracted by an enormous cobalt-and-white owl. With a wingspan larger than a condor's, it swooped down, picked up Olivia with its talons, and dropped her on the shore next to me. Completely covered with thick mud, Olivia said, "I'm a mess. Can someone help me?" A nearby elephant used his trunk like a garden hose and nearly flooded her with water, after which Olivia said, "Thank you. Now let's get out of here." We traveled back to my healing spot, where helpers led Olivia into the purifying water. Her now-vibrant, cord-free soul shell awaited, and when she emerged, Olivia put it on as if it were a second skin. "Now I feel like myself," she said. I returned Olivia to her soul.

Energy cords are like umbilical cords, but instead of being comprised of veins and arteries that transport food and remove waste products, they're filled with energy. Cords connect us to a person, place, thing, and even a belief, and provide a venue for our energy to travel away from us and merge with something else. This creates an energetic loss within our physiological system, as well as emotional confusion. Olivia was a brilliant woman attached to life's responsibilities, duties, and concepts her parents and culture found important and didn't know who she was without them. Free from cords and quicksand, Olivia was able to move forward in new and creative ways, ones that arose from her soul instead of cultural standards. I had a vision of her drumming and recommended she get a hoop drum and see what happens.

Energy cords are like umbilical cords, but instead of being comprised of veins and arteries that transport food and remove waste products, they're filled with energy.

DEPRESSION

Frank had a good life—a devoted wife, healthy children, and a beautiful home—but something was keeping him from living wholeheartedly. When he was eight years old, his younger brother, Reggie—two years old at the time—died, and instead of Frank's parents helping him process this traumatic event, they silently moved the family to another state and began anew, as if nothing had happened. Frank's intention was: "I'm free to be myself."

I was brought to the Death Gateway where an eight-year-old part of Frank was hysterically calling for his brother, "Reggie! Reggie!" While I remained on Horse outside the tunnel, as I always do when I find myself at the Death Gateway, I extended my arms and asked Frank if he'd like to leave and come with me. He refused. I looked to my Teacher for guidance, and he pointed to the right, where a being riding a large, white, winged horse had appeared. It was Reggie, all grown up! He called to young Frank, who immediately responded by grabbing my arms, moving out of the gateway, and joining me on Horse. Reggie said, "Don't worry. I'm fine. There's no reason to feel guilty. We were just kids. Live for both of us." The brothers hugged, and then the winged horse carried Reggie to the Light. Once they were gone, we brought Frank to the lake for healing. He loved being in the water and when his young vibrant self finally emerged, he declared, "I want to paint and draw." I restored little Frank into adult Frank's soul and shared the mystical story.

People can become so distraught at the death of a loved one that they try following them. This is what happened to Frank, and I imagine, to other family members. No one can move through the Death Gateway into the Light until it's their time. Grief-stricken soul-parts might try, but they only become stuck. People suffering from depression or who have attempted suicide commonly have parts in there. Some are so miserable, it takes an enormous amount of convincing for them to choose to return, others are confused and need an explanation about how they got there, while a few are aware they've become stuck and are thrilled to finally leave. Every situation is unique. After Frank's healing, his guilt over his brother's death receded, which opened space for his creativity. I like to imagine him painting and drawing.

Mirror Image

Patricia was in her late sixties. Tall, thick-bodied, and hunched over, she complained of weakness, pain, and sciatica. When I asked, "What can I do for you?" Patricia spoke without emotion, saying, "I've been working on myself my entire life" and "I don't want to speak about my past; it's too intense." Her intention was: "I am pain-free."

Patricia lay on my healing table and stared at the ceiling. I placed my hands on her feet, channeled Light, and remained still. It took a long while for the energy to move up her legs. When I was finally feeling the flow, my Teacher and Horse transported me to another realm where the only thing that existed was a hunchbacked, present-age part of Patricia's soul encased in heavy steel chains. They were attached at the front of her shoulders, wrapped around her back, encircled her waist, and then dropped down about four feet and connected behind her to a massive metal ball on the ground. Patricia was trying to walk. And while movement appeared to be an impossible task, her steadfast will and determination were unwavering. I asked, "Would you like me to remove the chains?"

"Yes," she replied, as no-nonsense in the Spirit Realm as she was the physical.

We freed Patricia and brought her to my healing spot where helpers escorted her into the water. She emerged refreshed, chainless, and upright. My Teacher proclaimed: *It is done.* I asked Patricia, "Are you ready to rejoin your soul?" After a barely perceptible nod, I called her healed soul-part into my hands, blew it first into her center, then into her crown, and rattled around her entire body. Patricia immediately sat up, smiling ear to ear. I smiled too… but something seemed odd, and as I watched her get up off the table, I knew what it was—she was no longer hunched over!

Patricia's soul-part had created an actual template for her physical body. Remember she had said, "I don't want to speak about my past; it's too intense." This might have been a reference to the metaphoric boulder she'd been chained to and was trying to lug. It had exhausted not only her physical body (can you imagine how tired she must have been?), but her emotional and energetic bodies as well. Patricia left my healing studio standing tall, fully energized, and in a delightful mood. I barely recognized her.

Spiritual Healing for Children

Children are ripe for Spiritual Healing. Their naturally expansive energetic state keeps them in a heightened connection with the Mystery, and because they're less caught up in their minds than adults, results can be rapid. Here's a soul retrieval story that took place from a distance:

A mother told me her daughter, Sara, "was born overly attached to me. Even as an infant I had to tell her before a change was going to occur because unless I prepared her first, she cried. For the next six years, we made sure she had time to adjust to new situations. The only way we were able to get her into school was because a progressive principal and patient teacher allowed me to remain in the classroom until she was ready for me to leave. When Sara was eight, she had a new principal and teacher. Neither was supportive of her needs, and both suggested I leave while she was upset. I tried this tactic, but Sara began backsliding on all the progress we'd made the previous two years and asked to be homeschooled every morning."

My Teacher shared: *Sara comes from a star system many light years away from any human-known systems, and all who incarnate from there have heightened, refined souls. This is both a blessing and a challenge. Sara must grow into her energetic nuances, for only then will she become comfortable being human and living with the density, suffering, and disunity of Earth. Sara sees and feels more than she can articulate. She travels in the night and receives enhancements to her energetic state, which is one of the reasons why it's difficult to awaken her.*

Specialized Beings don't necessarily fit in with our accepted organizations of family, culture, school systems, or religion. Easily misunderstood, they question authority, bore easily, and prefer to focus on creative interests instead of linear schoolwork.

Sara is what's often referred to as an Indigo child, or "Specialized Being" (the name I've been taught to call these wonderous ones). These are spirits that undergo a unique preparation for their benevolent life missions. These heart-based beings with heightened energetic frequencies relate from a place of Oneness and Unity, distinctions that make them vulnerable to the disunification of this realm. They're often called "old souls," because their expanded consciousness offers them—and us—powerful insights.

Specialized Beings don't necessarily fit in with our accepted organizations of family, culture, school systems, or religion. Easily misunderstood, they question authority, bore easily, and prefer to focus on creative interests instead of linear schoolwork. That's when labels and behavior-modifying medications come in, and while medicating these children may placate the family and generate compliant ease in the classroom, it doesn't always serve the child.

Pharmaceuticals shift a young person's core energetic essence, which contracts their hearts and diminishes their self-awareness and creative flow. These constrictions can lead to feelings of emptiness and are often followed by depression. Imagine a radiant golden heart. Now see it implode and collapse into itself. Our Specialized Being children might begin achieving higher grades in school, but does anyone notice their emotional shift? Hearts can become so deeply caved that suicide becomes an option. Sara chose an awake mother, perhaps an expression of her karma, and while her story is unique to her spirit/soul path, many children, aged from birth to the thirties, are here with similar blessings and challenges.

Sara's mother wanted to better understand Sara's fear of being alone. My Teacher explained:

The coarseness of the Earthly Realm was more than Sara's spirit overview had prepared her for. A separation occurred during your labor when contractions forced her to enter her small body and accept what she'd chosen. She needed more integration time. As a spirit, she had seen this, yet it's different when one is in the actual human experience.

It turned out that when Sara was born, an emotional survival switch—"It is not safe here; I have no control"—turned on and created fear, and this switch only releases when she feels safe. Spirit Sara knew she needed to learn about duality in this lifetime and incarnating on Earth was her conscious choice, but as she melded into the consciousness of this reality, the switch gained too much power, and she forgot her spirit-realm decisions—which, as we know, happens to everyone, not just her. My Teacher's guidance helped us arrive at the intention of the healing: "Safety."

I opened a ceremony, called in my helpers, and imagined Sara lying on my healing table with Light flowing through my hands into her body. As that was occurring, my Teacher and Horse took me on a journey to a cave. Just inside the entrance, an early-twenties part from Sara's future was acting as a fierce protector to multiple parts, of diverse ages. They all had one thing in common—fear of having no control. When I introduced myself, shared why I was there, and invited everyone to come with me and live inside Sara on Earth, a loud simultaneous, "No!" bounced against the cave's walls. I asked the protective mother part if she would be willing to peer outside. She agreed.

Her eyes alone explored a vista that showed particulars about her future. I was privy only to the final image—Sara as a beautiful, wizened, elder sitting on a rocking chair and knitting. After witnessing her upcoming life, she turned around, faced the cave, beckoned to the "children," and unified them into her body. Her power animal, a large white unicorn, awaited, and Sara sat on its back and flew with us to my healing water. After being attended to by the helpers, a fully empowered goddess, wearing a deep purple velvet cloak, emerged. She looked to the side and noticed her emotional survival switch in the "on" position, then glanced at me, grinned, and turned it off. My Teacher returned Sara and her unicorn to her soul.

"In the following days and weeks," her mother reported, "Sara began going to the bathroom alone.

This was a miracle. She also began getting dressed without needing someone with her. After a school break, I wondered how her first day back would be. When we walked into the classroom, her best friend wouldn't talk to her, and another girl was crying. Seeing a child upset was always enough to set Sara into extreme anxiety, but this time she didn't get lost in either experience. I knew she was nervous, but she calmly bid me goodbye, and at the end of the day, I was greeted by a smiling girl. Since then, she's stayed at both grandparents' homes overnight, without me or her dad. My daughter finally feels safe."

Children are teachers of love and Unity. Let's nourish their memories. Feed their individuality. And support them to flourish in their uniqueness and creativity. Every child is a Four-Petaled Flower role model who has purposefully chosen to enhance our collective awakening.

INTEGRATION

A restored soul-part is a multi-dimensional being that holds the heavy energy of the trauma, the reasons for dissociating, *plus* the refined energy we were unable to feel and express. After my six-year-old part was taken out of the cloakroom closet, healed, and restored to forty-year-old me, her young, vital energy became available to adult me. I can't begin to imagine the energetic shift Marc felt after the restoration of so many parts. Whatever abuse five-year-old Betty suffered that made her bury her voice to survive, and seven-year-old Millie endured that caused her to numb herself, the change in adult Betty's voice and Millie's body clearly showed that their original energetic health was restored.

Soulular integration is an exciting process. While results can be immediate, like Patricia's physical and emotional transformation (which to this day I believe was a true miracle), I've noticed that it can take three days (I don't know why) for the newly restored, refined energy to harmonize within the soul and body. As this balance unfolds, a person might find themself in any number of states—sad, happy, angry, exhausted, unable to sleep, dreaming, starving, not hungry at all…you name it, it's happened. The energy generally stabilizes by day four and continues harmonizing over weeks and even months. A client once described soul retrieval as "the gift that keeps on giving." Some parts require little attention, while others necessitate that we focus on them daily. And since soul retrieval stories can be linear, metaphoric, and/or allegoric, their specific symbolism is unique to the person, who may or may not fully understand it themself.

Dissociation and soul loss are common themes for the majority of my clients, whether they're physically ill, emotionally suffering, or energetically challenged. Trauma creates dissociation, or PTSD, which becomes soulular disunity. Soul retrieval, in its countless, worldwide creative forms, is a hallmark of all shamanic traditions. Its healing and unifying benefits continue to withstand the test of time.

SOUL RETRIEVAL
INTEGRATION SUGGESTIONS

GROUND. Place both hands on your heart/soul space. Breathe.

Use your imagination and call, one at a time, to each restored soul-part and lovingly welcome them home.

NOTICE THEIR BEHAVIOR. Is there anything she/he/they want to share? Listen to what they say, even if you think you're making it up. Choose to trust your experience.

And then (a little Heyokah humor here) ask the part, "What would you like for dinner?"

Most people are surprised when I suggest this and surprised again at the response they receive after asking the question. We all had favorite foods when we were young. If your part says, "chocolate cake," buy or bake one. You, the adult, can decide if it will be your dinner or dessert. The main thing is to connect with your part while eating it. (Little Annie wanted mint chocolate chip ice cream, so I ate an entire pint in her honor.)

A client called me two weeks after her soul retrieval to share a story. She'd been craving a McDonald's burger all week and couldn't understand why—until she had an "aha" moment. When she was nine years old, those burgers were her favorite food. Her reunited little girl wanted comfort food, and so, in an act of pure self-love, the forty-two-year-old vegetarian took her nine-year-old self to McDonald's.

CREATE AN ALTAR. Include your intention and if possible, pictures of yourself at whatever age(s) your restored soul-part(s) might be. If you received a power animal, find a picture, statue, or even a stuffed animal and place it there also. You might even decide to sleep with it.

CLAIM YOUR INTENTION, for as a student said, "the intention becomes an anchor for the conscious embodiment of the healing." Your entire post-healing experience unfolds in relation to this, and if you stay awake, and live "as if," your unification process might accelerate.

CHECK-IN WITH YOUR SOUL-PARTS DAILY. What do they want? Need? Can you accommodate them?

TRY THIS: Sit someplace where you won't be disturbed. Bring a pencil and paper. Ask one part at a time if there's anything it wants to say. Pick up your pencil with your non-dominant hand and begin writing. I learned this exercise in my early thirties while attending an inner child workshop. It was the first time I became viscerally aware of little Annie and discovered how scared and unhappy she was. (When a friend did this, her part responded by writing right to left, so when the process was complete, she had to hold it up to the mirror to read it!)

DON'T FORGET ABOUT YOUR POWER ANIMAL. What medicine does it offer? You can research this, but try asking directly. Here's a heart-warming power animal story. A client was in temple when the Rabbi suddenly began weeping in the middle of giving a talk. Once he somewhat composed himself, he explained to the congregation that his mother had recently died. My client became creative in a way that never occurred to me—she asked her lioness power animal to comfort the Rabbi. Within minutes, she said, he expressed that he suddenly felt a newfound calmness. She simply smiled.

Integration is a conscious, creative, self-loving exploration. Communicating with your retrieved soul-parts might make you feel a little crazy at first, but there will come a time when you'll notice you haven't checked in for a while. Do it.

Is everyone happy? If so, perhaps integration is complete.

Welcome to the WEST

THE PETAL OF ADULTHOOD

The maple leaves have turned multi-shades of red.
And as they dance in the Autumn breeze, gently falling and scattering on the lawn,
You're reminded of your childhood.
But that's the past. In the present, you're an adult
Walking the path of your career choice and attending to your family.
Are you ready to pause your day-to-day routine?
Get away for some much-needed introspection?
This is the home of Bear.
Ask her to take you into the lush, moist darkness of her womb-like cave,
Where pieces of your life puzzle await further exploration.
If these newfound discoveries ever begin to burden, tire, or bewilder you.
Take some breaks.
Crawl outside of Bear's lair, lay flat on Pachamama, and look up at the sky.
That's where you'll find Mother Moon, in all her phases,
Beaming unconditional love directly into your soul.

CHAPTER EIGHT
Yanantin:
The Union of Dissimilar Energies

Try not to become caught up in the human dilemma for too long,
for you are divine within the disguise of human being.

— MY TEACHER

The West petal is where you can explore your life from a place of no time. To notice where you feel unified and where you don't. Bear will be your devoted companion here. In many cultures, she's known as a healer whose medicine helps restore harmony and balance. Hibernate in her warm, nurturing cave as you immerse yourself in the dream of this petal of adulthood. Allow the introspective energies to awaken memories, remind you of who you are, and help you better understand your path.

The Milky Way Village spirits were the first beings who offered me a transcendent perspective for events in our human lives. Sitting Bear said:

For a spirit, the path is most significant. For a human, the body and life are paramount. Each has different perspectives and goals.

This wisdom motivated me to differentiate a little further, and I realized, for a spirit, there's no such thing as death, and life on Earth is a blink within the everlasting timelessness of existence, while for a human, life is everything and time is limited.

Spirit and human.

Purpose and tragedy.

Overview and present moment.

What is it to be *divine within the disguise of human being*, as my Teacher stated above? How do we integrate our spirit and human selves? These two different parts and perspectives? This is where *yanantin* comes into play, a foundation so essential for unifying that I've devoted an entire chapter to it.

In 1996, during the Peru trip where Phutu Cusi found a home within my heart, I learned about the Q'ero tradition of yanantin—"the union of dissimilar energies" or "complementary opposites." Yanantin describes us—unified spirit/human beings living two distinct paths. We are complementary opposites where the most significant contrast (other than a human has a body, and a spirit is formless) is this: a human can be a victim while a spirit cannot.

The *Merriam-Webster Dictionary* defines a victim as "someone or something that is harmed by an unpleasant event." How many "unpleasant events" deserve listing here? Physical, emotional, and sexual abuse, illness, tragic death, rape, hunger, war...I could go on and on. Each "event" involves trauma, suffering, and survival. Could there be another perspective or bigger picture at play? If, as the Milky Way Village spirits taught, spirits and humans have "different perspectives and goals," how do we, if we're even willing to, explore an all-encompassing human tragedy from a spiritual overview? Will we ever arrive at the truth? And if we do, will it bring us peace or further suffering?

The only way I can try to answer these questions is by sharing about a trauma I and over 27,000 others living in Paradise, California, and the surrounding towns experienced on Thursday, November 8, 2018.

The Camp Fire

It was just over a year after I moved into the first house I ever owned, and I loved my property. The flow of energy in the house was palpable, beginning at the front porch, moving inside through light-filled rooms, all the way to the back, where a sliding glass door opened to a one-acre, park-like setting. Multi-colored roses, intoxicating lavender, and eight-foot-tall pink, purple, and white hollyhocks delighted the senses, while purposefully placed statues of spiritual icons united the mystical with the physical.

A standout detail was the curved swimming pool. Constructed to resemble an Inka ruin (how perfect for me), it had a filtration system which on one setting sounded like a rushing river, and on another, a slow-moving stream. Apu was crazy about it. As soon as we'd return home from a walk, he'd jump in, swim, and excitedly emerge to run around the perimeter of the land.

Douglas fir, pine, redwood, and cedar trees acted as guardians of my paradise in Paradise, and on the far northern corner, a grandmother oak oversaw it all. This private world was surrounded by a tall, custom-made, redwood fence, and offered sanctuary, relaxation, and expansion to every person and creature that visited. I named it "Pachamama's Oasis."

I was sleeping in after leading a Healing Ceremony the night before in Chico, the city down the hill, and was rudely awakened at 8:30 a.m. by the blaring phone. Woozy, I picked it up, held it to my ear, and heard a friend say, "There's a fire near you. Check it out." I looked out the window, but it was too dark to see anything. When I went outside to the front porch, I was greeted by an apocalyptic vision of otherworldly colors—deep reds, oranges, grays, and blacks—encompassing the entire sky. The smoke was so thick I had to hold my breath. It was snowing ashes.

I got ready to leave, and gathered vitamins, dog food, and my black file box of important papers. I wore soft maroon sweatpants and a bulky sweater but as an afterthought, decided to take another sweater, just in case. I picked up my mesa, loaded the car, and pulled out of the long driveway. It would just be for a few days, or so I thought.

My road was still and quiet, but when I reached the corner where I usually turned right and easily drove into town, dozens of cars were sitting in motionless traffic. I didn't know what was going on and had to wait ten minutes before one let me turn. Meanwhile, shoeless pedestrians wrapped in blankets walked hurriedly down the sidewalk, and community members in wheelchairs, small dogs held tightly on their laps, urgently pushed themselves forward. The beds of pick-up trucks, normally empty or loaded with tools or gardening supplies, were packed with people. You could almost see the primal energy of desperation and panic filling the air.

I turned the corner, and after waiting another ten minutes in a long line of cars, I became scared and realized the only way to get anywhere was to drive down the empty left lane. That's when my entire focus became safety. I tried leaving town on my ordinary route, but helpers standing on street corners herded me toward side streets I rarely traveled. When I finally arrived at the Skyway, the only main road out of Paradise, I stopped at the light, and as soon as it turned green, was waved forward directly into a tunnel of flames.

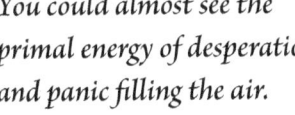

You could almost see the primal energy of desperation and panic filling the air.

Survival was the only thing that mattered.

Normally, there are two north and two south lanes, but on that day all four were southward bound. I tried not to drown in the sea of fleeing families all driving five or ten miles an hour. On my right, an orange inferno engulfed my friend's home. *Were Paula and Joe dead?* On my left, skyscraper flames were consuming every dwelling and rendering them charcoal. Majestic trees fell everywhere, including on the road, and the relentless wind blew their flaming limbs with abandon. Some missed my car by inches. The smoke was so thick it reminded me of fog. Vehicles were haphazardly deserted, not just on the side of the road, but *on the* road. The blaze was left, right, front, and center—an all-consuming, scorching inferno.

Survival demanded a sharp mind and expansive peripheral vision, so with sweaty hands hugging the steering wheel, I drove slow and steady while chanting aloud, "It is not my destiny to die in a fire. It is not my destiny to die in a fire..." I had to believe in something. Apu sat still and quiet in the back seat. Eyes wide, ears upright, all his senses were heightened. I made sure his leash was on in case we had to vacate. That is, if my car didn't spontaneously burst into flames. Anything was possible.

What once had been a simple, thirty-minute drive into Chico had become a four-hour, life-threatening escape—a living nightmare *impossible* to awaken from.

I landed at Kathy's where everyone was glued to the television. I prayed that my property was spared, yet as news filtered in, wondered if my prayer was a good idea. What if it was the only remaining home? After a few days of sketchy news reports, information finally showed up online—Pachamama's Oasis had burned in the Camp Fire, as had most of Paradise.

Shortly after learning this, two loving friends took me out to dinner and tried to distract me with expensive wine and food. A television crew entered the restaurant while we were eating, and we stopped at their table on our way out. The instant I heard they were going up to Paradise the next day, I begged, "Will you take me?"

I rendezvoused with one of the newsmen at ten the following morning, and we drove up the Skyway in the same lane I'd driven down exactly one week before. Ash and debris were everywhere. Did a bomb explode? Paradise was a toxic dump. My little street was littered with burned cars, trucks, and scorched, blackened trees. No more homes—only ashen remains.

Pachamama's Oasis was gone—the house, garage, sheds, trees, plants, and healing studio all part of a dream-like past. The entire kitchen had

The small icon of Horse, a gift from my son, remained unscathed and was sitting at his honorary place on top of the fire pit wall. The grandmother oak tree, slightly scorched, stood strong; what a story she has to tell.

sunk into the basement, and the place I'd lovingly named "Auntie Em's cellar" was now an open-holed junkyard. The skeleton of a metal table lay on its side on the broken concrete patio, and a murky swamp replaced the pristine Inka pool.

While my sanctuary had become a sea of rubble, the spiritual statues had survived and stood out like lights in the darkness. Guadalupe, now infused with fire medicine, rested on her side. She had gone from tan to multiple shades of black and brown. Angels looked up from the noxious ground with hope. Buddha stared compassionately at me from the center of a burned-out flower bed, while Saint Francis, still upright, waited for wildlife to return. The small icon of Horse, a gift from my son, remained unscathed and was sitting at his honorary place on top of the fire pit wall. The grandmother oak tree, slightly scorched, stood strong; what a story she has to tell.

I wore a mask to protect my lungs and booties to save my shoes, and slowly walked the perimeter of my property. The news crew filmed yet gave me space to absorb my new reality. They asked, "What are you feeling?" Barely able to speak, I thought, "I must be in shock." They wanted to know, "Who do you hold responsible?" Only an outsider would think I was grounded enough to consider that.

Maintaining sanity while integrating the present moment was my sole task.

I was alive, yet my home and all my treasures were gone. Where do I stay? What should I do? How do I remain lucid and healthy?

LIVING YANANTIN

I am a spirit in human form. As a human, I was the victim of a tragedy. As a spirit, what was the point? The expanded overview in relation to the present moment? And how do I integrate this union of opposites?

Two years post-fire (life for fire survivors has become pre- and post-fire), I was staying at an Airbnb in the San Francisco Bay Area and awoke in a panic. I couldn't understand what was happening until I rubbed my early morning eyes and noticed that the cottage was in the woods.

Almost four years later, strong winds still remind me of the swirling gale forces the day of the fire. The sight and scent of smoke invoke alarm. Driving with Apu anywhere away from Chico, where I now live, can rekindle my aloneness in the car with him that day.

Luckily, PTSD doesn't visit me for too long, for shortly after I become aware of its presence, I'm able to gain perspective and recalibrate. And, I've had several soul retrievals, of course. But no matter how much healing I've participated in, the Camp Fire continues to burn.

Will it ever be extinguished?

Suffering is real. During tragic circumstances, the only way one might consider that a bigger picture is involved would be to have a belief in Sitting Bear's teaching:

For a spirit, the path is most significant. For a human, the body and life are paramount. Each has different perspectives and goals.

The path of a human being is unmistakable regarding the Camp Fire. Each person affected was a victim. We not only had to flee an out-of-control wildfire, but lost our homes, most, if not all, of the objects dear to our hearts, our lifestyle, and pretty much the entire town. Everyone has had to create a new life, although not so for the over eighty-five people who died during the fire and the over fifty more who passed away because of it. (Exact numbers have never been agreed upon.)

The path of spirit is foggy. On a collective level, why did so many decide to participate in that human trauma? Was it part of our awakening? Did we have joint karma to complete? Why did some choose it for their deaths?

And on a very personal level, what were the individual teachings each person needed *so badly* we had to experience such a traumatic event?

THE POWER OF NOT KNOWING

It's rare for someone to believe there's a spiritual purpose for trauma. We ask, "Why did this happen to me?" "Why would God (or the Universe) create it?" If we were *physically* sitting together in my living room, and you asked me questions about the Camp Fire, I would remain silent for a long time. Then I might say, "I don't know why so many spirits chose to participate in it." If you then asked, "What teachings did *you* need to receive that necessitated escaping a wildfire and losing everything?" my answer would likely disappoint you.

My home at Pachamama's Oasis held everything I loved and deemed important for over sixty-five years. And yes, I miss my textiles, art, jewelry, photographs, and the mementos I saved from my son's childhood, but since I've never been a big collector of "stuff," I don't think I needed to learn non-attachment. I do know that ever since the fire, I have a newfound compassion for myself and others that has enhanced the importance of living with an open heart in every moment (I try my best). And I've gained a more conscious understanding of impermanence and Unity. Still, I continue in the "not knowing" regarding most of it.

However, if you changed the topic and asked if I had a spiritual understanding regarding my childhood abuse, I *would* have an answer; it was the initiation I chose that would make me the "wounded healer" I am today. My childhood birthed a Spiritual Healer who can assist others out of the unhealthy swamps of their lives and help them land on the mossy, stable ground of freedom.

In *Polishing the Mirror*, Ram Das wrote, "Life is an incredible curriculum in which we live richly and passionately as a way of awakening to the deepest truths of our being." If we choose to believe that all human events have purpose, how do we integrate our spirit and human selves? Come to terms with spiritual objectives and human tragedy? Unify overview and present moment? Live the union of opposites—yanantin —in an empowered way?

Sometimes we can't.

While the path of spirit is a continuous, everlasting unfolding, once we become embodied, we must be human first. Willingness to look at life from a spiritual perspective, whenever it's possible, helps us come to terms with our traumas, discover their teachings, and eventually heal and unify within. It doesn't mean we have to forgive everyone, and it's okay to "not know." Faith and Trust aren't automatic. What's most important for our hearts, minds, and overall health is to move out of the victim stance. Is this always possible? I don't know.

> *It's rare for someone to believe there's a spiritual purpose for trauma. We ask, "Why did this happen to me?" "Why would God (or the Universe) create it?"*

Either way, despite whatever trauma you may have undergone, love yourself as best you can and choose to heal. It might take years before you become ready to explore the spiritual objectives of a tragedy, if ever. As for me, it's only after I become emotionally solid that I *might* arrive at an overview.

I've been told self-forgiveness is the key that unlocks all difficulties. I've forgiven my spirit-self for creating the initiations and harsh lessons I believed I needed as a human and am aware the hurtful people in my life only acted out parts I needed them to play for my spiritual growth and awakening.

Yet I continue to wonder, "What in the world was I thinking?"

EXPLORE A DIFFICULT LIFE EXPERIENCE

Find a piece of paper and a pen, and sit in a safe, quiet, comfortable place. As always, ground.

When you feel ready, think of a difficult experience. Visualize it. Then call on our friend, Eagle, from the East petal. Imagine yourself sitting on his back as he soars over the event. Explore it as deeply and vividly as you can.

Ask your guides: "What was the point of this experience? What did I need to learn?" Write down whatever comes to mind. Try not to censor yourself.

Or, let the page remain blank.

Ask: "Have I integrated the teachings?" Again, write down whatever comes to mind.

Or, let the page remain blank.

Choose to trust whatever answers you might receive. Later, you can explore how your awakened knowings can assist you to alleviate your suffering, anger, guilt, or whatever reaction arises.

You may have been a victim, like I was as a child and in the fire, but understanding the spiritual overview can take you out of the *feeling* and into an experience of empowerment. This won't remove the need to know, but it might soothe the pain a little.

I've done this exercise many times since the Camp Fire and have been unsuccessful. During a few tries, all I've been able to do is cry. On others, I've sat on my cushioned rocking chair, looked at the pictures of Guadalupe and Ezekiel on the mantle, and gotten angry. I don't think I'm ready to emerge from Bear's cave on this one, so I'm choosing to trust that my knowing and not-knowing are a union of opposites themselves, another yanantin, and receive it as Bear's healing medicine.

Did you find yourself in a similar situation to mine? Let's place our hands on our centers, breathe deeply, and chant the prayer, "*The Light of Love is All.*"

It's the one thing we *do* know.

CHAPTER NINE
The Past Is Alive in the Present

Why think separately of this life and the next when one is born from the last?

— RŪMĪ, *Fountain of Fire*

No one is ever fully free from the past; experiences imprint themselves upon the books of our Living Library and affect us in the present. But are we bound by the past? Can we liberate ourselves and turn ordeals into personal power? Yes, we can—but to accomplish this it's important to make peace and create closure—from yesterday, and sometimes all the way back to a former life. Inner Unity depends upon this. If we want to live in the present with space for new ideas and experiences, it's vital we resolve ingrained themes that have replicated over time. I call these "soul patterns." I'm not talking about exceptional gifts—such as musical, intellectual, and artistic genius—rather, themes and patterns, such as addiction, abandonment, fear, lack of belonging, and self-hatred.

Take Carol for example. After finally leaving her abusive husband once her children were living on their own, she struggled unsuccessfully for years to understand why she had remained in the marriage so long. Carol had loved her husband and said she'd "embedded herself within his soul," meeting his

every need before he realized he had one. She'd engaged in the same pattern with her children, but her allegiance to him was first and foremost.

One night when she was asleep, a shiny book slipped off a shelf of Carol's Living Library, and in the morning, she awoke with a big realization, "I have a soul pattern of slavery!" Carol was finally able to name the belief at the center of her marriage— love equals slavery and service. She didn't remember when or why it had seeded within her soul but was positive the theme had repeated over many lifetimes. As Carol processed her new awareness, she realized that leaving her husband had been a gift in two ways: it facilitated her healing and allowed him, unhindered by her presence, to finally feel his own soul. Carol's guilt, shame, and remorse became themes of the past, and she developed new insights regarding what it is to love and be loved in a balanced way.

When we were in the spirit realm designing our lives, many of us committed to breaking free of a soul pattern, and to do so, we recreated it. Imagine that as spirit, Carol had said, "My soul pattern of 'love equals slavery and service' has been keeping me trapped in a low level of consciousness. In my next life, I want to repeat it excessively, so I'll become exasperated with its limitations and finally transcend it. I'm ready to experience healthy love." (A few years after her awakening, Carol met Frank and has been involved in a thriving, loving relationship ever since.)

Do you have a persistent theme? Take a minute, go back in time, and track its origin. Where did it begin? If you traced it to your childhood, that's a good start and might be all you need to know to heal and transmute it. If you choose to explore further, perhaps through shamanic journeying, hypnosis, channeling, or Spiritual Healing, you'll likely discover a former life where a significant, traumatic event occurred that seeded the theme within your soul. I call those "root lifetimes."

Root Lifetimes

A root lifetime is when a soul pattern began. It can be helpful to be aware of it, but it's not necessary for forward movement. Time is fluid. Once we realize a pattern exists, as Carol did, we've already begun completing the past and opening to the future. It's like dominos; when the lead is activated, the others ripple and fall. That's what happened with Arthur, whose guilt traversed multiple lifetimes and created a disunity so prolific that it caused prolonged suffering

Do you have a persistent theme? Take a minute, go back in time, and track its origin. Where did it begin?

in this one. He was haunted by the memory of being a man who went to work and upon his return home, learned that his young son had died in his absence. Arthur's healing intention was: "Self-forgiveness."

I journeyed on Arthur's behalf and was brought to an anguished, heartbroken soul-part named Ralph, who sat alone in a dense pine forest. The time frame was the mid-1800s. "I was a happily married father of a baby boy," Ralph told me. "I was gathering my deer skins to bring to the trading post, which I did once a month—but for some reason, my wife, Abigail, was reluctant to let me leave that day. My trading supported our family, and since nothing appeared unusual, I kissed her and the baby goodbye and left."

Two days later, unbeknown to Ralph, his son was overcome with a fever and died. Ralph had only been away for a week, the usual amount of time, but when he returned, heartbroken Abigail was unwilling to forgive him for being gone, and she withdrew into herself for the rest of their lives. Ralph remained guilt-ridden and tormented, even at his death.

I explained to Ralph that he was a part of Arthur's soul, and that Arthur needed to heal and move on. "Are you willing to help?" I asked. "Would you come with me?" Before agreeing to anything, Ralph brought me to his cabin, where I found Abigail lying in bed, blankly staring at the ceiling. She turned toward me, and once I explained what was happening, she wanted to know where her son was. I glanced at my Teacher, who pointed toward the window.

Everyone looked outside to see an elegantly dressed man in his mid-thirties playing with his three young children. It was their son! Abigail's grief-stricken face filled with joy when she realized her son's spiritual path had been unaffected by his early death. She got out of bed, took her husband's hand, and allowed us to bring them to my healing water. Once their healings were complete, my Teacher restored Abigail to the entirety of her soul, and I restored Ralph to Arthur's.

Arthur experienced a sudden sense of completeness and believed that once he integrated the story and reclaimed his soul-part, his grief would resolve. He wanted to fall in love, get married, and become a father again. And Abigail, whoever she is now, was unified with a formerly grieving and presently healed aspect of her soul.

Vows

A vow is a compelling statement that emerges as a result of a significant event and follows us through lifetimes until it has been resolved and its power dissipated. For example, someone unable to achieve abundance might have taken a vow of poverty in a former life. A person who lost a beloved partner in the past and made the vow, "I will never love anyone else," might still be living this declaration. These dynamic pledges emerge out of survival, claim space within the soul, and become soul patterns. Once again, noticing a current theme can offer insight, and if it no longer serves us, we can find the root, pull it out, and move forward. Vows are powerful energetics that can be helpful—like Ezekiel's vow to eternally protect me—yet can also be detrimental.

Timothy and Clara were unable to get pregnant. During our session, a past-life memory arose for Clara where she'd been the mother of an infant who was born with a birth defect and lived for only a few hours. Unlike Abigail, who became deeply depressed after losing her child, Clara made a vow to never become pregnant again. This statement might have served her then, but it was still alive within the dynamic of her soul and affecting her ability to become pregnant now.

I led Clara on a guided visualization to meet and converse with the soul-part of the grieving mother. Once she explained their interconnection and her current situation, the part empathized and immediately rescinded the vow. Clara then brought her to my healing water, after which she infused the healed mother from the past into her soul in the present. (This was all done by Clara herself; I acted as her intermediary or midwife.) A few months later... guess who became pregnant?

Then there was forty-five-year-old Amber, who liked to stay at home because it was the only place where she felt safe. One day, she decided her life had become too fear-based and limited, and asked me to journey on her behalf. Her intention was: "I'm safe wherever I am."

My Teacher and Horse brought me to the root of Amber's fear. In 1519, she'd been an adventurous man who left his wife and young child to join explorer Ferdinand Magellan's expedition to circumnavigate the world. The voyage lasted three years. When he (Amber) returned home, instead of reuniting with his family, he found a vacant town that had been wiped out by disease. His wife, daughter, parents, and friends were all dead, and in a state of horror, he declared, "I will never leave home again!" After much discussion, this distraught, guilt-ridden part of Amber's soul finally allowed me to take him for healing. I restored Amber of the past to Amber of the present, and she has been a traveler ever since.

ILLNESS

Unexplained illness can be rooted in the past, and I've discovered that sometimes completing the past can heal the illness. That's what happened to Sam, whose constant stomach pain remained undiagnosed, even after seeing three doctors and having an MRI. His healing intention was: "Radiant Health."

After about fifteen minutes of channeling Light for Sam, I was shown a former life where he'd been a samurai who was murdered by a rival. The samurai were military nobility, warriors of pre-modern Japan, who lived between 1185 and 1868. They were expected to adhere to a unique code of ethics, so the murder of one of their own was highly uncommon. Samurai Sam's killer had made a statement, not just by violating the code, but by leaving the large, sharp knife in Samurai Sam's stomach. This knife created an energetic imprint within the landscape of his soul and, 700 years later, had become the source of Sam's pain. I don't know why this book in his Living Library was activated—perhaps the karma between the men was complete—but Sam's past trauma had become a present-life disturbance.

I suggested that Sam keep his eyes closed, expand his inner senses, and search for the knife. Once he found it, he placed his physical hands upon the long, gleaming handle, pulled it out, and offered it to the helping spirits for transmutation. He then placed his hands upon the energetic wound and channeled Light while my Teacher brought me to his dissociated part. We found Samurai Sam in a meadow, lying in a pool of blood. My Teacher picked him up, brought him for healing, and once he regained his life force, I restored him to Sam. Both Sam and I were astonished when he instantly became pain-free.

PHOBIAS

A "phobia" is an irrational fear or aversion—irrational to the beholder because the experience is very real to the person suffering from it. A client's father had a phobia about needing to prove that his hands were empty, and he checked them dozens of times throughout the day. He'd clap them together and repeat aloud—to himself and anyone who might be around: "There's nothing in my hands. There's nothing in my hands." He had to make sure. I once watched a television show that did a segment on phobias and focused on a little girl who became intensely anxious whenever a storm was brewing. She wouldn't go outside and holed up in her room until the weather resolved. Her mother had tried everything to help her daughter, from psychological support to medications, but nothing worked.

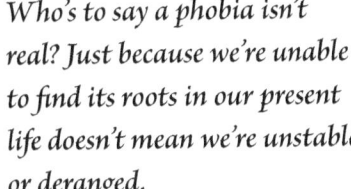

Who's to say a phobia isn't real? Just because we're unable to find its roots in our present life doesn't mean we're unstable or deranged.

Who's to say a phobia isn't real? Just because we're unable to find its roots in our present life doesn't mean we're unstable or deranged. Was it possible my client's father had a soul-part from the past that needed to prove there was nothing in his hands and was actively living and manifesting this traumatic experience in his present life? "I don't have the murder weapon. Look: there's nothing in my hands." Perhaps in a former lifetime, the young, storm-phobic girl experienced a cyclone, became caught in the vortex, and was thrown to her death. Soul loss would explain these present phobias. A germophobe might have a dissociated part trying to survive a plague. A person we presently label agoraphobic might have, in a former life, been taking an evening walk when he witnessed a tragedy so horrific, he never spent time outdoors again—and now, in another lifetime altogether, he rarely leaves home.

I was fanning my client Eliza with sacred Peruvian condor feathers, but instead of looking euphoric as most clients do, she appeared disturbed. When I asked her what was happening, Eliza told me she was afraid of all types of feathers, and the sight of birds triggered a fight-or-flight response. She said she'd been that way as long as she could remember and didn't know why. Her intention was: "My fear of birds is healed."

My Teacher and Horse took me to a former lifetime where Eliza had been a man who'd fallen ill, lapsed into a coma, and was pronounced dead by the medical people of his community. Since their traditional custom for death was sky burial, a wooden platform was built specifically for this purpose, and his body was laid down flat on his back, and bound and secured to the wood. When that was complete, a group of strong men lifted the entire platform and placed it high atop a tree where the body became an offering for the birds.

The man awoke just before the birds discovered him. His coma had been so deep he'd only appeared to be dead! Incapable of freeing himself, his piercing screams went unheard as dozens of large, hungry birds of prey picked at his eyes and devoured his body. He finally passed out and died.

My Teacher and I unbound the man and brought him to my healing water. He had a message for Eliza when he emerged, "It was all a terrible mistake," he said. I had a loving wife and many children. Don't worry. Now life can begin again—for you, and me, as a part of you." I restored the healed part to Eliza.

Who knows how many lifetimes the extreme terror of birds had been alive and active in Eliza's soul? Before I had the opportunity to share my experience, she got off the table, picked up my condor feathers, and began fanning me. I watched Eliza become an empowered vehicle for the same type of birds that had devoured her body in the past. Her phobia was over.

ANCESTRAL SOUL PATTERNS

Physical, emotional, or energetic themes can be inherited from our ancestors. The psychological word for this is "transgenerational trauma." Social Worker Elizabeth Dixon wrote on the *Psychology Today* website, "Transgenerational trauma refers to a type of trauma that does not end with the individual. Instead, it lingers and gnaws through one generation to the next. Families with a history of unresolved trauma, depression, anxiety, and addiction may continue to pass maladaptive coping strategies and distrustful views of life on to future generations. In this way, one can repeat the same patterns and attitudes of former generations, regardless of whether they are healthy or not."

Newborns are not born as blank slates. Instead, the Living Libraries of their souls are filled with books. Look at your family history. Has anything generationally repeated to you?

If you believe you're living an ancestral soul pattern, healing it now, in the present, will affect the past, all the way back to your ancestors, and simultaneously forward to future family members. This is what happened for Alexa, a story you'll read about in the Illness chapter. It's thrilling that one person's healing and unifying can have a positive ripple effect on an unknown number of others through both directions in time.

RESOLUTION

Each of us is a perpetual traveler upon what I call "The Eternal Spiral of Awakening." Our goal as spiritual beings is to progress from one level of the spiral to the next, but as human beings, when past themes and patterns are alive in the present, we persist in swirling around the same area repeatedly. How do we leave the past behind and move forward? Spiritual Healing—in all its myriad forms—supports us in becoming unstuck and liberates our spiral flow toward new, life-enhancing experiences.

Do all soul patterns radically shift and miraculously end? Not necessarily. Don't forget about the wild card of karma. But each opportunity we take to heal the past is valuable. Awakening to and then freeing ourselves from any form of soul pattern changes our lives for the better—in multidimensional past, present, and future time.

It's a gift to awaken to a soul pattern; remembering the root lifetime is wrapping paper and ribbons. Some people, like Carol, remember in dreams. Hypnotherapists skilled in past-life regression are wonderful resources and can assist us as we unearth buried knowings. Soul retrieval is helpful when the need for healing arises. Are you a shamanic journeyer? Ask your teacher and/or power animal to take you to the root of your soul pattern so you might gain understanding. Do you meditate? In your next meditation, open yourself to receiving what you need to know about a pervasive life theme. Are you plagued by patterns you're unable to change but have no memories of former lifetimes? Name the theme and follow through with one of the options above.

Awakening to the past can heal the present, as shown by Carol and new mother, Clara. Or we can begin in the present—like Sam's pain, Arthur's relentless guilt, and now—world-traveler Amber—to heal the past. All approaches work because the goal is the same—to awaken our consciousness, unify our souls, and not just live, but thrive in the Now.

THE PAST AS PERSONAL POWER

Stand tall.

Imagine a mesa—a brightly colored, naturally dyed, handwoven cloth—whose contents are past events and beliefs that disempower you in the present.

Place this medicine bundle on the floor behind you. Visualize it attached, via an energetic cord, to the rear aspect of your third chakra, in the center of your back.

Can you see it?

Place two clamps on the cord, one close to your body, and the other a few inches away.

Would you like to transmute your disempowered past into personal power?

State your intention, then cut the part of the cord that's between the two clamps.

Complete?

Now pick up the mesa of old disappointments, wounds, and unhealthy beliefs, and its long, clamped, and no-longer-attached-to-your-body cord. Bring it to your heart/soul space and channel The Light of Love into it through both hands.

As you do this, imagine the floating cord and clamp becoming part of the mesa.

Honor any images, memories, or emotions that arise in the transmutation process. Take your time.

When you're ready, infuse your Mesa of Personal Power into your heart/soul space.

Offer gratitude to everything you've been through that has brought you to this moment in time, where you're finally able to recognize that your wounded past has become your empowered present.

CHAPTER TEN

Systemic Energetics

The physician should speak of that which is invisible. What is visible should belong to his knowledge, and he should recognize illnesses, just as everybody else, who is not a physician, can recognize them by their symptoms. But this is far from making him a physician: he becomes a physician only when he knows that which is unnamed, invisible, and immaterial yet efficacious.

— PARACELSUS, *Selected Writings*

This is the final chapter in the West petal. Since you're still in an introspective dream space with Bear, I think it's a perfect time to introduce a concept I call "systemic energetics." This is a state where hucha grows, expands, and becomes so dysfunctional that it creates physical, emotional, and/or mental discord, all of which keep us from inner Unity. Spiritual Healing is the perfect resolution for what can be a crazy-making experience.

CONCEPTION

We already know that when we leave the Spirit Realm, we're as prepared as possible for our new lives as spirit/human beings, yet a spirit who travels through the Birth Gateway and is embraced within a loving conception, like Lisa—whose intentions with her mother were tenderly aligned—will have a different experience than one conceived in rape.

If the spirit and its guides determine that the energy of its conception will be an important aspect of the future spirit/human's awakening and growth, that energy can become intracellular.

A young friend once confided about his overwhelming shame regarding his pornography addiction. Before his mother had passed, she'd shared the experience of her son's violent conception with me, and I believed there was a relationship between this and his struggle. Hoping the information might bring him some understanding, I took a risk and told him what I knew. I held my breath... He was grateful. His conception was not a surprise to him and explained his addiction, which released his shame and brought him peace.

Seventy-year-old Indira had a different story, but the outcome was the same. She'd struggled with self-hatred and multiple illnesses her entire lifetime, and when I asked if she knew anything about her conception, she said her mother had been savagely raped and had not only remained in a relationship with her rapist but had held Indira responsible. During Indira's healing, I noticed that every cell in her body was saturated with this conception hucha. The Pleiadean healers infused her with their green-gold salve, which pulled the systemic heaviness out and created space for the cells to breathe. No wonder she'd suffered from so much illness. Indira felt the infusion as it was occurring, and said it left her relieved and optimistic about her future for the first time.

CELLS

Did you know there are over 37 trillion cells in the human body? Each is a universe unto itself and holds the template of optimum life force. Cells are a microcosm of humanity because, like us, they are individuated as well as part of a whole. They live in community clusters—the liver community, spleen community, heart, bladder, etc. However, their consciousness is not uniform, so the ones attuned to the highest frequency of awareness and purpose become the leaders. If these cells fall prey to an intruder—such as a virus or a rogue, cancerous cell—a cascade occurs, shifting all the members of the community.

There are times when lead cells, not unlike us, must be reminded of their tasks so they can awaken from whatever is weakening them.

When I was working with Tom, someone you'll spend more time with later, I learned we can communicate with cells in the same way we communicate with one another. His "intruders" were miscreants that had mutated in his brain and become cancerous. Once I contacted the leader and convinced him (the energy felt masculine) that living in the Light was a better option than Tom's head, the community began following him, an exodus that showed up on Tom's MRI as shrinking tumors.

A lead cell might fall into a cycle of slumber, a teaching I learned from Amanda, who was diagnosed with chronic fatigue. After sitting at her feet and channeling Light into her body and soul for quite a while, my Teacher showed me "sleeping" cells, as he called them, which I saw metaphorically as hundreds of "Sleepys," one of Snow White's seven dwarves. My task was to find the leader, focus Light on that single being, and awaken it. I prayed for the ability to accomplish this. My prayers were answered, and as it awoke, I watched the rest of Amanda's cells begin to match its frequency. Amanda experienced an immediate energetic shift, and I'm happy to say that the systemic illness of chronic fatigue is no longer an issue for her.

Oftentimes communication is unnecessary, and the flowing Light alone affects lead cells. Think about Sonja, whose lungs spontaneously healed, or how Lucy's cervical abnormality resolved. The lead cells in any area of the body need to maintain integrity so their community members can follow suit, which is why stem cells—specialized cells with the ability to develop into a variety of types—are a powerful healing tool. They assist sleeping cells to awaken and return to their pure state.

Stem cells are the mothers of all cells, and as we know, mothers are life-force beings.

PTSD

It's time to return to PTSD.

Since our cells store hucha, and trauma is hucha, when a person has a severely traumatic experience, even receiving monthly spiritual healings might not be enough to completely rid their cells of the fight-or-flight energy. It took me three years post-Camp Fire to discover this.

I had driven seven long hours through rain, snow, and fog to return home after visiting a friend. Following a good night's sleep under my soft, blue flannel sheets, I awoke engulfed in anxiety and tension. I didn't understand why I felt so agitated until I realized it was related to the Camp Fire.

While I was driving through flames, unbeknownst to me, my cells volunteered to store a limitless amount of fear so I wouldn't have to experience it all at once. The recent events of my somewhat perilous drive home the day before had triggered the stockpiled memories, and the cellular stress unpacked itself and became systemic. No amount of ashwagandha (an herbal adaptogen specific for stress and well-being), adrenal supplements, or

While I was driving through flames...my cells volunteered to store a limitless amount of fear...

centering, grounding, and releasing heavy energy could relieve it for very long. Even after receiving a healing and an acupuncture treatment, it took several more weeks for my system to calm enough to where I felt myself again. I had never thought of PTSD as systemic before this.

EARTHBOUND ENTITIES

An "earthbound entity" is a part of the soul that was either left behind intentionally by a deceased person or was lost due to a traumatic death. Like all soul-parts, earthbound entities are multidimensional beings. Some are called ghosts and reside in places they once loved, or bars they used to frequent, or wherever their death occurred. Either purposefully or by chance, others find homes in energetically depleted people where their unknown presence changes the person's thought patterns. Whatever their circumstance may be, all require understanding and assistance so they can choose to go to the Light and rejoin the rest of their soul.

Thomas was suicidal and his concerned wife sent him to me for a healing. He didn't believe in my work and, unwilling to surrender or relax on my healing table, watched every move I made. I closed my eyes, placed my hands on his feet, breathed to my center, and opened to the Light. After about fifteen minutes, I began feeling a presence near his left ear. I was silent for a while and then said, "There's a woman in your soul."

"She's older. Do you notice anything?"

"No," Thomas replied.

"I think she's an elder. Can you relate to that at all?"

"No."

"Let me see. She's sweet and appears to really love you. Does this make any sense?"

"No."

"She adores roses and has many varieties in her garden that she tends to daily."

"Oh my god!" Thomas exclaimed, "That's my grandmother!"

Thomas told me that he and Grandmother had been very close. She'd died a few years earlier, and one of his deep regrets was not being with her when she passed. I finetuned my inner senses and communicated with Grandmother. She told me she loved Thomas deeply and after her physical death had deliberately left a part of her soul within his so they would remain close. She said she spoke to Thomas every day, telling him how much she missed him. I reminded Grandmother that she had passed away and helped her understand she was creating an unhealthy experience for Thomas. I assured her that when it was Thomas's time to pass, she'd be with him again and even accompany him to the Light, where she now belonged.

I acted as an intermediary for a conversation between Thomas and Grandmother, in which they spoke of their shared love and good times together. Once they said heartfelt farewells, I called to Grandmother's deceased family members and asked them to escort her to the Light, where she would reunify her soul. Once she left, I filled the now-empty space in Thomas' soul with Light.

Grandmother's presence was an unhealthy systemic energetic that created a suicidal man, the opposite effect of her loving intention. When she was finally in her rightful place, Thomas was able to live without suicidal thoughts. Plus, he became a believer in Spiritual Healing.

CURSES

Believe it or not, "curses" are real, and their malicious hucha affects a person's entire energetic system. I'm living proof.

It happened during a bittersweet time—after living and working as a Spiritual Healer and teacher in Hungary for three months, I was going home. My dear friend, Csilla, and I sat in her rickety old van and began our drive from the small town that had become my home into the big city of Budapest. Across the road, a Romani man parked his brightly painted, carved, and decorated cylindrical horse-drawn wagon and went into a shop. This was not an unusual sight; I'd seen many of these unique, beautiful wagons, known as *vardos*, during my time in Hungary but hadn't taken any pictures and wanted to have one to show my friends. Csilla made a U-turn, parked near the cart, and I got out and innocently snapped a few photos from different angles. As we were getting ready to leave, the driver of the cart exited the store, looked up, pointed his finger at us, and ran toward me, furiously yelling and swearing, "That's *my* horse!!" (In Hungarian, of course. I had no idea what he was saying until Csilla told me later.) We both panicked. I frantically jumped into the van, closed and locked the door, and Csilla sped away.

We couldn't believe how scary the encounter had been. We imagined the man felt violated and threatened, but his aggressive behavior made Csilla and me fear for our lives. Once I got my bearings, in the spirit of Ayni, I decided to do something for him.

We stopped a few safe miles away. I grounded, called to my Teacher, and asked if we could perform a distant healing. He showed me that the man's wife was sick, so we focused on her. When the healing was complete and the unfortunate exchange balanced (or so I thought) Csilla and I took a few deep breaths, then continued our drive to Budapest. We had plans to stay with another friend for a few days and sightsee before I returned to the United States.

I immediately came down with a fever. This was surprising because even though I was tired, I hadn't been ill during the entire trip. My low energy and intermittent fever continued for weeks after returning to the US. I wanted to understand what was happening, so I took a shamanic journey where I was shown that the angry, finger-pointing man had put a curse on me! My Teacher said the way to undo it was by deleting the pictures of his horse and cart from my camera. Again, bittersweet. I followed his sage advice and slept well that night for the first time since returning home. The next day I finally felt like myself. The curse was gone.

Unlike me, Lily was aware of being cursed the moment it happened, and the heavy energy quickly infiltrated and traversed her body. She'd been traveling with a group to sacred sites in Turkey when, while she was sitting in a culturally significant cave, one of the men in the group stood behind her, placed his hands on her shoulders, and officially claimed her. "You are now mine," he declared. Lily had been under this spell for months before seeing me. She felt the man around her continuously, he appeared in her dreams, and even though it was difficult to admit, she had a repulsive desire to be with him. Lily tried removing him from her soul many times but had been unsuccessful. Her intention was: "I am safe and have my sovereignty."

Lily lay on my healing table with my mesa resting on her third chakra. I placed my hands on her feet, and as soul-purifying Light moved through me,

Unlike me, Lily was aware of being cursed the moment it happened, and the heavy energy quickly infiltrated and traversed her body.

I was astonished to notice large, energetic fangs on both sides of her solar plexus. My Teacher said we would use the mesa as a dialysis machine.

I continued channeling Light and watched my medicine bundle suction out the circulating curse. The heavy energy moved up from Lily's body, out through the fangs, and into the mesa/dialysis machine where it was transmuted into sami, which was then returned to Lily through the machine and infused directly into her body. The fang marks slowly faded during this process.

My Teacher and Horse then took me to the Hall of Records, also called the Akashic Records, the cosmic location where information regarding incarnational history is held. He showed me the page in Lily's "book," where an agreement between Lily and the man was written. I tore out the page and burned it.

Weeks later, Lily wrote, "I feel as if I'm nearly entirely rid of the systemic issue. I only say *nearly* instead of *entirely* because since my session with you, I've seen that man's face in the dreamscape, but it was only one or two times, and I no longer hold clear memories of the dream when I wake up."

BELIEFS

Beliefs play a huge role in our health, and like all energy, until we attend to them, detrimental ones can become systemic and grow as rampantly as fertilized weeds. This is what happened to fifty-year-old Edna, who told me her traumatic upbringing was causing her to feel more emotionally weakened than usual. Her intention was: "I'm centered, grounded, and empowered."

As Light moved from my center, down my arms, and out my hands into Edna, I was shown an energy of self-hatred within her bloodstream that was mirroring the flow of blood throughout her body. What could be more systemic than blood flow?

My Teacher said Edna needed a special transfusion, and immediately, an aspect of her higher self—a part of the soul that's more awake than we tend to express in our daily lives—appeared. She attached tubing from her energetic arm into Edna's physical arm in the same way a blood transfusion is done in this reality. I watched as two pints of self-loving "blood" traveled from Edna's higher self into her physical circulatory system.

Once the transfusion was complete, the tubing was removed, and Edna's arm was energetically bandaged. I was told that the homogenization of this new energy would take place over the next few days, and it was important for Edna to drink lots of water.

Edna knew this energy of self-hatred well. She said it was a remnant of her emotionally abusive childhood, something she'd always felt systemically affected by. A week after the healing, Edna called to say she felt more self-assured and had even begun feeling a little self-love.

Illness Averted

All people, no matter their gender, identification, or sexual orientation, are a blend of masculine and feminine energy. We can stereotype and say a man with a muscular physique and beard is masculine, and a woman resembling Marilyn Monroe is feminine. Those are external clichés. I'm talking about the yanantin of masculine and feminine energies, a union of opposites that creates Unity. People see feminine energy as intuitive, loving, and "being," and masculine energy as logical, controlling, and "doing." Is a man with an abundance of feminine energy weak? Is an active woman aggressive? Like most things, it's about balance.

Our uniquely blended masculine and feminine energies can become distorted. If a person has been deeply traumatized and emotionally wounded, their healthy masculine can warp within their psyche to the point they end up becoming a proponent of genocide. (Have you ever wondered about the childhood experiences of our world leaders?) Healthy feminine flexibility and gentleness can, for similar reasons, morph to such a degree that a person behaves like a doormat for others to walk all over. As we heal and unify within, our unique ratio of both energies finds its natural equilibrium and expression. Do pure masculine and feminine energy exist? Yes, in the natural world, where psychological wounding is not possible.

Most Indigenous people see the moon and water as feminine beings and the sun and fire as masculine. In Peru, where the Apus are foundational to life, there are male and female mountains. Phutu Cusi, as Juan taught, is the only female Apu at Machu Picchu. Her counterpart, Huayna Picchu, is a strong, masculine presence who is not only the tallest mountain at the ruins, but an important character in the events of autumn 1996—a prelude to my initiation four months later.

It was our third and final day at the ruins. The early morning sun was beginning to cut through dense layers of fog, a daily occurrence at nearly 8,000 feet above sea level. The previous day had been devoted to feminine energy. We'd hiked down to the subtropical jungle and spent time in ancient, carved caves—wombs of Pachamama—at the bottom of Huayna Picchu. Our focus this day was masculine energy and the group was going to the top. Apu Huayna Picchu, while considered masculine, is comprised of a balance of both masculine and feminine energies.

We began by standing in front of what many have named the "Sacred Rock," but Juan calls "the Pachamama Stone." About ten feet tall, twenty-three feet wide, and semi-flat on one side, this carved stone pulls in energy from distant mountains and represents Pachamama. We faced our palms toward her and offered our feminine energy for safekeeping, knowing she'd return it to us at the end of the day.

Juan led the way. The path up the mountain is made up of smaller-than-the-length-of-my-hiking-boots stone steps, some flat and others rounded, each purposefully placed by the Inka six hundred years ago. It was a little scary because they were uneven, and the narrow path became steeper and steeper the farther we ascended the 8,924-foot-tall mountain. With no guardrails to keep us from falling off the sheer cliff edge to our left, I walked with my right hand touching the mountain for what felt like hours until we reached the summit.

The top of Huayna Picchu had enough space for our group, plus several tourists, to gather. It's said that an Inka high priest and some local virgins once lived there, and each morning walked down what I consider a treacherous path to the center of the ruins to welcome the new day. The peak of the mountain is at the tip of a flat, angled stone. This is where our ceremony was held.

Each person took a turn and lay on this stone while Juan, standing across from them, raised his mesa into the air and collected the masculine energy from Huayna Picchu and four other significant masculine Apus in the surrounding area. He waved it around, calling, "Come. Come," then transferred the consolidated energy from his mesa by placing it briefly on the solar plexus of the group member. *On. Off.* After about a minute, the person stood up and walked away. It looked quick and simple.

When it was my turn, I lay down, closed my

Each person took a turn and lay on this stone while Juan, standing across from them, raised his mesa into the air and collected the masculine energy from Huayna Picchu and four other significant masculine Apus in the surrounding area.

eyes, and took some deep breaths. I immediately felt Juan's mesa. It was heavy. And getting heavier by the minute. Energy waves, a little like contractions during childbirth, began to slowly move through me, each becoming stronger than the one before. I rode the intensity with my breath (something I would later do at my initiation where the energy also felt like labor). As the ferocity inside my body increased, not unlike how an orgasm builds upon itself, deep moans instinctually emerged from my throat and mouth. The waves were relentless, and my voice became louder and louder as it matched the energetic acuteness building within me… Suddenly the energy peaked in such explosive magnitude that I released a primal scream.

My eyes flashed open.

There was Juan, standing calmly in front of me, his mesa still in his hands. It hadn't even been on my body! I tingled and pulsated. Every cell, from the tips of my toes to the edges of my earlobes, felt plugged-in and overcharged. I closed my eyes, took several deep breaths, and tried to integrate. It was impossible.

I bewilderedly looked at Juan, who reached his arms out to help me stand. My traveling companion, John, was waiting and took my hand and walked me to the other side of the mountain, where I sat and wept, transported to my six-year-old self. This occurred during the time I was in therapy healing my childhood. (Nine years before I was taken by surprise in the dentist's office.) How did I live with so much fear?

An hour later, when it became time for our group to descend the mountain, I was still feeling vulnerable. The "stairs of death," as they're called—the last rocky steps you walk up just before reaching the summit, and the very first steps you take on the descent—awaited. Over 8,000 feet of sheer free-fall was not an option, and I mustered every ounce of will to stay balanced. It felt like years before we finally arrived back at the Pachamama Stone, where I reclaimed my feminine energy and collapsed on a nearby patch of soft, fresh grass.

"What was that all about?" I wondered. Unbeknown to me, my body and soul had been systemically full—toes to earlobes—with my abusive father's distorted masculine energy. And it took the pristine, unadulterated masculine of the Apus to free it.

Anyone who has been abused will most likely retain the energy of their abuser(s). Distorted masculine energy, which can reside in both men and women, stagnates within our bodies, and eventually becomes so dense it manifests in our physical, emotional, and/or energetic systems. I believe if the hucha within me had remained, it's likely I would have become systemically ill.

I include this story not only because it's an example of systemic energy, but with the hope that abuse survivors gain further insight into their lives and seek the help they need. It's important we do our best to become free of latent energetic distortions before they become systemic and turn into illness.

CLOSURE

Heavy energy comes in various quantities and qualities, and too much of it—whether systemic or localized—can create havoc in a person's life. Western medicine can attend to systemic illnesses where communities of cells have forgotten their purpose and grown into tumors and masses, and surgery and chemotherapy save lives, but the stories in this chapter, which are more common than you might think, illustrate energetic conditions that medicine doesn't understand and is rarely able to treat.

If you struggle with an intrinsic feeling of physical and/or emotional discord that has been difficult to heal, consider that it might be a systemic energetic issue. From conception to abuse, to curses, earthbound entities, core beliefs, PTSD, and other situations not mentioned here, hucha within the body and soul can become so dysfunctional that medical doctors or weekly therapy sessions are unable to fully diagnose or resolve it.

Clearing our energy is not only necessary for health but is imperative to achieving inner Unity. This is why, after experiencing how often it's the only remedy for confusing and difficult physical and emotional states, I fall to my knees in gratitude for Spiritual Healing.

PILLAR OF LIGHT VISUALIZATION

Here is a beautiful way to clear heavy energy from the soul. You might not be able to transmute all of it, but you'll be surprised about how much is possible.

Hold this intention: I am in my own energy, and my Light is vertically aligned and anchored.

Center and ground.

Take a deep, oxygenated inhalation. Breathe all of your heavy energy—known and unknown—down and out your entire body. Release it from the top of your head, your neck, arms, hands, torso, and both legs—all the way to the tips of your toes. Push it all down. Remember, Pachamama receives our hucha as food. Imagine that she's voraciously hungry.

Take your time. Notice how you feel with each release.

When you're ready—centered, grounded, relaxed, and as energetically refined as possible—focus your breath on the Light within the center of your soul. You know it. The Light of Love. Breathe into this Light and envision it simultaneously growing up and down the central column of your energy system.

See it move out your root and crown chakras.

You've created a vertical ray of Light in the center of your body.

Now, with breath and focused intent, expand the ray horizontally, outside your physical body. Not too far. Make your entire body, inside and out, a Pillar of Light.

Explore your pillar with your inner senses. Do you notice any heaviness or energetic distortions? If so, release as much as you can into Pachamama.

Relish the feeling of being a Pillar of Light. When you feel complete, open your eyes, and re-center and ground one more time.

(If during this meditation you discovered heavy energy you were unable to release or transmute, consider seeking help from an experienced healer.)

Welcome to the NORTH

THE PETAL OF ELDER

It's Winter. Time to pour yourself a cup of hot tea,
Snuggle on the cushioned window seat under your favorite down comforter,
And celebrate the wisdom you've achieved
Since the beginning of your Four-Petaled Flower Medicine Wheel journey.
Here in the North, the human life cycle is completing itself.
Your spirit, escorted by loved ones, will soon leave your physical body
And travel through a wave-filled gateway back to the Spirit Realm.
Imagine the thrill when you recall what you may have forgotten:

You are an Eternal Divine Light of Loving Consciousness.

The inevitability of human death offers opportunities to release
what no longer serves
And encourages us to embrace entirely new perspectives.
As you read the following chapters, ask yourself…
Is a new way of life calling?
Buffalo lives here. Hoist yourself onto her thick, muscular back.
Take risks you never expected.
The stars will help you navigate.

CHAPTER ELEVEN

Illness

The beginning of healing starts with the restoration of your relationship with God, yourself, and others.

— Dr. Henry W. Wright, *Exposing the Spiritual Roots of Disease*

The first three petals of the Four-Petaled Flower Medicine Wheel awakened your sleeping wisdom. Now that these insights are an active part of your awareness, it's time to meet Buffalo. She joins us here in the North with teachings about prayer, gratitude, and abundance. Before you continue, take a breath. Sink even deeper on the couch or chair. And pray to the Mystery, offering gratitude for your beautiful spirit/human creation and life.

The *Merriam-Webster Dictionary* defines illness as "an unhealthy condition of body or mind." Here, I define it as "a teacher who arrives with offerings for spiritual awakening."

Do you know anyone who ever consciously invites this teacher for a visit? But if karma needs fulfilling or our sleepy-headed consciousness demands awakening, we might discover it standing at our door. Sometimes the knocks are barely perceptible, but if we ignore even the faintest sounds of our unexpected guest, they can become loud and persistent. And if we're stubborn and refuse to

open the door, this teacher might stop knocking and begin pounding, or even become a battering ram that barges in and makes itself at home, announcing, "I'm here!"

During a healing class in 1998, I asked that a being from the Light come through me and offer us a teaching about illness. A new, benevolent masculine presence entered my soul, and his energy felt so loving that I opened further and chose to relay his words to the group. He said his name was Djwal Khul. After the channeling, I researched and learned that D.K., as I discovered the spirit is called, is believed to be a Tibetan master of ancient wisdom. His teachings form the bedrock of this chapter.

This is how D.K. defines illness:

The nature of all illness is a set of complex karmic conditions. There is truly no need for illness upon Earth, yet it has become a powerful teacher for human beings as they ascend the spiral and further expand their souls.

For many, illness is a form of karmic punishment the individual spirit decides to take upon its human self. For others, it is a lesson in humility. For all, illness is a movement forward, a step spirit chooses to bring itself into more expansive consciousness.

The eternal Light within our souls is always calling, *"Look at me. Remember who you are."* Illness triggers an emotional vulnerability, and depending upon how severe it is, offers (or forces) an opportunity to pay attention to the Light.

When we first become ill, the initial step is deciding upon a healing path. Since most of us have confidence in Western medicine, that's the road we walk, which makes sense, because Western medicine can facilitate amazing results. Unfortunately, I've worked with several people who've explored it *to its end* and have not had that experience. Spiritual Healing was their last resort, and when they arrived in my healing room, most were physically and emotionally exhausted from their efforts. Why does one healing method work for some and not others? It depends upon the intentions of their illness teacher and is most likely, as D.K. taught, a blend of *"spiritual awakening and karmic necessities."* What I've found to be true is: with all its physical, emotional, and spiritual components, illness provides creative ways we, in partnership with Spiritual Healing, can work with our visiting teacher. The following stories illustrate this.

ILLNESS PREVENTED

There are times we can eradicate an illness in its beginning stages, which is what happened for Laura, who arrived at my healing studio in such an emotional frenzy, she could barely speak. Someone in her family was dealing with a health crisis, and Laura wanted to help so badly that she had worked herself into a chaotic state. She lay upon the healing table and rested while I channeled the Light of Love, and when the soulular purification phase was complete, my Teacher and Horse took me on a journey.

We arrived in a realm where a wide-eyed part of Laura was spinning out of control in the center of a cyclone. The rapidly moving, unmanageable forces were frightening—even to me—and I looked at my Teacher, hoping he would not direct me to enter them. Before he had a chance to say anything, Horse—who mostly acts as an unwavering transporter—surprised me by walking directly into the churning vortex. Horse stood calmly amid the chaos and with fearless, focused intent, watched Laura being swept around non-stop. Then, he tossed his head into the air to get her attention and patiently waited for her to notice. She finally spotted him, and after unsuccessfully trying multiple times to grasp onto his long, brown mane, Laura took hold. She clung tight, and once she'd hoisted herself securely onto Horse's back, he walked effortlessly out of the cyclone. I joined Laura astride my faithful power animal, who carried us both to my healing water where spirit helpers submerged her in its silky richness. She emerged grounded and ready to return to her soul.

As soon as I blew Laura's healed soul-part into her heart/soul space, she immediately sat up—but just as suddenly, fell back. Her physical equilibrium had become energetically aligned with the unsteadiness of her formerly dissociated part, and she needed time to recalibrate. After about ten minutes, she felt strong enough to sit and then stand. Laura was delighted to be back in her body and ready to serve her family, whose suffering had been so traumatic for her that it had caused soul loss! If she hadn't sought Spiritual Healing, Laura's disunified state might have created vertigo or worse in this physical realm.

SEIZURES

Louise began having seizures at six months old. Doctors wanted to put her on medication, but her parents decided to explore other options and brought their six-month-old daughter to see me. I held calm, trusting Louise on my lap, and as she slept, I channeled Light and journeyed into the landscape of her soul.

My Teacher and Horse brought me to an area of the Spirit Realm where Louise's spirit/soul family—a group of beings that resonate at a similar energetic frequency and level of consciousness and often incarnate together—were gathered. I learned that spirit Louise was their teacher, and before she had entered the Birth Gateway for a new life, intentionally left a part of her soul with them. This formed an energetic cord that was attached from the group soul to human Louise's crown chakra, a connection that allowed her to visit and continue teaching. The problem was—cords become roads between one energy system and another, and Louise's connection with her soul family had become a well-traveled freeway with no speed limit. I explained to her soul-part that each time she focused on her grouping, part of her incarnated soul made a rapid exit out of her physical body, which ignited a physiological electrical current and resulted in a seizure.

Louise hadn't fully incarnated and, teacher that she was, understood it was time to do so. She lovingly departed from her group, cut the cord, and placed clamps on both sides, just as midwives and doctors do to the umbilicus at birth (and how you disconnected from your mesa that was filled with disempowering former events and beliefs). This separates the energies and redirects the flow where it naturally belongs. I restored Louise's soul-part and disabled the freeway by placing a time-soluble, energetic coating around her crown chakra and reshaping it to its appropriate size.

Louise was the first client to teach me about the seizure phenomenon, and I can happily say others have been served with this information. While all seizures involve rapid out-of-body exits, their reasons differ. Not everyone is a teacher within a spirit/soul group. Some might leave their bodies to visit deceased loved ones. Others are spiritual explorers. Western medicine offers pharmaceuticals that help many people remain in their bodies, yet I expect that most have expanded and possibly misshaped crown chakras, one or more energetic "freeways," and soul loss. Spiritual Healing can help seizure sufferers understand the particulars of their phenomenon, change the energetics, unify the soul, and offer tools for remaining embodied.

I'm thrilled to say that Louise's seizures resolved.

Multiple Sclerosis

When I was in Hungary, I worked with a loving couple, Vilma and Istvan. Vilma had multiple sclerosis, a disease where the protective covering of the nerves is attacked by the immune system. Her symptoms had accelerated over the years, and when we met, her legs and arms were elastic, and numbness was spreading from her abdomen throughout her body. Vilma's parents had divorced when she was three, and she'd been raised by her alcoholic mother and abusive grandmother. She remembered being sexually abused at five and six years old and raped at fourteen, which is when she became pregnant and had an abortion she still regretted. Vilma wasn't asking for or expecting a miracle healing; instead, her miracle was to understand the roots of her illness.

While Vilma lay upon my healing table and received the Light, my Teacher and Horse escorted me to an arid piece of land where a burial site awaited excavation. I called for spirit helpers to exhume the remains, and once the wooden casket was on top of the Earth, I carefully opened it. Inside lay a fourteen-year-old part of Vilma's soul enveloped in white satin sheets and surrounded by red and pink blossoming roses. My Teacher put sacred water on her face, and she startled awake, looked directly at him, and said, "I'm better off dead." I persuaded teenage Vilma to allow us to bring her to my healing water. While spirit helpers attended to her, I was taken to a five-year-old soul-part who also needed healing. Once both girls were revitalized, I reminded them of who they were and spoke about the life awaiting them with adult Vilma and her devoted husband. The parts were willing to re-join her, and I blew them into Vilma's soul.

Vilma was extraordinarily cognizant. She knew her first dissociation had occurred when she was sexually abused as a young child, and when it happened again at fourteen, she told me she'd literally "died" of shame. That "death" is what ultimately shut down her immune system and created space for illness. Vilma and I spoke at length about self-love. I encouraged her to put pictures of her five- and fourteen-year-old selves on a special table and surround them with roses. I also suggested she design a ceremony for her unborn child so she might

That "death" is what ultimately shut down her immune system…

feel a sense of completion with her abortion.

Vilma was grateful to finally understand her illness and said she felt unified for the first time in her life. A woman of strength, courage, and insight, Vilma's story teaches us not only how trauma and soul loss can systemically affect the entire body, but that healing is not always about physical health.

GENETICS

This is an important topic, and I'll address it by sharing something that happened to me. For too many years, whenever I got sick or felt an unusual body sensation, I thought it might be fatal, a belief born from the unsafety of my childhood. In my fifties, I started feeling as if I wore layers of thick, energetic overcoats made up of family illnesses. I *desperately* wanted to be rid of them, so I asked my trusted friend, Joy—mother, farmer, and healer—if she would do a distant healing for me.

Joy opened a ceremony and requested the participation of our spiritual allies. When her teacher arrived, he called to the Star People, new beings to both of us, who surrounded my soul, placed their hands upon me, infused me with Light, and said:

We will speak with you about overlays. All people are eternal, vibrant, Light beings. Everything overlays this. The experience of the physical body within the entire earthly dimension is one large overlay.

You live and focus on the dimension of Earth where birth, growth, decay, and death all overlay the physical experience. Each exposure one has while in the body is a result of everything that individual has ever witnessed, heard, or believed. This includes family ailments. It is important to let concepts and memories of someone else's physical and mental experiences go. Your family's illnesses were theirs. Whatever each person created in their body and unique life has nothing to do with you or with genetics.

In my case, these overlays were my mother's breast and colon cancers, my father's Parkinson's disease, my Grandma Tillie's arthritis, and my healthy-his-entire-life, non-smoking Grandpa Louis's sudden death from lung cancer. On my father's side, there was leukemia, diabetes, and high blood pressure—but perhaps because I was never close with his parents, I wasn't wearing those coats.

Joy said the Star People peeled and removed multiple overlays from my soul, and it wasn't long after that I began noticing a difference in my thoughts. Grandma Tillie's curled arthritic fingers no longer held a charge for me, I understood that my mother's cancers and father's Parkinson's were theirs, and the sudden death of Grandpa Louis—which had instilled a very real fear of the same thing happening to me, especially since it had happened to my sister—calmed. Now, when I feel an unfamiliar pain or discomfort, I sink into it, discern what it is, and try to understand its teaching. If I come up empty-handed, I call a friend for perspective.

Perspective was something that served Alexa

as well. Breast cancer ran in her family, and at forty-four, she was so fearful it would happen to her, she was considering the prophylactic removal of both breasts. During her healing, I was shown a matrilineal soul pattern—Alexa's great-grandmother, grandmother, mother, and aunt had all died from breast cancer. From a human perspective, this is genetics. From a spirit perspective, in Alexa's family, it was what you chose if you wanted to belong, like the dues one pays to join an exclusive club. Because it was part of her karma and overall spiritual development, spirit Alexa had made that choice. I spoke with the part of Alexa's soul wedded to club membership and explained that it was no longer necessary to accept the conditions. Plus, if she wanted to, she could shut down the entire organization.

Now, when I feel an unfamiliar pain or discomfort, I sink into it, discern what it is, and try to understand its teaching.
If I come up empty-handed, I call a friend for perspective.

My Teacher and Alexa's soul-part teamed up and summoned the entire lineage to us. All women—past, present, and future—that had been, or would become, a club member stood in a line so long I could barely see the end. My Teacher raised his hands, faced his palms toward them, and streamed healing Light. Once a woman received it, she faded away. When no one was left, the ancestral cycle—which had included not only Alexa, but her daughter, future granddaughter, and all unborn women yet to join the family—was healed and complete. I returned Alexa's part and shared the story. She decided not to have the surgery, and as far as I know, remains cancer-free.

Something similar happened with Elek, a talented woodcarver I met in Hungary. He had polycystic kidney disease—actively growing cysts on his kidneys—something his father died from at forty-seven. Elek, now fifty-five, was on a kidney transplant list. His intention was: "My kidneys are strong, and I'm a good example to my sons." During the healing, the Pleiadean surgeons arrived and drained and salved Elek's cysts, and once this was complete, my Teacher and Horse brought me to a seven-year-old aspect of his soul.

Little Elek sat on a log, watching his father split wood, admiring every little nuance—from his worn flannel shirt, torn faded jeans, thick, mussed-up, wavy brown hair, to his uninterrupted focus and calm response when the wood didn't split exactly the way he planned. When his father looked up and smiled at him, Little Elek's heart expanded, and he thought, "I want to be just like my daddy." And at that instant, I watched the father's destiny imprint itself upon the young boy.

After explaining my presence to father and son, I asked little Elek's father for permission to take his son for healing. "Do whatever you think is best," he said, "I trust you." Their embrace moved me to tears, and when they finally separated, little Elek's father watched his son mount my horse and leave. We traveled to my healing spot, where the mystical alchemy of the water erased the soul imprint. I restored a healed, refreshed child into adult Elek's soul.

Elek and I spoke for a long time, and as he understood that being like his father had meant taking on his illness, he became concerned for his two young sons. I suggested he do a few things post-healing: perform an honoring ritual for his father to release his need to be like him, have a conversation with his sons about what it means to emulate another, and communicate with his kidney cells, reminding them how to function properly. My Teacher said that, as a result of the spiritual surgery, Elek's urine might be brown for a few days, so I recommended he drink lots of water until it became clear. Elek embraced his healing and said it provided new freedom for him and his sons. Although I never saw him again, I'm confident he followed through with my suggestions. I hope he received a new kidney, but it's also possible he died. Either way, Elek's healing ended the pattern of the "genetic" illness.

STAGNATING HUCHA

D.K. taught:

What appears to be incurable to medical science are masses of energetic frequencies that have become bound and tangled. These need to be sorted out, in combination with the soul's agenda, and the person's psychological state and willingness to heal.

This was certainly true for Tessa. When she was twelve years old, Tessa accidentally discovered a secret her father had been keeping—he was having an affair. He made her swear not to tell anyone, especially her mother. Tessa never said a word, but lying to her mother and absorbing her father's shame created internalized stress and resulted in a brewing stewpot of hucha. When she was twenty-five, the "stew" was given a name, Crohn's disease, an inflammation of the digestive system.

Tessa lay upon my healing table, and once she was in a deeply relaxed state, I asked if she could locate the core of her disease. She breathed deeply, opened her inner senses, and said, "A huge, red-eyed snake is enveloping my intestines." Tessa used her physical hand to firmly grab the energetic snake (which only she saw), and with the power of a warrioress, pulled it out in one swift movement, and thrust it to my spirit helpers, who took it away for transmutation. She then placed both hands directly upon her second and third chakras, filled them with love, and emphatically reclaimed her intestines: "Only my energy can live here." Tessa fearlessly discovered, unbound, and sorted out *masses of energetic frequencies* that had been stored within her body since childhood and was astonished at how spacious she felt. She called a few weeks later, saying the doctors had declared her illness in remission.

And then there's my mother, who suffered from various illnesses, including COPD—chronic obstructive pulmonary disease—the result of a lifetime of cigarette smoking. In addition to maintaining the secrets of our childhood, my mother chose to be estranged from Susan and me. We were never told she was ill and weren't invited to her bedside as she was dying. The depth of her emotional wounds held her prisoner, but unlike Tessa, she did not choose to address them. I believe my mother is a classic example of profound inner disunity, a woman for whom stored hucha created a universe of its own and ultimately claimed her body before she reached seventy years of age.

BLENDED ENERGIES

According to D.K.:

Physical illness seems mysterious much of the time, yet it is not mysterious at all. If you could only see how energetic frequencies blend, merge, shift, and become beings of unknown origin to human doctors.

This is how it was for Deborah, a fifty-seven-year-old woman who struggled with fear, self-sabotage, and disunification her entire life. Her *"beings of unknown origin"* showed up as depression, exhaustion, and irritable bowel syndrome—a chronic disorder affecting the large intestine. Deborah, an only child of Holocaust survivors, had been brought up in an environment of such anxiety and separation that when I asked if she remembered a happy time, after a long silence, she replied, "No." Deborah's intention was: "I am whole and feel my Light."

As Deborah lay upon the healing table and received the Light of Love, I noticed she was cloaked within other people's energies in addition to what looked like hundreds of cords that were attached to her solar plexus, the area of digestion. When my inner vision traveled up a few of the cords, I saw that each one was connected to a person, who was connected to another person, and another, and another. No wonder Deborah was ill. Spiritual ally Archangel Michael—protector and transmuter of the heaviest of energies—arrived and efficiently cut and clamped the cords, and then brought the displaced beings to the Light. A simple task for him became a healing for many.

Afterward, my Teacher and Horse brought me to the upper world, where a four-year-old part of Deborah's soul sat upon a throne radiating love and Light to an infinite number of beings. Because her parents had been unable to express affection, their young daughter, desperate for love, decided, "If I take on their pain, they'll love me," and like many neglected and needy children, brought the energy of her parents' suffering into herself. This was bad enough, but there were soul-parts of other Holocaust survivors living within her parents' souls, and mistaking Deborah for the Light, they joined her as well. This energetic debacle made Deborah dissociate further, and at four years old, she'd become the "Queen of Heaven" for an infinite number of lost souls. To make matters worse, her parents continued recreating their suffering, which made Deborah's job ongoing.

I explained to the child that she was part of adult Deborah's soul and asked if she'd like to come with me. Little Deborah loved the idea, and once she joined me on Horse, my Teacher emptied the palace by escorting the Holocaust survivor souls to the Light. Little Deborah's task was finally complete. I left her in the care of spirit helpers at my magical healing spot, while I was brought to the Death Gateway to meet another aspect of Deborah's soul—a mid-thirties, suicidal part. I spoke with the young woman about present-time Deborah and the little girl, and although it took a while, convinced her to return. She reached for my hand, stepped out of the tunnel, and joined me for a ride to the healing water.

To my surprise, my Teacher informed me there was more to do, so I mounted Horse once again. They brought me to a calm, flowing, sunlit river where, per my Teacher's instructions, I stood on a large, flat boulder, held out my arms, and called, "Deborah. Come, come..." Iridescent bubbles, like the ones that form when a child places a wand in a container of suds and blows, instantly surrounded me. I gathered them in my arms (one of many things possible only in the shamanic realms) and they merged and transformed into a shining, rainbow quartz crystal. At last, my Teacher said: *It is done* and returned me to my healing area, where Deborah's power animal, a large Elk with ten-point antlers, awaited. Once all of the parts emerged from the water, I gave the crystal to the four-year-old

and blew her, the mid-thirties part, and Elk into Deborah's heart/soul space.

As you might imagine, after this immense energetic shift, Deborah had to become familiar with an entirely new way of experiencing herself. Her emotional integration took months, but her physical health improved immediately.

COMPLEXITIES

D.K.'s teachings were especially relevant to Tom:

Curing an illness is a complex task, for the psychodynamic nature of the individual enhances or detracts from the cure. It is always of vital importance to determine whether the individual wishes to be cured. Speaking the words: 'I wish to heal' is not necessarily the deeper truth. All illness is curable, yet who is manifesting the illness? Why? What is the purpose?

Tom was in his mid-thirties and blessed with a loving wife, two healthy children, a beautiful home, and a supportive extended family. Unfortunately, he had aggressive brain cancer, and one round of chemotherapy and two surgeries did not stop his tumors from growing. Tom was offered a second round of chemo, but doctors told him he was going to die with or without it. I was his last resort.

I saw Tom twice a week for six weeks. We didn't talk much; everything took place on the healing table as I channeled Light, and he slept. By the end of our time together, a new MRI showed a reduction in the size of his tumors and no new growth.

Tom's family was ecstatic, but Tom was not. This coincided with the "emotional exploration" phase of Spiritual Healing, a consciousness-awakening experience that would transmute more heavy energy. Tom was disinterested. I soon discovered he did not have a will to live, so after what looked like a miraculous prognosis, Tom chose to end our sessions. He passed away six months later.

D.K. reminds us: *There is a spiritual purpose for all human illness.*

Tom was the first human teacher to show me the complexities of participating in someone's healing. Who knows what anyone's purpose for a visit from their illness teacher is? Tom appeared open, but on deeper levels, he wasn't, and while standing at the crossroads between living and dying, he chose death. Was that his karma? Or was it his highest healing path? Tom taught me that healing does not necessarily mean living.

Is this why one person heals, and another doesn't? The dilemma of being spirit/human beings and simultaneously walking two paths, each with their unique intentions, consistently gets in the way of our linear understanding. Choosing an illness for spiritual growth sounds like madness to a human. But to a spirit? Once again, this is yanantin, the union of dissimilar energies.

When a Teacher of any form of illness or disharmony arrives, no matter what healing modality you choose, make the most of it by including the Spiritual Healing perspective: identify as spirit, remember your inner Light, attend to your emotional state, and unify what might be disunified. And of course, choose Faith and Trust.

And finally, as D.K. put it:

The consciousness of spirit must and can evolve past the need for illness. And when there is no more need, illness will no longer exist.

Understand Your Dis-ease

First of all, be patient. In an ideal world, answers arise from within, so begin your exploration there. Then, if you need greater understanding, ask for help.

As always, center and ground.

Create a goal such as "I want to gain perspective about why I have this illness." Or "I want to explore my soulular overlays." Or "I want to discover the hidden emotional reasons that contributed to my dis-ease."

Meditate about it.

Consider hypnotherapy to help you bypass your linear mind and access hidden knowings.

Journey with your teacher and power animal.

Visit a Spiritual Healer.

Sit with an experienced channeler and ask questions.

Talk it out with a friend.

And if you never arrive at an understanding or perspective, consider that an opportunity has arisen to choose to trust your situation and deepen your faith in the Mystery.

CHAPTER TWELVE

Coma

We—each of us—are intricately, irremovably connected to the larger universe.
It is our true home, and thinking that this physical world is all that matters is like
shutting oneself up in a small closet and imagining that there is nothing else out behind it.

— EBEN ALEXANDER III, MD, *Proof of Heaven*

Coma is mysterious. According to my Teacher: *For a human being to live, at least fifty percent of their soul must be present and intact.*

Coma patients have extreme soul loss, which leaves them in varying states of energetic disunity and physical unconsciousness. Much of the time they lie in bed as if asleep but are unable to awaken. Where are they? Do they hear our voices? Can they feel our loving touch? Will they ever come back to us? Every comatose person I've assisted had one thing in common—*all* were spiritually conscious—and when given an opportunity to communicate, they took it. Connecting with people in comas supports their empowerment, unification, and spiritual evolution, as well as has the benefit of helping families heal.

Janika and her mother are examples of this.

JANIKA

I was working in Hungary when my friends Csilla and Roberto and I walked up creaky, wooden stairs to an apartment on the ninth floor of a decrepit, concrete building. Sarah, Janika's mother, opened the door and graciously welcomed us in. I tried not to gasp. Her daughter lay in a hospital bed near a large window, and instead of looking as I'd expected—a young woman sleeping peacefully (this was my first coma encounter), Janika's body was emaciated and distorted. Her head rolled non-stop from side to side, and her slightly open mouth exposed a twisted jaw filled with a jumble of protruding teeth. Her open, wandering eyes appeared empty.

We sat on the couch and drank tea and ate butter cookies while Sarah spoke about her daughter. Janika's bed was close, and I believe on some level, she was aware of our conversation.

Janika was in her early thirties and had been a professional beautician. According to her mother, she'd always been healthy, but over a period of two months, she developed both appendicitis and a stomach ulcer. Ten days after a routine appendectomy and normal recovery, Janika had the first of three seizures. High fever accompanied the third, and Sarah brought her back to the hospital, where X-rays revealed an inflamed lung. Janika was given antibiotics, but the seizures continued, so her doctor ordered medications to calm her nervous system. A charting mistake changed everything. Suddenly overmedicated, Janika plunged into a coma. Her doctor said there was nothing he was able to do and discharged her into her mother's care. Sarah's prayer was for Janika to return to her body and enjoy life again.

I am a distant star, fallen to Earth by mistake. Where I am now, I can fly and be the free soul I was meant to be.

We opened a ceremony, called to our spirit helpers, and prayed for a miracle. I sat next to Janika, gazed directly into her vacant, meandering eyes, and introduced myself: "I'm Annie, and I'm going to try to help you." With my hands upon her feet and the Light of Love flowing, Roberto drummed a steady, repetitive beat, and I journeyed on Janika's behalf.

My Teacher and Horse took me far away in the upper world to a star that, he said, was part of a constellation in a galaxy yet to be discovered by human beings. A healthy Janika greeted me. After reintroducing myself and explaining why I was there, I asked, "What can I do for you? Is there anything you need?" Janika said, "I've always been misunderstood. No one has ever known me, not even my mother or sister. I am a distant star, fallen to Earth by mistake. Where I am now, I can fly and be the free soul I was meant to be. They have repressed me, but here, I am free, and they are repressed. I feel their love, but I don't care. The stars are my brothers and sisters. I'm free with them."

I told Janika how much her mother missed her and tried persuading her to return to her body, but she didn't want to leave the stars, especially because of her distorted facial abnormality. (I wondered how she knew...) I suggested that surgery might be able to correct things. Plus, I assured her that coming with me didn't mean she'd be stuck in her body; she could always leave again. Janika paused, contemplated her options, then decided, "yes," but only because returning to the stars was a possibility.

Janika joined me on Horse, and we traveled to my healing spot in the lower world. She was brought into the water, and once she emerged, I restored Janika's strong, healthy part back to her soul.

My Teacher advised: *Tell Sarah that Janika will begin having dreams. This is all right. It is through the dream state she will gain the support to reclaim her body, although once she feels it again, she may not remain. There is a great amount occurring here. She is strong-willed and will determine her fate, as well as the fate of the family.*

I shared my experience and delivered the message to Sarah who, between sobs, said she felt and recognized her daughter.

I had an experience I didn't reveal to anyone that day. After the healing was complete, on my way to the bathroom, I discovered Janika's father sitting in the tiny kitchen, which happened to be adjacent to the living room in the meager apartment. Unbeknown to me, he'd been there the entire time. Lurking. Listening. Not joining in. When I was in the star realm with Janika, I sensed a secret that might have contributed to her original illness and felt the energy of "lurking," which I understood only after encountering her father.

According to her mother, Janika never dated men and spent most of her time with one close woman friend. Did Janika have secrets? Had her father violated her? Janika made it clear she had anger toward her family. When she was alive and healthy, she felt powerless, yet in her weakened physical state, she relished having all the power.

Three days later, Csilla received a frantic call from Sarah saying that Janika was restless and seemed to be reacting to dreams. Csilla reminded her that Janika was exploring how it feels to reclaim her body and making decisions about her future. It took only one week post-healing for willful Janika to return to living as a free soul in the stars and a semi-comatose woman on Earth.

ROD

Alicia's boyfriend, Rod was in a severe motorcycle accident that left him in a coma, and she implored me to visit him in the hospital. When I arrived, Rod's eyes were closed, and he had a breathing tube in his throat and several intravenous lines connected to his veins. I opened a ceremony, placed my hands on his feet, closed my eyes, and was immediately escorted to the part of his soul that had dissociated during the accident. I tried communicating with him, but he was shaking fiercely with anger and emotionally unreachable. My Teacher said: *Let it be.* This was the first time I was unable to break through a soul-part's emotional experience. I completed the hands-on aspect of the healing and shared my struggle with Alicia, who said anger had always been Rod's default emotion.

As Alicia put it: "Rod was in recovery from heroin and alcohol addiction and had been sober for two years. He struggled daily, wondering, 'Why am I here? Why is life so hard?' A few months before the accident, I sent him to Annie for a healing. Following the accident and her initial hospital visit, she did three more healings for him, although those were done at a distance. Rod's anger abated after the first one, and he told her he wanted me to sing to him at night—which I did. When the second was complete, Annie relayed that Rod loved listening to my voice and recommended I continue. In the final healing, she said Rod was participating in a life review and receiving teachings, and that his spirits had given him a timeframe, two weeks in linear time, to decide whether he was going to return to his body or let go and move on.

When the 'deadline' was a week away, I went

to the hospital every morning, desperately looking for a sign, and stayed all day, noticing the slightest changes in his demeanor, facial expressions, and activity. Then, pre-deadline, Rod technically came out of the coma. While he didn't seem present and was unable to maneuver any body parts, his slightly opened eyes could track your finger if you moved it in front of them. On 'deadline' morning, I anxiously rushed to the hospital to see what change there might be. The instant I entered the room, Rod turned his head and looked directly at me with a smile so big it lit up his entire face. Rod was finally present and in his body.

I missed visiting three days in a row during the Christmas holiday. When I arrived, Rod was sitting in a wheelchair outside his room and burst into tears the moment he saw me. Angry tears. He made such a commotion that the nurse ran over. Since the accident, Rod hadn't displayed vocal emotions, but his loud sounds and flailing arm gestures showed me his frustration and anger."

Rod stayed in the hospital for two more months and was discharged into an assisted living home. Physical therapy helped him walk again, but he never regained his speech. The situation was difficult—not just for Rod, but for Alicia as well. A few months after his hospital release, she came to accept that she didn't feel the depth of love necessary to maintain their relationship.

Rod and Alicia eventually broke up.

JACK

Former student and successful businessman, Jack was a wise, kind-hearted man, and whenever I was in his presence—even though I was technically the teacher—I learned something significant. Jack had been suffering organ failure, and a recent heart attack thrust him into a coma. His eyes were closed, and his body was attached to several machines. He wasn't expected to live. His wife asked me to help in whatever way I could.

My Teacher instructed:

Human beings believe machines keep them alive, and without them, a person will die. How is a machine more powerful than a spirit? Is the machine Divine? Yes, of course, for it is the Divine manifesting in the form of a machine that stimulates body responses and makes the body appear alive.

I placed my hands upon Jack's feet, told him I would try to meet him wherever he was, closed my eyes, and channeled Light. *The Light of Love is All... The Light of Love is All...* were my only thoughts as my Teacher and Horse escorted me to the realm where part of his soul was lingering in a state of confusion. Jack was delighted to see and recognize me and asked if I would explain what was happening. I pointed to the energetic cord attached to his third chakra that was traversing the mystical realms all the way to the physical, where it connected to the third chakra on his body. He could travel down this cord, I suggested, and try to inhabit his body again, or he could cut it and let go. "What do you want to do?" I asked. Jack didn't realize he had decision-making power and said he deferred to his wife on personal matters. (I found it interesting that this pattern was active in his coma experience.) "Do whatever you like," I said, "It's up to you."

Jack integrated this information and chose to cut the cord, a decision that transformed the formerly confused energy of his soul-part into empowered clarity. He called out for a sharp knife. When a Light being appeared with one in its hands, Jack grabbed it and then liberated himself from his body by severing the energetic connection. I imagined that this resoluteness had been an integral aspect of his entrepreneurial success.

Once the cord was no longer an issue, angelic beings arrived and enveloped Jack within their midst. He looked at me with an elated smile, said goodbye, and ecstatically floated off with them. It was a beautiful sight. I asked my Teacher how long it would take for this to manifest in physical reality. My linear mind thought it would be instantaneous, but I was told no, it might be several days or even longer. Jack was officially pronounced dead within two weeks. A few months later, his essence came to me in a dream; Jack was delighted to be free.

My Teacher offered this wonderful explanation of what happens to the soul when a person is a coma:

In a coma, the soul can become numb, yet it appears to be asleep. Is it possible to awaken a sleeping soul? Yes, although the human body is its own force, with a physiological system that must perform to house the spirit and soul. If the body has gone beyond functionality, it can no longer support them; thus, it will not be possible to awaken a sleeping soul and expect it to live. Once the body no longer functions, the soul merges within its spirit and exits.

ROBERT

Robert was on his morning bicycle ride around town when he was hit by a drunk driver. Witnesses called 911, and an ambulance immediately arrived and brought him to the hospital. Robert's injuries were so severe that to protect his brain, doctors placed him in a medically induced coma, a temporary coma brought on by an anesthetic drug. For many weeks, it was unclear whether he was going to live, and during this time, Robert's wife asked me to do a distant healing for him.

My Teacher and Horse took me on what felt like a never-ending journey to the upper world, so far away from anything remotely tangible or familiar that I questioned what was happening. When we abruptly stopped in what felt like mid-air, my Teacher shared that it wasn't safe to take me any farther. He explained that since Robert was a world traveler in the physical realm, he was taking the opportunity for further exploration during his dissociated state. "Ah…" I thought, "his basic nature and uniqueness are alive and well." (Qualities that each comatose person I've related with had in common.) I was able to sense Robert's blissful energy but couldn't see him. My Teacher said Robert hadn't yet decided if he was going to return to the confines of his physical form, and it was not my task or right to interfere. Robert awoke from his coma weeks later, and while it took many months for him to heal, his overall health has been restored. He does not remember anything from his comatose escapades.

Dr. H

Dr. H was a sixty-three-year-old family practitioner who was beloved within his community, a place he'd lived since birth. He had a devoted wife, three grown children, and several grandchildren. A month before we met, Dr. H had arrived home from work, suffered a heart attack, and collapsed on the living room floor. Paramedics tried to revive him for twenty long minutes, but eventually pronounced him dead. Two minutes later, Dr. H began breathing on his own.

I walked through the door of Dr. H's private room, where he was semi-sitting in bed. His eyes were open, and a tracheotomy tube extended out from his throat. Paralyzed from the shoulders down and unable to move his head, Dr. H was in a form of semi-coma, embodied just enough to try coughing up mucus.

His wife told me, "He's between worlds. I want to know what he wants me to do."

My job was to communicate with her precious husband on her behalf. I sat on a chair next to Dr. H's bed, looked directly into his eyes, and told him who I was, why I was there, and that I hoped I could be of service to him and his wife. I closed my eyes and prayed that he would allow me to enter his soul.

He did.

Dr. H shared how wonderful it was to arrive home from work each day and be greeted by delicious dinner smells and his loving wife. He was ready to die, he told me, and "be in the arms of our Lord." Dr. H believed I could bring him back, but instead, asked his wife to let him go. He wanted her to have a high quality of life while she still could, and not be tied down caring for him. He said she should focus on the children and grandchildren, and even suggested she take a trip and enjoy herself.

Dr. H was confident they would be together again in heaven.

It was a blessing and privilege to be the vehicle of communication between Dr. H and his wife. He was a man who understood and made manifest the sanctity of life, and whose legacy of service to his patients and family continued even in his semi-comatose state. Three weeks after our visit, Dr. H left his body while being held in his wife's arms. Again, healing does not necessarily mean living.

CONSCIOUSNESS

The human soul maintains its humanness in dissociative states. Rod, Dr. H, Jack, and Janika all had emotions and awareness, and Robert, who I was unable to reach and connect with, was reveling in his explorations. Some coma patients successfully return to their bodies on their own, others choose a release from their physical forms, but too many remain in limbo like Jack had been—confused and lost within the spiritual realms. In each communication, clients gained an understanding of their experience and were offered options that empowered them to make choices regarding their future.

The benefit of Spiritual Healing, not only to coma patients but to their loved ones, cannot be overstated. All family members—Janika's mother, Rod's girlfriend, and Jack's wife—were comforted by the information I gave them. Even Robert's wife, while disconcerted, was glad to hear about her husband. They each needed to know *something* so they could understand and support their cherished one's choices. The bridge of communication I was able to facilitate between Dr. H and his wife benefited both and was exactly what she'd asked for.

People in comas live between worlds, as Dr. H's wife so eloquently stated, and are in extreme experiences of soul loss and disunity. Their fates are determined by a variety of spiritual factors, with karma, teachings, and incarnational decisions at the top of the list. It's not yet commonplace for them to have an opportunity to communicate. To know they're not alone. Understand what's happening. Realize they have options. Perhaps in the future, as more people re-vision what has been culturally taught about coma, an experienced Spiritual Healer will be called to the bedside of each person trapped within this dilemma.

I'll leave you with this: A website called "A Guided Passage" posted a story about a seventy-year-old comatose man in a European hospital where the medical staff allowed his dog, a beige mixed breed, to remain by his side and snuggle next to his head. After a month, the man awoke, regained consciousness, and asked, "Where is the white angel who constantly whispered that everything would be all right?"

COMMUNICATE WITH SOMEONE IN A COMA

Have a witness. It might be the person's wife, husband, mother, father, son, daughter, friend, etc. Someone who will share their questions and provide you with more if you end up getting into a dialog with the person.

Make sure you won't be disturbed for an hour (unless there's an emergency).

Center and ground.

Open a ceremony.

If you're a shamanic journeyer, travel with your power animal and teacher to the person, as I did in each of the stories I shared above, except for Dr. H. If you're not, or you feel like trying something new, follow the suggestions below.

Sit beside the person.

Once you feel ready, close your eyes and ask your known and unknown guides to come and help. Tell them you intend to communicate with (the person's name).

Breathe. Stay calm and trusting.

Take the person's hand and speak. Do this in your head or out loud, whatever feels right at the time. If they know you, say a few personal things. If they don't, introduce yourself. In both instances, let them know why you're there and what you're going to try to do. Remember, the person is present and listening.

Say, "I'm here for you. Is there anything you'd like me to tell your loved one?" Or "Is there anything you need?"

In the same way as when you communicated with the Birth Guardian, allow yourself to feel the subtle or dramatic shift of energy.

Everyone's inner senses are different. You might see the person talking to you. Hear their words.

Or notice and hear nothing, but sense what they're communicating. The most important thing is—however you receive the information—trust it.

If speaking aloud is too scary, write down any answers you receive. Remember, this is not about you. You're doing a service. A communication that might not make any sense or seem insignificant to you, such as, "He's saying something about the color red…," could result in knowing laughter upon relaying this to the family member: "He always loved that couch!"

Be as interactive as the exchange allows, even if it becomes difficult. Remember how I was confronted with Rod's anger? It was easier with Janika, Dr. H, and Jack because they were ready and willing. I was unable to contact Robert at all.

Make sure you let the person know that they're in a coma and anything else that might be pertinent. When the time feels right, ask if they want to return to their body. Whatever the answer, do what you can. If their needs exceed your scope, tell them you'll find someone with more skills to help.

When the communication is complete, thank the person. Even though their eyes are closed and they *appear* unconscious, you're speaking to someone with a spirit and soul, and as we know, spirit is consciousness. You'll discover the best way to complete the exchange. Once you have, step away.

Breathe. Re-center. Ground one more time. And share your experience with their family or loved ones.

Close the ceremony when everything has been accomplished.

CHAPTER THIRTEEN
Death: A Return to the Mystery

And what is it to cease breathing, but to free the breath from its restless tides, that it may rise and expand and seek God unencumbered?

— KAHLIL GIBRAN, *The Prophet*

We've nearly completed our exploration of the North petal and are now in the place of literal and metaphoric death and rebirth. Has your hair become gray yet? Before you continue, stop for a moment and *once again*, honor the wisdom you've achieved. And then consider: Is anything dying within you?

All religions have ideologies about what happens when we die. Christians and Catholics believe we either end up in heaven, where we meet God and live forever, or go to hell to be eternally punished. Muslims also believe in heaven and hell. Seventh Day Adventists say that upon death we fall into an unconscious slumber until Christ returns and awakens his believers, an awakening that allows them to be with God in heaven. Many people of the Jewish faith also accept that a heaven with God exists, while Buddhists, Hindus, and Sikhs have a variety of beliefs about reincarnation. Native American ideas about death vary tribe to tribe—from people becoming Earth or star spirits, to living in the spirit world where they communicate with the living (like the Milky Way Village Spirits), to immediately reincarnating into their original family. In an article by Kitty Edwards in *Natural Transitions Magazine*, Q'ero elder Don Francisco Chura Flores said, "After death our physical body returns to the Earth. Our wisdom returns to the mountains. Our soul returns to the stars." And then there's the Tibetan saying, "Everyone dies, but no one is dead." I think that whatever a person believes, at the very least, once a spirit leaves its body, the mesmerizing human mirage of separation from Source dissolves.

In the mid-1990s, I designed a three-day shamanic workshop called, "The Death Gateway" where participants have a safe place to discover (and maybe come to terms with) this inevitable passage. I've offered it several times.

During one, Ezekiel shared a profound teaching with the group, and since my understandings about death are tiny drops in the ocean of knowledge, his perspective will ground this chapter.

I'll begin with this:

Everything is conscious energy in a perpetual state of transformation. Therefore, all appearances of death—people, flowers, trees, insects, animals—are illusions.

THE AFFINITY OF BIRTH AND DEATH

In 1984, I had the honor of being present at my Grandma Tillie's passing. At the time, I'd been attending childbirths for three years, and my presence at this sacred life passage affirmed an affinity between birth and death.

Both involve "labors" that flow in their own purposeful timing outside our human concept of control. In childbirth, the early phase can last for days, while in death, it might go on for years. Things get equally serious when we enter the active phase, where we realize "this is really happening" and must choose to either resist or surrender. I've been at births where women became so angry and fearful that they fought their labors, which only tightened their muscles and made the experience worse. Similarly, a friend told me that while her mother was dying, instead of opening to loving support, she battled until the very end. Both situations created suffering.

The transition phase of labor can be frightening. Energy flows throughout the body with the intensity of a river just before reaching the ocean, and a woman's body becomes so unified with the current, that unless medicated, she's unable to jump out or go back. Transition during death is the opposite; energy slows to the gentle trickle of a seasonal creek. One day, my grandma and I were in the bathroom: she sat on the toilet, and I sat cross-legged on the floor directly in front of her with my hands on her feet. As I lovingly gazed at her beautiful, wrinkled face, she looked directly into my eyes and asked the universal question of laboring women, "Why is this taking so long?"

Labor energetics change again when full dilation occurs. The body is ready to push the baby out, and the "living energy," as Juan might say, of these contractions—forces of nature in their own right—compel women to fully engage. The mystical movement of spirit out of the body demands no physical strength. Only a surrender, perhaps the deepest we'll ever experience, to the inevitable. And in the end, where the birth of an infant is a tangible, joyous event, the birth of a spirit from form into formlessness is invisible and too often, sad.

No matter how kind, loving, and supportive you are, some people will suffer while vacating the form. Worry not about this. Love them. It is part of their evolution. All spirit/human beings have experienced this at least once. Continue enhancing love and Light. Once they have broken free, they will receive the healing they need.

GRANDMA TILLIE

I was sound asleep on the living room couch. The pre-dawn, morning light was just beginning to peek through the cobalt sky when I was startled awake by voices and movement upstairs. I jumped up and said, "Something's happening in Grandma Tillie's room" and ran to the staircase, grabbed the oak railing, and sprinted up the carpeted steps. This was it.

I walked in to see my frantic mother, desperation flooding her face, sitting on a chair next to the bed. "Mother, Mother!" she called loudly, leaning in and holding her mother's hand tightly. Could her loud voice and physical strength keep death at bay? My father, completely out of his element, stood at the foot of the bed, a worried look on his face. I positioned myself behind my mother and near my grandma. Her eyes were closed.

It was all about her breath.

At birth, we look and listen for the infant's first breath, and as soon as we hear it, breathe a sigh of relief ourselves. During death, we look and listen for the last—the blank space between inhalation and exhalation.

Grandma Tillie inhaled deeply. After what felt like an endless pause...her breath released. Again. And again. Until...stillness. I sensed a presence in the upper left corner of the room and looked. My outer eyes perceived nothing, but I knew—the unfilled gap of Grandma Tillie's breath was the expression of the birth of her brightly lit spirit out of her frail, ailing body. There she was, near the ceiling. Ecstatic. A feeling of bliss and freedom filled the room.

Upon death, spirit, as conscious awareness, experiences a release from form. A second ago, one was contained in a body, and now one is not. Some become elated, while others feel fear, disorientation, or chaos. All are enveloped by celestial realm beings, a cocooning that creates a loving, contained, and soothing presence for those in fear, and heightens the joy, wonder, and freedom for others.

THE SOUL DURING DEATH

The journey from spirit to body and back again is all about expansion and contraction. At birth, a spirit leaves the expansive nature of the Spirit Realm and contracts into form. (Do you remember my client who felt that?) Once embodied, its soul-seed expands. Upon death, the soul no longer has a body to be concerned about, so it contracts and transforms into a seed within its spirit. And then this expansive spark of Loving Consciousness journeys back to the formless Spirit Realm to continue its awakening.

During this mystical process our Birth Guardian arrives. The spiritual midwife who accompanied us when we left the Spirit Realm takes on a complementary role and becomes the Death Guardian who safeguards us on our return. There may be others as well.

Post-death experiences depend upon the individual spirit's state of awareness. Some are accompanied through the gateway by relatives. Others call to a spiritual master to escort them to their version of heaven. Some even choose to visit a hell realm, for that is where they feel they belong. No matter what occurs, all are lovingly encapsulated and tenderly spoken to by their guardian, who brings them to the area of the Spirit Realm appropriate for their level of awakening. There, the spirit can rest, learn, and grow.

Once we've returned to the Spirit Realm, we participate in a life review with our teachers, the beings who originally helped us plan our lives. Did we accomplish our goals? Become too caught up in the human dilemma? What did we learn? When we rejoin our spirit/soul grouping—a circle of beings at similar levels of consciousness, like the one infant Louise was part of—we expand our knowledge even further and prepare our soul seed for its future germination and growth. It's likely our spirit teachers, in partnership with Divine timing, determine when we're ready for a new incarnation, which is when reincarnation will deliver us, not only to new lives, but back to the human illusion of spiritual separation.

The good news is we don't necessarily start from scratch. Unless we choose otherwise, perhaps for karmic or altruistic reasons, our conscious awareness remains at the level of awakening we attained in our previous incarnation. Ultimately, we'll no longer need to continue the remembering process,

because Unity—even in the face of the extreme collective disunity that is manifesting in our world right now—will be solidified within our souls. And finally, it's worth repeating what spirit guides Alura and Athena shared:

As one moves through and completes its cycle of spirit/soul evolution, one becomes a co-worker within the spiritual realms and can assist others in the awakening of consciousness.

IDA'S SURRENDER

I first met Ida when she came for a personal healing and then again when she participated in a group Healing Ceremony I facilitated. Our mutual friend, Sharon, invited me to visit her at the hospice center where she had been staying for a few weeks. Ida was in bed when we arrived and looked warm and comfortable under her baby blue flannel blankets. Her eyes were closed, and her breath so still and quiet I was unable to discern whether she was conscious. Sharon sat at the foot of the bed, placed her hands upon Ida's feet, and channeled the Light of Love. I sat near her head and gently shook a rattle. After a few minutes, I felt surrounded by angelic beings, a magical configuration that had been encircling Ida, and by sitting close to her, I'd unknowingly entered. They seemed to be awaiting her surrender.

Amid the rattle's rhythmic tones, the angels used my voice to share their messages with Ida: *Your family will be fine. Trust this. Let go any time. You are safe. You are loved.* Sharon and I stayed for an hour. Just before we left, I placed Ida's hand gently in mine, and she opened her eyes, looked directly at me, and smiled. Ida passed the next day.

Aldous Huxley wrote in *Island*, "So now you can let go, my darling…Let go…Let go of this poor old body. You don't need it anymore. Let it fall away from you. Leave it lying there like a pile of worn-out clothes…Go on, my darling, go on into the Light, into the peace, into the living peace of the Clear Light."

SAMUEL'S BELIEFS

While some people live with a specific spiritual belief structure regarding the afterlife, others believe their human life is all that exists. Those who hold the latter belief have surprising death experiences, which often are delightful, but can also be disorienting.

Robin's father-in-law, Samuel, had always been an atheist, certain that death completely extinguished consciousness. When a terminal illness rapidly overcame him at forty-seven years old, Robin watched Samuel move in and out of emotional distress… until the day Samuel began seeing deceased family members. His wife and children thought he was going crazy, but Robin knew differently. She believed her father-in-law had passed through an energetic veil and was discovering life beyond the limitations of his mind. Robin said Samuel was thrilled when he began seeing angels, and the euphoric smile that filled his face as he took his final breath led her to suspect that he died in their embrace.

SOUL LOSS

Soul loss is common at death. It might be the result of a trauma, as illustrated by Eliza's story of the birds, or purposeful, like when Thomas's grandmother left a part of herself in her grandson's soul. Each situation is unique, yet what's universal is that if the soul is in pieces—dis-unified—the life of the future spirit/soul unit will be affected, and when it reincarnates, it will be missing a part. But no worries. Although it might take multiple lifetimes for karmic resolution, you can count on Unity to prevail.

My friend Lizzi was raised in an unconditionally loving family. After her father died, Lizzie devoted her life to caring for her ill mother for eight years. One month after her mother's death, Lizzi became distraught, disoriented, and uninspired, and no longer knew who she was. We, her friends, created a Healing Ceremony for her, but since Lizzi was still focusing on her mother, she asked us to make sure she hadn't left any parts behind.

After drumming, rattling, and praying, my Teacher and Horse brought me to the Death Gateway. Lizzi's mother was inside the tunnel, weeping so intensely I was unable to get her attention. Then I noticed Lizzi, also inside the tunnel, trying to calm her. I call this part of Lizzi's soul "Caretaker Lizzi." My Teacher spoke directly to Lizzi's mother: *It's time to go now.* She was startled, not only to have a visitor, but for it to be my Teacher in his human form. He said: *Look over there. Do you see him?* Everyone turned to see Lizzi's father just outside the gateway where it merges with the Tunnel of Light, beckoning his wife to join him. Lizzi's mother looked at her husband, then at my Teacher, and then at Lizzi. My Teacher encouraged her, saying: *Go, my dear. It is time. Your family will be well.* Lizzi's mother paused, sent her daughter a kiss, then turned toward her husband and surrendered to the gateway currents. As they gently moved her into his embrace, two lights unified, formed a figure eight, and flowed into the Tunnel of Light.

I reached my hand out to Caretaker Lizzi, still in the gateway, who grasped it and joined me on Horse. My Teacher placed his hands on her shoulders, channeled Light, and restored this open-hearted part back into Lizzi's soul. Her role was complete. With her mother's fully intact soul in the Light with her father, Lizzi was able to rest, recuperate, and allow a new aspect of life to unfold.

A WE-SOUL DEATH TEACHING

I lost two long-term friends while I was writing this book. These remarkable people probably knew me better than I know myself, and were support beams in the house of my soul. The next two stories relay gifts and teachings they offered me, which I now offer to you. They wouldn't want it any other way.

Chris left first. He had been my partner in Healing Quest, a week-long ceremony you'll read about shortly, as well as a supportive friend for over twenty years. I didn't learn about his death until the day after he passed. He visited me on two consecutive nights, his loving presence so clear and alive I wanted to reach out and touch his smiling face. After that I no longer felt him, and when I asked Ezekiel about this, he told me Chris was participating in a life review.

Ten days later, I went to sleep as usual but awoke in the middle of the night panicked, my heart pounding so furiously I wondered if it was going to explode. I looked up and noticed my closet door open (which was unusual) and a dark figure standing inside with his back to me. I turned on the bedside light, and to my relief, saw a closed door and no one in the room. My hands immediately went to my heart/soul space. I breathed deeply to calm my galloping heart and then called to my spiritual helpers and asked them to purify not only the room, but the house and entire property. I chanted *The Light of Love is All* nonstop. Eventually my heart eased, and my Teacher said: *It is done.*

Then he explained—Chris and I were part of a "spiritual partnership we-soul"—two human beings so spiritually connected over multiple lifetimes that an energy bubble had formed. When he died, his physical absence created an opening that allowed my Light to be seen in low-consciousness realms where an entity—a being that has completely forgotten it is Light—was attracted to it and joined me in my bedroom. I held my mesa to my heart and continued chanting while the Pleiadean surgeons mended my soul. When my Teacher said *It is done* one more time, I was finally calm enough to fall asleep.

A week later, Chris showed up again, although his presence wasn't as tangible as it had been in his earlier visitations. This time he used all the energy he could muster to be present. We shared a deep gaze, after which he gave me a message for his wife. Then he was gone.

When a we-soul of any type shifts, either by death or another life change, everyone in the bubble is affected. If there are many people, such as a workplace we-soul or belonging to a group that shares a common cause or purpose, the affect might be minimal. When there are just two, as in my case with Chris, the energetic shift can be devastating. After this experience, I understood why it had taken me so long to heal after my second husband left. At the time, I'd thought, "We were on a path together, and now I'm on it alone." But what I called "a path" was actually our drastically torn we-soul.

We've all heard stories of long-term relationships—we-souls—where, when one partner passes, the other soon follows. If their karmic timing is aligned, they're successful, but if it's not, a part of their soul might end up stuck in the Death Gateway—unable to go to the Light or return to their body.

It takes considerable energy for a person who has died to manifest in this reality. Chris wanted his wife to know, *one more time*, how much he loved her. I believe he chose me because he knew I'd be receptive and utilized the final energetic remnants of his soul to relay the message before fully merging back into his spirit.

When a we-soul of any type shifts, either by death or another life change, everyone in the bubble is affected.

MY BELOVED FRIEND

We met in 1979 in a childbirth preparation class. I was twenty-six and pregnant with what came to be my only child. She was thirty-five—a "geriatric pregnancy" in those days (they moved it up to forty now)—pregnant with her second. Her first child was five. It was the beginning of a long-term friendship I never would have predicted and didn't nourish—we were so different—but she did, and the rest is history.

I've chosen to share this story in present tense, and out of respect to the family, keep my friend nameless. (I had permission from Chris's wife to use his name.) The following is a summary of our visits during the final days of her life.

She has no hair. First, the chemo took it. Then her eight-year-old granddaughter cut the rest. Now she's bald—a smooth, pale-pink head embraced by elfin ears. Like a newborn. But the hairless head of a newborn is natural. Healthy. My friend's head is a diseased distortion.

She's in bed, disoriented as she tries to put an esoteric experience into words. I'm the perfect one to help. She says: "I woke up today and realized that I lost my will to live. Lost. That means it must be somewhere. Where could it be? How do I find it? Do I want to find it?"

And then: "I'm on a boat in the vastness of the ocean. Alone. Big waves are taking me someplace. I don't want to go there."

I recognize that she's in the waves of the Death Gateway and assure her there are others on the boat. Right now, I say, her vision is cloudy, and she can't see them, but I guarantee her that once they become visible, she'll be in ecstasy.

The first thing she says when she sees me the next day is: "Remember the boat? I decided to change its course."

I wish I could see how my face responded to her earnest statement.

"That's a joke," she says. "As if I had the power to do that."

My bald friend is skin and bones. At seventy-seven, cancer traverses through her blood like a freight train rolling down the tracks, dropping boxes of poison cargo at every station—heart, liver, lungs, bones, brain... A freight train, chugging along, just doing its thing, touching every inch of railway that was ever built, one she lovingly—and ironically—attended to daily.

I ask: "Have you seen your brother and sister-in-law lately?" *No, I haven't visited with them in a long time.* "Do you think you'd like to?" *That would be nice... Is it time?* "Yes, I think it might be time." *Yes, I think it is time.*

We sit on the deck, where majestic Mount Shasta directly faces us. She's bundled up on the lounge chair, a velvet, multicolored, patchwork blanket covering her body and a purple velour hat protecting her vulnerable head. The sky is clear blue, and the bright sun flits in and out of the cotton-candy clouds. We're quiet for many minutes when she breaks the silence: "You know what my favorite thing in the whole world is?"

"What?" The friend who accompanied me that day asks her.

"When children are playing at the edge of the water and start making up songs. I think that's great." We silently envision that.

Her frail body soon chills, and we go inside, where she returns to the couch, lies down, and gets as comfortable as possible. I ask her if her bed is cozy. "My bed is a mess!" she says. "No one has changed the sheets in weeks!" I breathe deeply and embrace her hand tighter. My visiting friend stands up and goes into the bedroom, where she removes the soiled sheets and replaces them with clean, soft, sage-green flannel ones.

Each minute I spend with her is a gift, and as the hours pass it soon becomes time to leave. We kiss lovingly on the lips. "I'll see you tomorrow," I say. "I'm so glad you were here," she replies.

The next day when I arrive, she is asleep on the living room couch. I make a mug of tea and bring it outside to the deck, where I sit on a cushioned chair and look at a *National Geographic* about Mount Everest. Like yesterday, the blue sky is dotted with white, puffy clouds, and the bright sun feels like medicine penetrating deep into my body. Mount Shasta, in all her snowy glory, stares at me while the resounding creek sings melodious water songs.

I skim the magazine, then go inside and try waking her. She's not ready. I walk down to the creek where a perfectly placed chair (I wonder when she last sat there?) awaits. I inhale and receive the healing waters, her daily soul food.

Fifteen minutes later, I try again, and again she needs more time. "Just a little," she says. She soon awakes, ready to eat. She tells me she feels weaker today than yesterday, while at the same time, I watch her devour fish soup and grains and vegetables.

I had already decided to entertain her this day, so I talk about my book and show her design ideas. "What do you think?" I ask. She's an artist, after all. Her focused intensity surprises me, and I welcome her feedback. "Would you like to hear a story?" Yes, she replies. I pick the chapter entitled "Unity" and begin reading the Crystal Kailash story. Twenty-three years ago, she was a huge support to me when I returned from that pilgrimage.

I read with dramatic emphasis and look at her often, the way one does when reading to a child. Her eyes never leave my face. Enraptured, she follows every nuance of every sentence of every paragraph. Our unified hearts and minds dance to word music.

It doesn't take long before her eyes slowly close, and she fades back into a semi-awake slumber. I read a few more lines and say, "this is a good place to stop." She agrees, then looks directly at me and says, with astounding passion: "I love it. Your writing is amazing. I was with you in every moment."

I'm delighted.

It's time to leave, so I gather my computer and purse and lean down to hug and kiss her. "See you later," I say. Our eyes lock. "I love you," she says. "I love you too," I reply, and walk out the door.

The next day I leave town for my home, two and a half hours away, where I wait to hear some news. I am so sad.

In two weeks, her daughter calls and tells me to come. My friend has taken a turn. Breathing difficulties. Oxygen. More meds.

The blood, lunar eclipse decorates the sky that night, its transformative energy blessing everyone. I wonder if she'll leave in its wake.

I drive without stopping and am greeted by the immediate family. Everyone is here. Her forty-two-year-old daughter, her husband, and their two young children. Her forty-seven-year-old son—a resident helper—and his wife and teenage children, newly arrived from Hawaii that morning. The couch she had lain on in the large, light-filled living room has been replaced by a centrally located hospital bed. Expansive windows bring Mount Shasta's potent presence into the house with us.

She lies on the official bed, looking asleep, as daily life flows around her. Sounds and scents of food preparation, dogs milling about, and spontaneous laughter create an illusion of normalcy. Her hearing is acute, and she sometimes has a tender smirk on her face or makes a comment about what's being said around the dining table.

Her daughter sits on a chair on her left side. I stand at the end of the bed in direct line of vision with her entire body, place my hands on her chilled feet, and say hello. She startles awake, and her wide-open eyes peer deeply into mine. Her facial expression speaks surprise, happiness, and dare I say? Relief. In a flash, her eyes close again. I believe she's aware of more than everything.

I remain at her feet and channel Light: *The Light of Love is All, The Light of Love is All.*

When her daughter gets up, I sit in the chair. Her hand reaches for mine and grips fiercely while her labradoodle places his large head as close as he can get between us. I lean down and whisper: "Are you still in the boat?" *Oh yeah.* "Is anyone with you?" *Yes.* "Who is it?" *You.*

Ahhh. I was wondering if something like that might be going on.

I stay at the house for about three hours, until she suddenly decides she wants to go into the bedroom. Her son and husband physically support her and help her get settled. My friend's weakness is staggering.

That night I'm unable to sleep. A strong headache inflames my entire forehead, and I wonder if I'm

That night I'm unable to sleep. A strong headache inflames my entire forehead, and I wonder if I'm getting a migraine, something I've never had but she suffered from for years.

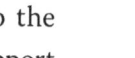

getting a migraine, something I've never had but she suffered from for years. I go into the pantry for some crackers and eat them with two ibuprofens...do I need three?...and lie still on my back. Then I remember:

I'm on the boat with her, ebbing and flowing in the energetic waves of the Death Gateway. I see it. Feel it. And realize it's time to get off.

We used to talk about death. I'd say: "Since you're older, it's only natural that you'll go first. Then, when it's my time, you can meet me in the space where the Death Gateway merges with the Tunnel of Light."

She'd say: "I imagine we'll be laughing hysterically, remembering all the spiritual realities we thought were real and then finally experiencing them in their true, expansive fullness."

I call to my Teacher and power animal and they immediately manifest. "What should I do?" I ask. My Teacher says: *I will replace you. She knows me. Don't worry. It will be fine.*

The boat is a large, wooden rowboat without oars, free-floating in the stillness between waves. It's grounded, steady, and somehow anchored in that mystical moment. My friend and I simultaneously stand up and hold one another in a full-bodied embrace, two separate beings merging into one. Time stops. A second, minute, hour, or an eternity passes, and then, in mirrored motion, we pull apart.

I instinctively step backward off the boat and watch my Teacher replace me. Before I can think or feel anything, they're gone.

I fall asleep.

My phone chimes me awake at eight o'clock the next morning. Her daughter says her mom passed about two hours earlier. Her daughter also had a headache in the night, and I wonder: did the three of us merge so we could absorb her mother's final physical pain? She wants to anoint the body and dress her in a beautiful outfit. Can you wait for me? I ask. Of course. There's nothing else to do.

I arrive at the house amidst hugs and tears. Her son shows me my friend's final communication to me, written in her hospice paperwork: "I request that Ann Fuller serve me and my family as my end-of-life midwife, should she be available."

Throughout our friendship, as my life wove in and out of turmoil, hers appeared solid, and whenever I was in a period of suffering, she would remind me: "You and I have been with one another many times before, in different roles and relationships. I know your path because I've walked in your shoes. And you've walked in mine. We made a plan together for this life and decided it was your turn to be the healer and mine to be the householder. We arranged it this way. That's why you can teach and heal and guide, and I can support you in ways no one else can possibly understand. And as I fulfill my part, yours is to keep reminding me of life's spiritual realities, memories I put aside so I might have all

that goes with family and privilege. I am certain of these things."

I wasn't just her end-of-life midwife, but her lifetime spiritual guide. That's why I was on the boat with her. Who else but me?

They told me that the previous night, my friend requested dinner—her Last Supper—and not only ate more than she had in weeks but was specific about the food and actively engaged in conversation that was both sensical: "Don't put the tofu on the plate. I need a separate one." And expansive: "What do you think would happen if the walls just dissolved from the room?"

She slept until a little after six in the morning, when she awakened and demanded to use the port-a-potty. Her son and husband assisted her, and like a woman during the pushing phase of childbirth just before the baby emerges, she expelled waste. After that, she collapsed, took a breath, and birthed her spirit out of her body.

We arrange her body neatly and symmetrically on the bed. Her eyes are closed, and long legs, arms, hands, and fingers perfectly placed. Her daughter mixes coconut oil with gardenia essential oil, her favorite, and family members and myself swim together in the love-filled ocean of her bedroom and tenderly massage her still-warm skin. The scar where her right breast once was is barely noticeable, but the breast's absence, lost to cancer many years ago, is. Her daughter chooses a cobalt-blue dragonfly skirt with a matching sleeveless top, and when we're complete, we dress her oil-infused body. Two fiber-art necklaces she'd created over half her life ago are placed around her neck.

Her young granddaughters adorn her with rose petals.

The day unfolds, and we take turns sitting with her, eating with one another, engaging in profound and trivial conversations, and taking walks. Then it's time. Everyone, including the children, gather around her blessed body and one by one, reveal what she means to them, each word a drop of love in the limitless water of memory.

The mortuary person arrives during dinner and, assisted by her son and husband, respectfully wraps her in a sheet, removes her from the bed, and places her on a gurney, which they roll out to a car. And just like that, she's gone.

Postpartum

Although her diagnosis came as an unwelcome surprise, my best friend of forty-two years surrendered to her path with grace and dignity. She was Clear. Purposeful. Her bald head transformed from a manifestation of illness into one of empowerment, and she became a role model for all of us—a living template of conscious dying.

One week after she passed, I awoke in the night to see her in the far-left corner of my bedroom. Somehow the walls were extended, reminding me of her last conversation with family and showing me the intermingling of the physical and energetic realms. She was smiling. Beaming. Vibrant. Fully in the Light.

Cremation took place two weeks later, and although I lit a candle that morning in honor of the occasion, my experience during the day took me by surprise. As someone who knows we are spirit in form, who escorted a friend in the Death Gateway as far as it was safe, who anointed and dressed her lifeless body, who saw the mortuary person leave with it, who spent two weeks getting used to the fact that she was gone, it was something else to envision her body becoming ash. *She really is gone.* The vessel, her costume of form, was no longer needed.

I felt the dilemma of yanantin strongly. And understood that however much I or anyone knows about spiritual realities, the greatest power of life is the heart. Honor yours during the deaths of loved ones. The "she's in a better place" comment I heard from some doesn't cut it when a person you love is no longer physically present—when you can't see them, call them on the phone, or just know that they're out there somewhere, living their life as you are yours. Honor your heart. Don't be afraid to feel the pain and loss. Yes, we are spirit, yet it's our hearts that make us human.

My Father

Just a little over three weeks after my friend died, my father passed. He left in the wee hours of the morning, at 3:00 a.m., and I received the call shortly after. I wasn't surprised—he was ninety-two, after all—yet the timing helped me understand the fitful restlessness and inability to sleep I'd been experiencing since I'd gone to bed that night.

For weeks, I'd had a feeling a third death was coming. After I got the call, I realized I was glad it was him and not another friend whose life would be cut short. I consciously connected with my spiritual "posse" and said a prayer of gratitude for his peaceful journey, something I knew he had wanted, and I wanted for him. I believe he flowed easily through the Death Gateway into the Tunnel of Light, where he was lovingly greeted by his wife / my mother and his siblings and parents.

I wasn't sure about my sister.

I've never been able to truly forgive my father for his role in Susan's life and early death. Or my own life. I stated earlier that as a spirit, I chose him for the initiations I needed so I might become the healer I was meant to be. While I do understand this, his actions created a need for what has often felt like *too much* awakening for me as a human being. Excessive physical and emotional healing and restructuring of core beliefs can be exhausting. Not everyone can flourish when their seeds are planted in poisoned soil. Susan couldn't. At times I barely have.

Did we need to experience that much wounding and separation?

So, amidst the waking songbirds and soft, early morning glowing light, I decided to speak to him. Somehow his death must have dissipated my anger, for the words that flowed from my mouth surprised me. "I forgive you." And then suddenly, out of nowhere, I felt a doorway open into a boundless chamber of my heart where further forgiveness and eventual compassion can grow.

My intention is to use my father's final gift—one that came from a man who rarely gave any—to restore and enhance the Unity of all life.

A Reminder

I'd like to conclude our exploration of physical death by sharing an important reminder from Ezekiel:

A spirit is never alone, either in or out of the body. Does the spirit realize this? Not always, but all will eventually, for it is part of spiritual awakening. Once one experiences this Unity, it becomes a foundational awareness, and when the time arrives for its next incarnation into form, it will remember. If you presently have this awareness, you experienced it in the past and have retained the knowing.

SHAMANIC REBIRTH

Now it's time to think about death from another perspective—the metaphoric. At the beginning of this chapter, I asked, "Is anything dying within you?" If you answered "yes," then Shamanic Rebirth—a ceremony that offers an opportunity to "die" without releasing our physical form and then "reincarnate" into a new life—is a perfect venue to explore.

In the summer of 2000, I created and led a weeklong ceremony called Healing Quest, which took place in Southern Oregon for fifteen years during the August full moon. Groups of up to twenty people gathered for a week on pristine property that had been identified as sacred, vision-quest land by Agnes Baker Pilgrim, a Native American elder and spiritual leader of the local Takelma tribe. Some participants were called to be Mountain Questers and others, Camp Questers, and all were connected within the yearly theme of Unity.

Each "season" we created a village that included a sweat lodge, tepee, kitchen, shower (with hot and cold running water!), and healing clinic. Everyone participated in hauling in and organizing food, water, cook stoves, kitchen supplies, camping equipment, and the twenty-two-foot tepee. My now deceased friend, Chris, was my Healing Quest partner for most of those years.

This powerful ceremony offered Questers a framework in which to explore the emotional landscape of their souls to discover and then heal the layers where unhealthy childhood wounds had been inflicted.

The template of Healing Quest was Shamanic Rebirth. This powerful ceremony offered Questers a framework in which to explore the emotional landscape of their souls to discover and then heal the layers where unhealthy childhood wounds had been inflicted. By participating in this courageous act, they not only improved their Individual lives, but each healing enhanced the emotional health of the Collective.

Do you remember how the outer layer of the soul directly affects us? Its energy radiates down through the Living Library landscape, reaches the emotional and physical bodies, and informs our entire existence. If the energy of low self-esteem abides there, you likely see its manifestations throughout your life. It's the same with uncertainty, fear of all kinds, doubt, shame, abandonment, and so on. The purpose of Shamanic Rebirth is to free that hucha and replace it with something positive.

This is how it works. First, we state an unhealthy theme or pattern we've been struggling with and call it "a life that is dying." Some Questers named theirs: Shame. Expectations. Judgment. Insecurity. Fear of manifesting. Needing acceptance and approval. Resistance. Entanglement in habitual behavior. The guilty self. Identification with childhood wounds. Anguish. Low self-worth. Resentment.

Once we become clear about the dying life, we decide what new life will be born to replace it. For example: Enacting magic. Unity. Self-love. Inspiration. Enlivening passion. Freedom. The peaceful, harmonious wild woman. Emotional strength.

Then it's time for the *Khuya* ceremony.

Khuya means sacred object in Quechua. This ancient ritual is part of their heritage and has been kept alive by Juan, my teacher of the Andean path. The intention is to purify a person's soul, or energy bubble, as the Q'ero call it. This leaves them in their own energy and personal power and is sometimes the first time in their life that they experience their energetic uniqueness. Special stones are used to open, cleanse, empower, and connect the seven major centers of the body via a series of energy belts. I was initiated to perform this ceremony in 1997 by Juan and a few years later, discovered that it's a powerful means of facilitating Shamanic Rebirth.

The Khuya ceremony officially begins once a person becomes clear about their old and new lives. We stand across from one another, and I ask, "What is the life that's dying?" After the person names it aloud, I make certain, "Are you sure you're ready to let it go?" It's important to be fully committed. Then I ask, "What is the name of your new life?" Once they declare it, I open the outer skin of their bubble by literally pushing it away with my left hand and releasing the impression of the old. (Imagine a snake instantly shedding its skin.) This creates space for the new to emerge (which was there all along, just

like the snake's new skin) and embed. The rest of the ceremonial actions align each center to one another and "solidify" that potential. When everything is complete, the person lies down and rests in their purified, reborn soul.

While the Khuya ceremony is traditionally performed by an initiate and takes only twenty minutes (for me), what I call the "Resurrection-of-Self Phase" begins right away and can last up to nine months. This phase can be a little tricky. After the Khuya ceremony, we return to the life we'd been living pre-ceremony, which has now become a *former* life. But since change is challenging, it can be easy to revert to familiar patterns and forget that a miraculous opportunity has occurred. In times like those, we must grow courage, trust, and above all, willingness—minute to minute or day by day—so we can let go of the old and allow the new to unfold.

THE WAY IT WORKED FOR ME

On the new moon of January 2022, I chose to end an old life of Suffering and be reborn into a new life of Abundant, Flowering Joy. (Do you remember that Flowering Joy is the translation of Phutu Cusi's name?) Since then, every morning when I'm out with Apu, I claim my new life. I breathe into my center, and as I exhale, say aloud, "I'm Rays of Light, Ezekiel's Daughter" (the spiritual name given me years ago), "and I'm living a life of Abundant, Flowering Joy." I smile every single time because I can almost literally see my Four-Petaled Flower blossoming.

Birth and Death as a Full Circle

First, we leave the Spirit Realm, travel through the Birth Gateway into conception, grow bodies, and become spirit/human beings. Then, when our time on Earth is complete, we leave these bodies and travel through the Death Gateway, back to where we originated. It sounds simple. Natural. But the "modern" world has become afraid of these mystically infused transitions, and this fear has polluted their organic processes. Too many of us are born, give birth, and die in sterile hospitals. Original cultures, each with specific traditions regarding the natural cycles of life, are far more evolved than what's called the "modern" world.

Spiritual Healing supports us to come to terms with and accept our inevitable passing. It facilitates interconnection with the visible and invisible worlds, reminding us that we're never alone and are instead part of a marvelous spiritual reality. It restores inner Unity by recovering lost parts of our souls, and it consistently awakens our consciousness. All of this heightens the opportunity to have an empowering death journey. Most people don't experience death the way my beloved friend did. Or my grandma—home with loved ones by their side. (I respect my mother, lover of all things medical, for adhering to her mother's wishes.)

Here are final thoughts from Ezekiel:

The Universe is Benevolent and Unified. Evil, separation, and aloneness exist only in the minds of humankind as reflections of inner disunity. There is no such thing as death, for all are spirit, and spirit is eternal consciousness.

Live from your hearts.

Heal your souls.

And trust and believe in Oneness.

Explore Shamanic Rebirth

Rumi said, "Forget safety. Live where you fear to live. Destroy your reputation. Be notorious… I have tried prudent planning long enough. From now on I'll be mad."

Would *you* like to explore Shamanic Rebirth?

Put thought into naming the life that's dying. Ask yourself, "Am I happy?" "Is there a soul pattern I can't seem to resolve?" "Do I have unfulfilled dreams?" "What are they?" "Am I willing to live them?" "Can I commit to releasing the past and beginning anew?"

Then, consider what you'd like your new life to be, the one gestating right now in the East petal of your future Four-Petaled Flower Medicine Wheel.

Take as much time as you need; it might be weeks before you become clear.

Once you're ready, ask a friend to witness and support you. (Don't be surprised when after explaining the process, they want to explore Shamanic Rebirth themself.)

Create an altar that includes a candle, paper, pen, and any important personal items.

As always, center and ground.

Light the candle and open a ceremony in your sacred way.

Call to your healing guides and teachers. You don't have to know who they are or even feel them. Put out the intention and trust the results. They'll be there.

Write down the name of the life that's dying. Say it out loud. Be definitive and committed. For example, "The life that is dying is Shame. I am over it! Done! Complete!" Express gratitude for how it's gotten you to the present moment, and then tear the paper, and place the pieces on one side of the altar.

Write down the name of your new life. Say it out loud. For example, "I am living a life of Empowered Creativity." Be passionate. After all, you're designing your future. Place this paper on the other side of your altar.

Stand tall. Re-center and ground. Spread your arms wide, out to your sides in a position of openness, receptivity, and power.

Ask your invisible guides to remove the template of your old life from your outer soul skin. Help them by imagining the entire process. Breathe it off. Begin at the top of your head and visualize it peeling back. Do the same thing at the front of your head and see it peeling forward. Attend to each side.

You might feel a little naked when the old life is gone. That's okay. Call to your new life. Breathe it in through your heart/soul space and as you exhale, let it infuse your entire soul. Do this until you feel saturated from your center, all the way to the edges of your outer skin.

Take the torn-up bits of your old life and infuse them with Light and gratitude. After all, they brought you to this moment in time. Then, release them—burn, bury, or even throw them in the garbage or toilet if that feels right.

When you're complete, close your ceremony with prayers of gratitude, and blow out the candle.

Place your altar someplace in your home where you'll easily see it. Make sure the statement of your new life is visible. You might even cut out pictures to make it feel more alive.

Then treat yourself to a yummy birthday treat.

Remember, you're an infant. Be patient, and most of all—love yourself—as you align with your new reality.

Welcome to the CENTER

UNITY

Congratulations!
You've completed your walk around the Four-Petaled Flower Medicine Wheel.
Now enter the Center.
The place all four petals: East, South, West, North,
And their distinctive colors: Yellow, Red, Black, White,
And themes, seasons, animals, energies, and teachings,
Meet, Merge,
Unify,
And create the energy and scent of the entire Flower.
This is the home of all life forms.
Take a breath…
And look inside your soul.
Can you see the Light of Love ablaze within your Center?
Admire the fully blossomed, multi-colored petals of your distinctive Flower.
Inhale its fragrant aroma…
And as you exhale…
Send the purifying, healing Love Essence
To every being, realm, and reality that exists.

CHAPTER FOURTEEN

Unity

We are already one. But we imagine that we are not. And what we have to recover
is our original unity. What we have to be is what we are.

— THOMAS MERTON, *Asian Journals*

Welcome to the Center of the multidimensional Four-Petaled Flower of Wholeness. It's time to rest for a while. Put your feet up and enjoy that hot cup of tea or glass of wine I suggested you drink (way back in A Letter to You) when first we met. And while you sip your favorite beverage, honor yourself for your commitment and all the work you've done to arrive here. Then, when you're ready...since we're still gathered in my living room...grab a pillow, lie on the carpeted floor, and get comfortable.

I'm going to tell you a story about how I awakened to Unity. It began in late 1998 and culminated in early 2000—which, to put things in context, was over six years *before* the dental dam exploded my world and led me to Teotihuacan to meet the Four-Petaled Flower. It's a tale that belongs right here, at the center of the flower. Imagine I'm reading aloud...

I love mail. You never know what you'll get. And one stormy, rain-drenching day in October, I grabbed an umbrella and ran down the stairs to

see. I opened the mailbox to discover a small, mysterious package. I had no idea what it was, but the return address showed a student's name. Surprised, curious, and excited, I brought it into the house and sat down on my favorite, purple-cushioned rocking chair. Once I'd opened the box and disentangled the bubble-wrapped gift from its tightly taped, cellophane coating, I held a two-inch-long, one-inch-in-diameter, brilliantly shiny, pitch-black crystal in my hand. One end came to a perfectly smooth point and the other was roughly flattened. The enclosed flyer said it had been mined by monks in Tibet and hand-delivered to the merchandiser. I held my new friend up to the light, admiring its gleaming perfection, until I was interrupted by a masculine voice. There was no denying it came from the crystal: *Put me in a clear glass jar with rainwater for seven days and seven nights. After that, I'll be ready to work with you.* I nearly fell off my chair!

I had exactly the right size jar for the crystal person. I put him inside and then placed them both on the wide porch railing, where I'd be able to watch the jar collect the pouring rain. When it was full, I picked it up and carefully walked to the backyard. The only honorable place to leave this special being was in the nook at the center of the Spirit Tree, the grandmother acacia who witnessed my initiation less than two years before. I positioned the jar so it wouldn't tip, said a prayer, and went back into the house.

On the morning of the eighth day, I brought the jar containing the water-infused crystal indoors and placed it on an altar. Four friends arrived to support me in channeling the mysterious person. Who was he? What did he mean by *"be ready to work with me?"* Up until then, I'd only given voice to teachings from invisible spirit teachers and had never thought about channeling a physical object. Would I be able to do it?

My friends believed I could. They made themselves comfortable on the couch, and I sat directly across from them on the rocker. Between us was our altar, a small table covered with a multi-colored alpaca cloth woven by my Q'ero friends. On top of that was a white candle and the crystal, still immersed in rainwater. I nervously took the cool, wet crystal out of the jar and held it securely in both hands. A sense of calm immediately infused me. We lit the candle, grounded, and opened a ceremony. I closed my eyes and prayed for the ability to communicate the crystal's message.

My prayers were answered.

Our new friend informed us about a wellspring of love energy that was flowing inside the Earth and vibrating at a potency so refined, it had never been exposed to humans. Every person on the planet needed this energy now, he said, in preparation for upcoming, turbulent years. Then he pleaded—yes, *pleaded*—that we release the energy into the atmosphere. He said the crystal people (it appeared he was the voice for many) and human beings were partners in this endeavor—they knew the task, but it was our job to accomplish it.

When a participant asked, "Where are we supposed to go?" The crystal replied, *It is not my place to say, but Annie's to discover.*

The intensity of the crystal person made such a strong impression, it never occurred to me to say no, which was the same response I had to Phutu Cusi's request. Once everyone left, I put my investigator hat on and set off on an exploratory path.

I knew it would lead to Tibet because that's where the crystal came from—but where? Sarah, a former student who had become a dear friend and was my housemate at the time, and I spent hours in bookstores and libraries researching Tibetan crystals and mountains. We found many possibilities... but nothing felt right. Then one day, as unexpected as the crystal's arrival, I saw a flyer stapled to a telephone pole announcing an upcoming slideshow about Nepal. A wave of chills indicated I needed to attend. Sarah was working, so I asked another friend, Jeanie, if she'd come.

The show was located at a local mountaineering store and hosted by a traveler who'd recently returned from Nepal. He was an extraordinary photographer. We saw families dressed in traditional garb—wearing huge, turquoise and coral jewelry—Buddhist temples and the monkeys that inhabit them, and tall, snowcapped mountains. Even the food—sour and spicy fruit treats, yak cheese, and fried dumplings called *momos*—looked artistically prepared and scrumptious. But when a pyramid-shaped glacier called Mount Kailash appeared on the screen, chills—this time, rivers of them—flooded my body. Mount Kailash is in Tibet, not Nepal, but there it was, part of the slideshow, as if it had appeared just for me. I'd never heard of this mountain before, but I knew, without a doubt, where we needed to go.

Mount Kailash is one of the most sacred mountains in the world and is seen as the Axis Mundi, or spiritual center of the universe, in Hindu, Buddhist, Jain, and Bon cosmology.

Mount Kailash is one of the most sacred mountains in the world and is seen as the Axis Mundi, or spiritual center of the universe, in Hindu, Buddhist, Jain, and Bon cosmology. The place where heaven meets Earth. This remote and not easily accessible mountain lives in western Tibet near the borders of India and Nepal and is almost 22,000 feet tall, which is smaller than other mountains in the Himalayas. It is the source of four significant rivers that are said to divide the world into four regions. Mount Kailash stands alone. It is so uncommonly shaped—a four-sided, glacier-capped pyramid with each side facing one of the four directions—that some Russian scientists believe it is too perfect and symmetrical to be considered a natural occurrence.

Nobody climbs Mount Kailash. Instead, pilgrims circumambulate the perimeter along two concentric circles called "koras." You don't walk the inner kora unless you've circumambulated the thirty-two-mile outer kora thirteen times. Each circumambulation can take from one to three days to complete unless you're doing full-body prostrations—an act of supreme devotion where you lie face down upon the ground, arms outstretched the full length of your body, then get up and begin again at the place where your hands touched the ground. Each prostration serves as one step, and a pilgrim might prostrate over 20,000 times to complete the thirty-two-mile kora. Traveling to Mount Kailash is the most sacred pilgrimage a Hindu or Buddhist can take. It's said one circumambulation around the outer kora frees you of a lifetime of karma.

Five months after the crystal first arrived and a good deal of research, channelings, planning, and life changes later, Sarah, Jeanie, John (from my first Peru trip in 1996), and I, all passionately drawn to the crystal's message and vast undertaking, left on our mission for the planet. We flew from San Francisco to Kathmandu and traveled for two months in Nepal and northern India, preparing for our three weeks in Tibet. We purified our souls at the power spots of the Buddha—Lumbini, Nepal, his birthplace; Bodhgaya, India, where he attained enlightenment under the Bodhi tree; Sarnath, India, the location of his first sermon; and Kushinagar, India, where he died. We released hucha at each sacred site and filled with vibrant sami.

Getting to Mount Kailash was a big deal, and we couldn't do it on our own, so I pre-arranged as much as possible and was fortunate to find Jamie, an experienced organizer, trekker, and Mount Everest summiteer. He coordinated everything regarding our Tibet expedition and even gave our trip a name: The Crystal Kailash Pilgrimage—which, second only to the birth of my son, remains the most phenomenal experience of my life.

A few days before we were to leave Kathmandu for Lhasa, Tibet, John was wandering around town and "by chance" found the missing piece that completed the jigsaw puzzle of our trip—a book about Mount Kailash. In *Circling the Sacred Mountain*, Robert Thurman, renowned Buddhist author, scholar, and teacher, wrote: "Lama Govinda told us that he had discovered an ultimate place of power on the north face of the mountain, a place where one could place one's deepest wish for the world, and all the Buddhas and gods and Dakini-angels would see to its accomplishment. Mt. Kailash could be that powerful." Before John read us this

passage, we hadn't yet known where at the mountain our ceremony was going to take place, but after hearing Thurman's words, we were clear—the north face.

Our journey to Lhasa officially began in the Kathmandu airport, where we boarded a plane that flew so close to the Himalayan mountains, we tried to reach out and touch them. I watched the wind blow clouds horizontally off the peak of 29,032-foot-tall Mount Everest and wondered if we were in heaven.

The Chinese government was (and continues to be) a strong presence in Tibet and decided we needed a guide. They matched us with Migma, a twenty-something, English-speaking, deeply spiritual Tibetan man who accompanied us on the entire mission. Migma was a wonderful addition to our group. Originally from Dharamshala, India, home of the Dalai Lama and the Tibetan government-in-exile, Migma knew we weren't traditional tourists, and while he didn't understand what we were doing (and at times was a little afraid of it), he respected our mission and wanted us to have the best possible experience. In our eyes, Migma wasn't a required guide, but a gift from the Dalai Lama.

We spent a week in Lhasa, sightseeing and acclimating to the altitude—12,000 feet above sea level. This is where I had the collective human soul experience I wrote about in the South Petal. We recommitted to our purpose—to circumambulate the outer kora of Mount Kailash and release a wellspring of love energy for all the world to absorb. The day we left for the Tibetan plateau, Sarah, Jeanie, John, Migma, and I piled into a Landcruiser with driver extraordinaire, Mr. Lee, a trustworthy, big-hearted character who knew the roadless route. Jamie traveled with a group of porters in another vehicle. The plan was to meet up with a flatbed truck filled with supplies—various types of tents, sleeping bags, water, and food—in one of the small towns.

In the first town we drove through, we were greeted by an excessively barking, unfriendly looking dog, tightly chained and staked to a post. Soft-hearted Mr. Lee instantly stopped the car, got out, and walked over to the underweight creature. We were afraid for his safety, but when he reached out to pet the dog, it excitedly wagged its tail and licked Mr. Lee all over his face. *Whew.* He found the dog's owner, engaged with him in what appeared to be a negotiation, and just like that, we had a dog! Mr. Lee stopped at each patch of roadkill he came upon and gathered meat for "Dog," who sat happily in the front seat with his new master.

At night, we stayed in ramshackle 1950s single-story stucco hotels that were so drab they were a little frightening to enter. But once we braved the unknown, as we were doing in each moment, we'd unexpectedly be greeted by colorful furniture and spotlessly clean, ice-cold rooms. Thick woolen bed quilts kept us warm at night.

Ezekiel and our council (disguised as porters and local mechanics) unified, set up a bank of battery-operated lights, and stayed awake all night fixing the truck.

The supply truck met up with us on the third evening, but there was a problem—it had a broken transmission. Jamie said that for any other group, this would have signaled the end of the trip, but my traveling companions and I knew we were guided and protected and would reach our destination. Ezekiel and our council (disguised as porters and local mechanics) unified, set up a bank of battery-operated lights, and stayed awake all night fixing the truck.

It took five days for our caravan to reach the final town, which was located at the edge of the breathtaking, moon-like terrain of the Tibetan plateau. It was literally the end of the road, and where our official circumambulation began. Our supply truck was traded for yaks—amazing animals related to cattle with three times the lung capacity—used for farming, hauling, hides, fur, and food. And since there are no trees at 16,000 feet above sea level—the roof of the world, as it's called—yak dung is dried and used for cooking and heating.

The next phase of our odyssey was about to begin. Sarah, John, Jeanie, and I embraced fun-loving Mr. Lee, gave multiple pets to Dog, and then left the vehicles behind and set out on foot with Jamie, Migma, and the porters. We planned to walk about ten miles a day for two days, which would get us to the north face of the mountain, remain there an extra day and night to fulfill our ceremonial mission, and complete the outer kora on the fourth day.

Our journey took place in mid-April, the very beginning of the "season" for circumambulation. Along the way, we met devoted spiritual pilgrims who were prostrating around the mountain, wearing tennis shoes on their hands and leather aprons to protect their bodies. Nomad families and communities were abundant. The daytime temperature could be a wonderful sixty degrees, but in the evening, it dropped to near or below freezing.

Our first night on the plateau, the porters set up camp below a red-rock butte which adventurous John, still energized from the day, decided to climb. At the top, he found a charnel ground—an above-ground cemetery where bodies are left in the elements to decompose and become part of the Earth. Migma told us that Milarepa, the beloved Buddhist saint known for his miraculous acts, had once flown across the Himalayas to that very place to give a lecture.

Milarepa's history is unclear. It's said he was born between 1028 and 1053 to a loving, financially privileged family. When he was seven years old, his father died and left a will naming his brother and sister-in-law guardians of his estate until Milarepa came of age, an edict that placed Milarepa and his mother under their care. But his father's wishes weren't honored, and the aunt and uncle kept the wealth and made Milarepa and his mother work as their servants. His mother was enraged and wanted revenge and insisted Milarepa learn black magic

to punish them. He complied and ended up killing many people but soon became filled with remorse and sought out a Buddhist teacher to help him heal and purify. He found Marpa.

Tsangnyön Heruka wrote in his book, *The Life of Milarepa*, "Marpa was absolutely clear in his mind that this big-hearted little man whose mind was completely shamed and shattered could not gain the desired transformation by any normal training." Marpa's purification methods included physical and emotional abuse, and it wasn't until Milarepa became suicidal that Marpa relented and offered him the teachings he'd originally come for. Milarepa studied with him for many years after that, and then left to visit his mother. When he arrived home, he found a broken-down house and his mother's bones scattered on the dirt floor. This began Milarepa's lifelong lesson in impermanence, and he retreated to the mountains to meditate.

Milarepa ultimately achieved Buddhahood, a state of awakened enlightenment, and had many disciples who, even after his death, experienced and shared miraculous stories of his teaching adventures. He, on the other hand, considered himself an ordinary person, not unlike you and me, who was able to awaken to wisdom and compassion with the help of Buddhist teachings and meditation. Milarepa's gift to us is: *If I can do it, so can you.* We felt his presence throughout the entire Crystal Kailash Pilgrimage.

The second night, we camped directly across from the icy, pyramidal north face of Mount Kailash.

A smaller mountain behind us housed a monastery that had been built by hand in front of a natural cave. That night, the eve of our ceremony, a Buddhist monk invited us in. Once we safely navigated the vertical, rocky path up, he led us through the small, ornate monastery, which led into a connecting cave, then to a tiny, cramped area in the back of the cave. A shrine filled with sacred Tibetan artifacts was off to one side, and Sarah, John, Jeanie, and I scrunched together on the clean, freshly swept dirt floor and tried not to disturb it. We sat in silence. After a while, the monk began drumming and chanting in Tibetan, and as sounds echoed off the low ceiling, I was lulled into what felt like an ancient, supernatural state. I have no idea how long we were there; it might have been hours. I do know we received many blessings—not only from the monk, but from Milarepa, the original occupant of the cave (the monk showed us his footprints on the ceiling), as well as from Mount Kailash itself.

After breakfast the next day, we left the kora route and walked directly toward the mountain, wondering just how close Mount Kailash would let us get. There was no path, so we wandered along the untrodden, rocky terrain, which led to a frozen pond we had to carefully cross. Suddenly, the four of us simultaneously stopped and gazed at one another in awe. Colors had heightened, and the energy around us, already so pure, refined even more. I was in such a profoundly invigorated state, I didn't know if I was reacting to the thin, 11.4 percent oxygenated air (sea level is 20.9 percent) or if I was no longer on Earth and had entered another reality.

Apu Kailash showed us our ceremonial place.

Ice was everywhere, and we found our special dry spots upon the large boulders. Our intention had already been decided: to sit in prayer, connect with the mountain and energy below it, and free the love in whatever ways we'd be shown. I closed my eyes and prayed to the Mystery of the Universe...to my usual spiritual helpers...to Milarepa...to the Buddha...the crystal people...and to Mount Kailash.

Once everyone felt ready, with overly expanded inner senses gifted to us in that uncommon realm, we each focused on our task. That's when I journeyed with my Teacher and Horse into the Earth beneath the mountain.

To me, the well-spring of love energy looked like a large, bottomless lake. I sat beside it, prayed, and asked Pachamama to dissolve anything blocking the release of this love—her love—up through the mountain. I waited patiently, and after a while, began to feel movement. The lake rippled as if there'd been an explosion underneath, and suddenly, a volcanic eruption of love water began spiraling up from its depths, through the base and peak of Mount Kailash, and out into the atmosphere. Sarah, John, Jeanie, and I all opened our eyes at the same instant and watched the invisible release.

None of us were able to say how much time we'd spent in meditation, but the thing we knew was this: we, the crystal people, Mount Kailash, and multitudes of invisible spiritual beings had been unified in purpose, and this mutual effort resulted in a successful mission, one that was set in motion on the rainy day the crystal arrived in my mailbox. (By the way...the very same student who sent the crystal was the one who awoke me the day of the Camp Fire. Thank you again, Krissy. I hope you enjoyed reading the story of the planetary healing that evolved as a result of your inspired gift.)

While I might have been the human guide of the Crystal Kailash Pilgrimage, Ezekiel and my spiritual council were the true guides. The crystal person had been the initial messenger and teacher, and while I did channel him once along the way, his task was to live in and energetically radiate from my mesa. We felt his presence daily. Ezekiel's teachings, guidance, and expanded overview grounded and supported us, and Sarah, John, Jeanie, and I routinely witnessed the manifestations of merged mystical and physical realities—the gift of Migma, John "coincidently" finding the book, and of course the broken truck—where we almost physically saw Ezekiel and the council busily working. And these are just a few.

I awoke early the next morning, our last day on the Tibetan plateau, and poked my head out of the tent to see a hint of rising sunlight flashing upon the sapphire sky. It was still and quiet, except for the gentle, rhythmic purr of John's snore. I lay back down and happily inhaled the crystalline air, while at the same time feeling warm and relaxed in my down sleeping bag. Even though we had an entire day of walking ahead of us—including over the 18,471-foot Dolma La pass—nothing concerned me.

Amid this high-altitude serenity, I became aware of the presence of my spiritual council. This was not unusual. I was used to feeling them nearby and seeing them embodied in the many helpers who crossed our path. I tuned in... Ezekiel lovingly thanked us for what we had accomplished and then surprised me with an instruction: *We want you to complete your initiation.*

I didn't understand. I thought I had. But he was clear: *We want you to journey, this time consciously and without fear, to and through the energetic waves of the Death Gateway, to and through the tunnel of Light, all the way until you reach the Expansiveness of Light.*

He continued: *You will return with knowledge for all people. This will be the full circle of your initiation.*

Was he crazy? We had just achieved something most people never imagine. Can't I rest for a while? And more important, I'd already survived two initiations.

Wasn't that enough?

While I might have been the human guide of the Crystal Kailash Pilgrimage, Ezekiel and my spiritual council were the true guides.

Shamanic Initiation: Part Three

If you surrender to the wind, you can ride it.

—Toni Morrison, *Song of Solomon*

From that moment on, Ezekiel's request plagued me, and I resisted it for five months after returning home. When I finally surrendered (as I always do to these kinds of things), the pieces began falling into place. There was no mystery about when my third initiation would occur—January 21, 2000—three years to the day from the events I had thought would be my *only* initiation. I'd been infused with fear and doubt then, and in my deeply disunified inner state, fell victim to believing I was all alone fighting threatening spiritual powers. This time, I decided, as a willing participant with conscious intent, the experience would be a healing for me, as well as a blessing for everyone I would share the knowledge with.

So much occurred during the preparatory months. Milarepa paid me a surprise visit in the dream state one night. I took several shamanic journeys with my Teacher and Horse for support and insight. I lost count of the number of conversations I had with Ezekiel.

There was no mystery about when my third initiation would occur—January 21, 2000—three years to the day from the events I had thought would be my only initiation.

I prayed for trust and courage daily.

I invited a small group of friends to witness and support me. Jane, who'd performed the soul retrieval during the second part of my initiation, arrived with Jean, my oldest friend and biggest champion. We ate well, took walks, and focused on the upcoming task. John and Sarah from the Crystal Kailash Pilgrimage, and Elaine, representing the Buddhist perspective, arrived a few days before the ceremony. Our small group had passionate, esoteric conversations lasting long into the night, and during one of them—when no one could assure me I wasn't going to die—I got so upset that I canceled the entire thing.

I changed my mind in the morning.

That day, Jane did the Khuya Ceremony—the ancient Inka tradition that purifies the landscape of the soul—for each of us, and during my turn, so much hucha was freed that I fainted! When all our preparations were complete, we entered the healing room, created an altar, and opened a ceremony.

Jane drummed while the rest rattled. We called "Spirits, Masters, Healers, Teachers, Shamans of the Light, Come. Come." Each person visualized energetic filaments of Light extending out from the fabric of their souls and covering the entirety of mine as a way of keeping me grounded.

I felt safe.

I lay on my healing rug, a sacred red, white, yellow, and black fabric I designed, wove, and offered to the Milky Way Village spirits eight years before, and placed an eye pillow over my eyes to block out light and strengthen my inner vision. The rhythmic drumbeat was the only sound. I called to my Teacher and Horse, "My intention is to journey through the Death Gateway to the tunnel of Light to the expansiveness of Light and return with medicine for the people"—exactly word for word what my council asked me to do.

Nothing happened.

"My intention is to journey through the Death Gateway to the tunnel of Light to the expansiveness of Light and return with medicine for the people."

I repeated this over and over and over, but nothing changed.

I panicked. *What's going on? Why isn't the energy shifting? I'm an experienced shamanic journeyer. I know how it feels to be taken someplace. I'm not feeling anything.*

Why isn't my Teacher taking me where I'm supposed to go?

Why can't I do this?

The drumming continued. *Bom, bom, bom, bom, bom, bom.*

I changed the wording and said, "My intention is to journey through the tunnels, to the Light, and return with medicine for the people."

My Teacher was present but silent.

I shortened things again, saying, "My intention is to journey to the Light."

Nothing.

I'm desperate.

I cannot believe I'm unable to do this. After so many months of preparation, I don't understand what the problem is. Everyone is going to be so disappointed.

Out of supreme despair, the words "My intention is to journey to God" came into my head.

What? I never use the word 'God.' Why am I using it now?

Wait.

The energy shifted. I felt movement. My Teacher was finally taking me someplace.

This is weird. I'm moving but not moving. Going somewhere and nowhere. Not up, down, or out.

Ahh...they're taking me in?

Where am I?

I exploded with laughter and was unable to stop.

I'm in the center of my soul!

The drumming continued.

Then I heard my Teacher...

Everything is within you, my dear. This is the Light. This is God. This is Unity. It is who you are.

I roared with laughter.

There's no place to go. It's inside of me. It is me! I'm home.

Can I live here forever?

Oh, I do live here forever.

The drumming began to sound strained. *Jane must be tired. This has probably been going on much longer than a usual shamanic journey, plus I'm lying here in a fit of laughter. What must they be thinking?*

I sobered up from my spiritual delirium, breathed deeply into the center of my soul, and said to whatever beings were listening, *"I'll never forget this blessed knowledge. Thank you for making it possible.*

I shook the eye pillow off, sat up, placed my hands on my heart/soul space, and breathed.

The drumming stopped.

It was time for the karpay, an energetic transmission of my experience. John lay down in front of me. Immersed in my awareness of Unity...I felt an invisible, loving hand gently pushing my head downward.

I'm confused. Am I going to kiss John?

Inches away from his chest, my hands instinctively encircled his heart/soul space, and I blew my experience directly in. *Woosh.* His light illuminated so brightly I backed off.

I returned and placed both hands directly on his center, recalled my freshly awakened awareness, and energetically transferred everything I knew to him.

The karpay was complete, and I released my hands. John moved, and Sarah lay down. I repeated what I had done. Then Jane. Elaine. And Jean.

Everyone received a transmission.

My eyes opened to see rays of love beaming from the hearts of my beloved friends. We sat together in silence for what might have been an eternity, then closed our ceremony.

Inches away from his chest, my hands instinctively encircled his heart/soul space, and I blew my experience directly in.

Post-Initiations

Earlier in the book, Lucy asked: What is the point of this exercise? If the point of being here as spirit/human beings is to awaken from our spiritual slumber and remember our unified identity—that we—*everyone and everything*—are spirit, part of the Mystery, Light, God, Goddess… let's do it!

But can it be so simple?

Awakening often involves healing, and healing takes courage. Particularly now, during this exceptional, evolutionary time where Pachamama is in a vortex where she's transmuting her outer soul skin from duality into Oneness. Remember, we not only live and walk upon her body, we also live within her soul. Pachamama's crisis and mission are ours.

Ever since I participated in the Hatun Karpay and the personal initiations that followed, all of which brought me deeper into the fourth level of love and Unity, I try my best to recognize places within myself where disunity might be hiding. But I'm not conscious all the time. And then there's the news; I could do endless distant healings and still be unable to transmute the pain and suffering of the world's injustices.

In the end—when so many individual actions appear primitive, narcissistic, and selfish beyond belief—we remain as One, just each in different stages of awakening to that truth. Which excuses nothing, but when all else fails, it can be helpful to remember Ezekiel's wisdom:

Unity and separation walk hand-in-hand, side-by-side.

Is it necessary to have an esoteric experience to remember Unity or travel anywhere in search of God? No. The divine spark of the Mystery lives within the center of our soul. It's each person's responsibility to release the heavy energy creating the blinders that keep us bound within the illusion of separation.

Do you remember when my council spoke with me on the final pilgrimage morning and shared the higher purpose of the third part of my initiation?

They said: *You will return with knowledge for all people.*

This means *you.*

THE KARPAY

I invite you to receive the Unity karpay.

Transport yourself from my living room floor to my healing room floor. I've just completed my initiation, and it's your turn to receive the energy transmission.

My sacred rug awaits you. Lie down upon it, directly in front of me, and breathe into your heart/soul space.

Feel the heat as my hands surround it.

My head is moving closer and closer to your chest, and then...

Woosh! I blow my experience of Unity into you.

I now place both of my hands directly on your center, breathe deeply, and energetically transfer everything I know to you.

Inhale. Enhance your luminous, glowing Light.

And as you exhale, fill your entire being with the awakened knowing of Oneness and Unity.

Lie there as long as you like. You're home.

AFTERWORD
The Four-Petaled Flower Revisited

The wheel is come full circle.

— WILLIAM SHAKESPEARE, *King Lear*

I was savoring a mug of my favorite Mexican coffee—*café de olla*—a distinctive blend of ground coffee, piloncillo (dark brown sugar), and Mexican cinnamon made in a large, round, clay pot called an olla. I drink it when I'm in Mexico, which is where I was, sitting with Emily at her round kitchen table in San Sebastian. In a few days, we'd be driving to the airport to pick up a group of ten women traveling from all over the United States to join us in a weeklong exploration at the ruins of Teotihuacan. I love working with Emily. While we each have our special roles, our mutual respect allows us to lead together in what feels like a synchronized dance, instead of as two separate people. We create the day according to what's happening in the moment and inspire one another to teach and heal in more expansive ways than if we'd been alone.

As the flavors of café de olla merged in my mouth, Emily and I discussed the upcoming journey, the same one I wrote about at the beginning of the book. "We already know the Four-Petaled Flower will be the true leader," Emily said.

"Yes," I agreed, and then pointed out the obvious, "but other than that, we haven't scheduled much."

As our conversation meandered back and forth, the ancient ones took us by surprise and simultaneously infused us with the same awareness. "We're not just going to learn more about the Four-Petaled Flower, as we had originally thought!" Emily exclaimed.

"No," I said, "We're being tasked with awakening it…"

"Yes!" Emily interjected, and we finished the vision together, *"…and then integrating its healing medicine into universal consciousness."*

"How in the world are we going to do that?" I asked in amazement, then stopped, took a sip of my sweet café, and closed my eyes: "The human soul is part of the soul of Earth, and since the Four-Petaled Flower is a symbol of Unity and Wholeness, activating it will naturally release that energy into the atmosphere. Once that occurs, all life forms will be affected."

"True," Emily said, "and because all are One,

the integration will happen as a matter of course."

"Absolutely," I replied. "It's the same principle as removing the seal from Phutu Cusi and releasing the love energy underneath Mount Kailash."

Emily had been to the ruins hundreds of times and envisioned our group exploring them in a new way. "There are several different entrances," she said. "You know how on the first day we usually go through the main gate and walk directly into the large courtyard?" She was referring to the pyramid of Quetzalcoatl, the feathered serpent deity, and the route that takes us from his courtyard down the Avenue of the Dead—the one-and-a-half-mile, North/South main street lined with more courtyards and temples.

"What if we don't visit Quetzalcoatl first?" Emily asked. "Instead, we can walk into the ruins from a side entrance and begin in the center of the complex, directly in front of the Pyramid of the Sun, the location of the hidden Four-Petaled Flower cave. If we consider the cave as the center of the flower, we can connect with it every day, and from there, intuitively wander along the unseen petals in the four directions—East, South, West, and North—as far as the energy under our feet leads us."

I was nodding like crazy. "And once we find the center of each petal," I added excitedly, "the group will activate it."

This unique, four-petaled route would entail being outside the gated area of the ruins and within the surrounding communities, and as far as we knew,

no one in our lifetime had ever explored Teotihuacan from this perspective. While Emily and I weren't sure what it would end up meaning, we knew in our hearts it was the right thing to do. "This," we said, holding one another's gaze, "must have been the way of the ancients."

We shared our plan with the other pilgrims, and they committed to the challenge. Each day after breakfast (where café de olla was a staple), we sat together in meditation with the intention to become attuned to the ancestors who had lived in an area much larger than the officially designated archeological site. We prayed for guidance regarding where to go, asked to receive wisdom from the spirit of the flower, and when we were ready, walked to the ruins and beelined to the cave underneath the Pyramid of the Sun. Once each person was satisfied with their connection, we traveled together in that day's direction.

With Emily's extensive knowledge of the local communities, our group entered towns, villages, and neighborhoods that had formerly been part of the ruins, but were now inhabited by families, animals, shops, ornate churches, and community plazas. We explored as a group, yet each woman was guided by her intuition—something akin to being in the collective environment of the Spirit Realm—while maintaining our individuated selves.

Once we began feeling the energy of the petal we were dedicated to, we united even further and were led, perhaps by the flower itself, to an area that felt right to everyone—a local church, caves in a cactus garden, the stone remnants of an old ruin with ancient multi-colored murals, and even the Pyramid of the Moon at Teotihuacan itself. It reminded me of when John, Sarah, Jeanie, and I were seeking the right place to perform our ceremony at Mount Kailash.

Since this is the same trip I wrote about in an earlier chapter, let me refresh your memory about what happened next. On the fifth and final day of our unique mission, the group climbed up the two hundred and forty-eight steep steps to the very top of the Pyramid of the Sun. After adjusting to our remote distance from the ground, and intimate proximity to the sky, we made a circle in the middle, right above the hidden carved Four-Petaled Flower cave. We sat down, placed our mesas in the center, and held hands.

This is where Sarayna offered us the original teaching, which is worthy of repetition:

The Four-Petaled Flower is a symbol of the Unity of All Life. It is Wholeness, Beauty, Fragrance, Bounty, Harvest, and Union. The energy of each petal imparts uniqueness, and the center of the flower is a combined fusion of all four petals and creates the energy of the entire symbol, which is Unity.

In a similar approach as when I connected with Phutu Cusi and Mount Kailash, our group first envisioned the uniqueness of each petal. Then, we imagined the merging of all four petals coming together. When it became time to activate the center of the flower—the Unity energy—we visualized it emerging from the depths of the Earth, rising up through the cave, and moving through the pyramid into our physical bodies. That's when a collective inhalation spontaneously arose, and with a unified exhalation, we released the energy of the Four-Petaled Flower into the atmosphere for all beings to receive.

The trip lasted another few days, and after the participants had gone home, Emily and I sat at her kitchen table and processed the events—this time drinking strong mango margaritas. "As expansive as our vision was," I said, "it was also limited. I can't believe I completely forgot that planetary missions require personal purification."

"Yes," Emily replied. "It's too bad we were taken by surprise by the huge need for emotional release that walking this unknown path stirred up."

The experience of opening and activating the flower had created a lush opportunity for internal disunities to ripen, arise, and seek healing and unification. Group members transmuted individual, as well as collective, heavy energy—and thanks to their high integrity, each person arrived at a newly awakened internal balance. Participants shared that they felt more "themselves" than when they'd first arrived, and one even said, "We all experienced a sense of grace and satisfaction that we were able to accomplish our task."

Emily had a mystical vision during one of the petal activations. She saw that the universal image of the Four-Petaled Flower was originally brought to us by our star family ancestors who embedded it within the center of Earth as an infinitely spinning, energetic imprint. This whirling rotation creates a complete sphere, and its physical manifestation is what we perceive as our planet.

In other words...*Earth is a rotating, radiating Four-Petaled Flower.*

And since the human soul is part of the Earth's soul, if she radiates the Four-Petaled Flower, we do also.

One of the ways Pachamama manifests her Four-Petaled Flower rotation is by offering us wildflowers. We see their colorful faces at a river's edge, in sprawling meadows, on the desert floor, cascading down hillsides, and even popping up in concrete cracks next to deserted buildings. There are thousands of distinctive varieties, colors, shapes, and sizes growing all over the planet. Even in the Arctic, where the growing season is only three months out of the year, you'll find spectacular, multi-colored displays.

Wildflowers ask nothing of us. From the tiniest, velvety yellow buttercup to the thirty-six-inch-tall purple coneflower to the intoxicating fragrance of a soft lavender lilac—no matter how many petals they have, each one is a gift from Pachamama.

One person alone can't cure the world's addiction to duality and separation, but we can attend to our own. I'm not saying this is easy. Separation has been pervasive in my life. As an abused and neglected child, a disowned daughter, a mother who had to share custody of her son with a power-hungry ex, and a grown woman, I've lived and replayed separation more times than I care to remember. And even after awakening to it that day at the river, it's taken years for Unity awareness to consolidate within my mind and heart.

My Teacher said:

Unity exists always, even in the direst manifestations of separation.

And while I believe his words are the most important in this entire book, it can still be difficult to view it in this way.

I must.

We must.

There's no rightful order to awaken and live Unity. We can start by walking the Four-Petaled Flower Medicine Wheel to notice and heal our personal disunifications. Or we can begin in our minds and simply choose to see life from an expanded perspective. Remember the Shamanic Rebirth teachings? Now is a perfect time to participate in that life-changing ceremony. Whatever your way of living Unity might be, it's important to know that it not only enhances you, but feeds the collective, which in turn supports Pachamama within the healing vortex she's entered on our behalf.

At the beginning of this book, I invited you to gather in my living room with other like-minded spiritual seekers. Think back to that moment and marvel at the changes that have occurred. Your multi-layered soulular Living Library has refined and purified and you've awakened to Unity in lasting ways.

How do you feel?

Receiving the Unity karpay was the completion of our mystical journey together. So much has been born, relinquished, and re-born—and like snakes, you've repeatedly shed skins and grown new ones. We may not all know one another, yet over the duration of our living room time together, we've become a spiritual family. Now it's time to close the ceremony we opened at the beginning of this book and for everyone to disperse into their own lives.

Let's tend to our altar, the one that's remained in the center of our circle during the entire Four-Petaled Medicine Wheel walk. The white candle is still burning. Can you see it? Let's stand up, hold hands, and blow it out together. Hug one another deeply and fully. Then reclaim the medicine item you originally placed on the alpaca cloth: the crystal, picture, rock, owl feather. *Your* special item. It's infused with everything you (and everyone within our spiritual family) learned and experienced and is fully potentized for the next phase of your journey.

But wait... Consider one last thing.

We know the center of the Four-Petaled Flower represents Unity, but are you aware it's also the eye of the flower?

Breathe into your heart/soul space.

Each individual awakening becomes an elixir that infuses the collective, spiritual slumber and stimulates it to stir, stretch, yawn, and awaken.

Feel the energy of the karpay fill your center and all four open petals. Focus on the center again and make a conscious choice, "I am a Four-Petaled Flower of Wholeness who sees life through the eye of Unity." And when you feel the depth of your new truth, do as Sarayna suggested:

Become the energy of the flower and feed it to all humanity.

Your initiation (did you realize you were in one?) is complete. You have evolved into a new form of living energy, not unlike the waves of Earth, or the ones we encounter in the Birth and Death Gateways. You are a Four-Petaled Flower wave, a force of nature that affects everything.

I visualize you walking out the door as such.

Everyone has the power to feed and invigorate the shift Pachamama is engaged in. Do you remember the magic?

Each individual awakening becomes an elixir that infuses the collective, spiritual slumber and stimulates it to stir, stretch, yawn, and awaken.

Let's do it for ourselves, one another, and all future generations. One day we'll return to the Spirit Realm, yet our children and grandchildren will remain on Earth. As energetic waves of Unity, we can make the transformation happen now—*for them*—so the lives of every future human being will be more awake and consciously unified than ours have been.

Gratitude

Wherever I have knocked, a door has opened. Wherever I have wandered, a path has appeared.

— ALICE WALKER, *In Search of Our Mother's Gardens*

I thought long and hard about these pages. How can I possibly list everyone to whom I'm grateful? You'd be reading for months. Years. So, I've decided to give you a little background on this book first.

I was born pregnant with an unwritten book—and finally, at twenty-nine years old, became ready to nourish, grow, and birth it. I left my husband and three-year-old son to fend for themselves for a week and went to a cabin in the woods near Mendocino, California. It was a beautiful and secluded place, high in the mountains, yet close enough to the ocean to hear sea lions barking. I brought healthy food, copious notes, paper, pens, and big intentions. (No computers back then for me.) During that time of my life, I was a childbirth professional—a labor coach, apprentice homebirth midwife, and teacher of all things birth related. My "book baby" was about labor support.

I carried my gear—a full cooler, bedding, clothing, and toiletries—up the hill and settled in for a nurturing week in the perfectly sized, one-room log cabin. It had a double bed, compact kitchen area with a table and chairs, and a small oak desk. Fresh well water was available at a nearby pump, and a perfectly clean outhouse completed the rustic environment.

On my first night, I lay in bed and read a novel by flashlight, then fell asleep to absolute silence. Melodious songbirds awakened me early the next morning, and after heating water on my camp stove, I sat outside on the Adirondack chair and drank my tea. The forest was enchanted. Later, following a gratifying breakfast of yogurt, granola, and blueberries, I sat down at the window-facing desk and gazed at the trees. It was my first official writing day, and I was excited, until…a surprise visitor arrived at my open door.

The owner of the land had just received a call from my husband and found himself in the unfortunate position of having to tell me that Grandma Tillie, my favorite person in the world, was dying. That was it. I packed, moved out, drove back to Berkeley where I lived, and flew to the East Coast.

My book pregnancy never left my soul. Malnourished, it was barely noticeable on some days, but made itself known on too many others by shouting, "I'm still here!" There were lots of beginning books—entire folders of notes, chapters, and stories—and while I did self-publish a handbook in 1995, called *Healing Hands: Energy Work for Pregnancy Through Postpartum*, I knew that wasn't it.

Students were forever asking where they could find a book about whatever I happened to be teaching at the time, and my answer remained the same, "There is no book." They wanted to know, "When are you going to write it?" Then they'd push on my invisible guilt strings, "We need this information in the world." My consistent response was, "I have to support myself. I don't have the time or luxury to write. If someone wants to sponsor me, offer a place where I don't have to pay rent... Well, then I'll reconsider."

Fast forward to November 8, 2018—the Camp Fire. Then to early March 2020—the Pandemic. Two events that made it difficult for me to work. No person sponsored me, but homeowners insurance helped, and unemployment (briefly) after that. What I had in abundance was "the time and luxury to write."

The first being I want to thank is the spirit of this book, the one I was always meant to write. Somehow, no matter the mood I was in, when I sat in front of my computer to give you attention, every time I was complete—pushed back my chair and stood up—my mood was elevated. Your spirit shifted me out of exhaustion or sadness or disappointment or...more times than I could ever count. I've said to many people over these past years that your gestation and growth has not only been a vehicle for new learning curves and creative expression, but an anchor of sanity—particularly during the isolating pandemic years.

Now for the rest.

The Milky Way Villagers, my Teacher, Ezekiel, Guadalupe, Mary, Energeesa, the Pleiadean Healers, Horse, and all the other "people" in the known and unknown gang: Your wisdom continues to awaken my consciousness and through this book, will do so for others.

My two remarkable friends who passed while I was writing: Your love, support, and belief in me over all the years of friendship, travel, ceremonies, love, heartache, craziness, and just plain life gave me the confidence to grow into the Spiritual Healer I am today. I don't know what I would have done, or who I would be, without either of you.

Lisa: You were solidly there in the beginning of it all.

Michon: You saved my life on that pivotal day, and have become a lifelong friend.

Jane, Dawn, and Nicole: You saved it again on the days that followed. I believe my life would never have unfolded in such a balanced way had each one of you not been there offering your time, hearts, and medicine.

Janice: Every Thursday night after I made what I hope was a delicious dinner, you let me read different chapters aloud and offered priceless feedback. You, who live Unity, are my teacher of social justice, and a consistent presence in my life that I never take for granted.

Salita: Sister from another mother. You never stopped letting me know how proud of me you were. I don't think you realize how much I appreciated that.

Kathy: You took me in for all those months after the fire and made it fun. I will never forget your open-hearted, generosity.

Joy: Your solid friendship and extensive wisdom and healing abilities are continuous gifts.

Linda Jean: You stayed on the phone with me for hours, helping with whatever I happened to need that day.

Marita: You were a consistent source of wise, empowering comments. And wine.

Jayme: You were my personal cheerleader.

Janice, Jayme, Marita, and Sara: You gifted me by agreeing to be readers of the initial manuscript, and I took each of your wise suggestions to heart.

Susan. Sarita. Sue. Paulita: Whenever any of you asked, "How are you doing?" I would say *what* I was doing, and you'd listen to me talk nonstop about the book.

John: The Crystal Kailash story would have been flat without your excellent memory.

Juan: Your wise teachings and support are integral aspects of this book.

My Q'ero friends and family: *Unity Begins Within* would lack backbone and dimension without your generous knowledge and life-changing karpays.

Clients, students, and travel participants: Your contributions to my life are priceless.

Editors: First, there was talented Katheryn, who turned me on to her teacher, Kate (WordWorks.xyz), who, through her extensive and patient knowledge, taught me the foundations of writing. After that, through some mystical perfection of timing, I found Alice (AlicePeckEditorial.com), whose wisdom supported me to enhance the manuscript, and when we deemed it complete, introduced me to brilliant copyeditor, Crystal (WritersVoiceEditorial.com).

Yes, it took a village.

From beginning to end, your big hearts, professionalism, and uniqueness of medicine helped me grow into a woman who loves to write. (I must always make sure I'm sitting up straight when I'm writing because each one of you is on my shoulders.)

Emily: Longtime friend and phenomenal artist, (EmilyKGrievesArt.com), your consistent, flowing creativity is a model for life. Where would my words be without your art?

Chris: Book designer, (ChrisMoleDesign.com). When I saw your first vision, I leaned back in my chair, smiled, and breathed a sigh of relief. I knew my book was going to be beautiful. You have been a blessing to collaborate with.

And finally, my family:

Susan: I'm so grateful I got to know you a little bit during your short life. I miss you every day. Thank you for staying true to your knowing and leaving the world—and me—the gift of your son, my nephew, Troy. How miraculous that we found one another.

My precious son: Thank you for coming into my life, receiving my love, awakening the "little league mother" in me, giving me a beautiful daughter-in-law and a light-filled grandson, and being another Teacher with a capital T.

My "book baby" has been born!

May All Beings Heal, Awaken, and Live Unity.

A Few Inspirations

Once you stop learning, you start dying.

— ALBERT EINSTEIN

Anderson, Eben. *A Neurosurgeon's Journey into the Afterlife.* New York: Simon & Schuster (2012).

Brennan, Barbara Ann. *Hands of Light: A Guide to Healing Through the Human Energy Field.* New York: Bantam (1988).

Eliade, Mircea. *Shamanism, Archaic Techniques of Ecstasy.* New Jersey: Princeton University Press (1964).

Gordon, Oakley E. *The Andean Cosmovision, A Path for Exploring Profound Aspects of Ourselves, Nature, and the Cosmos.* Oakley E. Gordon (2014).

Harner, Michael. *The Way of the Shaman.* New York: HarperCollins (1990).

Heruka (Author) and Lobsang P. Lhalungpa (Translator). *The Life of Milarepa: A New Translation from the Tibetan.* New York: Penguin Books (1992).

Ingerman, Sandra. *Soul Retrieval: Mending the Fragmented Self.* New York: HarperOne (2011).

Mini, John. *The Aztec Virgin: The Secret Mystical Tradition of Our Lady of Guadalupe.* Sausalito, California: Trans-Hyperborean Inst of Science (2000).

Newton, Michael, PhD. *Journey of Souls: Case Studies of Life Between Lives.* Woodbury, Minnesota: Llewellyn (1994).

Parisi Wilcox, Joan. *Masters of the Living Energy: The Mystical World of the Q'ero of Peru.* Rochester, Vermont: Inner Traditions (1999).

Roman, Sanaya and Duane Packer. *Opening to Channel: How to Connect with your Guide.* Tiburon, California: HJ Kramer (1987).

Sams, Jamie. *Sacred Path Cards: The Discovery of Self Through Native Teachings.* New York: HarperCollins (1990).

Tafur, Joseph. *The Fellowship of the River: A Medical Doctor's Exploration into Traditional Amazonian Plant Medicine.* Phoenix: Espiritu Books (2017).

Weiss, Brian L. *Many Lives, Many Masters: The True Story of a Prominent Psychiatrist, His Young Patient, and the Past-Life Therapy That Changed Both Their Lives.* New York: Touchstone (1988).

Wright, Henry W. *Exposing the Spiritual Roots of Disease: Powerful Answers to Your Questions About Healing and Disease Prevention.* New Kensington, Pennsylvania: Whitaker House (2019).

About the Author

ANNIE FULLER has been a spiritual seeker since she was a young child growing up in a household of secrets and separation. After the homebirth of her son in 1980, she spent the next twenty years supporting families as a homebirth midwife and childbirth educator, a passion that fueled a desire to heal her childhood experiences and unify her soul. Along this healing path, Annie became inspired to learn shamanism, channeling, soul retrieval, and hands-on healing, all of which evolved into a Spiritual Healing and Teaching practice.

Annie sees people of all ages for individual Healing Ceremonies. She creates and teaches a myriad of shamanically based classes and workshops and leads Healing Ceremonies for communities. With over forty years of experience, Annie's steadfast intention is to assist every person she meets to heal their soul, awaken from the pervasive virus of separation and its resulting afflictions, and experience inner Unity.

An avid traveler, one of Annie's favorite pastimes is bringing people on spiritual journeys to Mexico, where she first encountered the Four-Petaled Flower, and to the mountains of Peru, where her almost three-decade relationship with the land, people, and teachings has become foundational to her life. She served as the visionary leader of Healing Quest for fifteen years, received the energy of ancient pyramids, led a high-altitude pilgrimage for the planet in Tibet, sat on the mountaintop and inside the caves of the tallest mountain at Machu Picchu, and created a three-month healing clinic in Hungary.

Annie lives in Northern California, where she enjoys daily hikes with Apu, her cheerful, constantly-sniffing-everything, corgi-mix companion, roasting garlic-encrusted leg of lamb for meat-eating friends (and artichoke quiche for the others), reading novels, and watching movies with dramatic themes.

To schedule a Healing Ceremony, attend a Class, or participate in Spiritual Travel—
Visit Annie at: www.FullcircleSpiritualHealing.com.

www.ingramcontent.com/pod-product-compliance
Lightning Source LLC
Chambersburg PA
CBHW041509120626

46551CB00018B/2367